Table of Contents

Chapter 5: Superintendent/School Board Relations (cont.)

Chapter 6: Female Superintendents 77

Chapter 7: Ethnic Minority Superintendents 103

Chapter 8: Professional Preparation and Training 127

Chapter 8: Professional Preparation and Training (cont.)

Foreword

School superintendents at the start of the 21ˢᵗ century work under intense scrutiny from parents, teachers, board members, and elected officials. They are held responsible for the progress and achievements of the students in their district's schools. Their hours are long; their critics are many And yet this ninth national study conducted by the American Association of School Administrator finds that the majority of superintendents derive satisfaction from the job and would enter the profession again given the chance.

What are the challenges and satisfactions in this most visible role in public education? Who are the men and women leading the nation's 13,500 schools districts, which range in size from fewer than 300 students to more than 1 million? What is the traditional career path to the superintendency, and where might future superintendents come from?

These questions, and others, are answered in this comprehensive survey of America's superintendents. This *2000 Study of the American School Superintendency* presents responses from the largest sample of superintendents of any of AASA's 10-Year Studies; nearly one in five superintendents is represented. We explore a spectrum of issues that affect education and leadership, and take a close look at just who are the superintendents of education in the new millennium.

Superintendents today find themselves in a role markedly different from even a decade ago. Several profound shifts in American life and culture have compelled schools – and their leaders – to rethink some of our basic premises of public education. The rapid increase in both number and diversity of students in our nation's largest urban areas demands new skills of teachers and administrators. The information and knowledge explosion made possible by widespread use of the Internet makes national boundaries meaningless, even as a "digital divide" threatens to widen the gap between mainstream society and the poor. Add to this mix the national commitment to high standards and accountability, and the potential for stress in the superintendency becomes clear.

The national press makes much of the short tenure of superintendents, particularly in urban districts where politics may take precedence over education. While this study finds that the average tenure for all superintendents is between 5 and 6 years, rather than the widely publicized 2.5 years, the fact remains that frequent shifts in leadership can and do take a toll on districts and impede reform efforts.

We thank Tom Glass, Lars Björk, and C. Cryss Brunner for conducting this study. We are all the beneficiaries of the time these individuals devoted to data collection and analysis.

This study of the American school superintendency was researched and written against a backdrop of intense interest in the future of public education. While it is clear that change is inevitable, it is not yet clear what direction that change will take. The superintendents of the 21ˢᵗ century have the opportunity to play a pivotal role in shaping the structure and content of education for the next generation. They must provide the vision and collaborative leadership to meet the challenges ahead. We hope that the profile of the profession offered in this study is a resource for the men and women carrying out these important tasks as well as those charged with preparing and assisting them.

Paul D. Houston
Executive Director
American Association of School Administrators

Acknowledgments

This study has been conducted in collaboration with the Joint Program Center for the Study of the Superintendency, a part of the University Council for Educational Administration. Professors Lars Björk of the University of Kentucky, and C. Cryss Brunner of the University of Wisconsin, co-directors of the Center for the Study of the Superintendency, have joined with Professor Thomas Glass of the University of Memphis, author of the 1992 Study, to sample over 2,000 practicing superintendents about important aspects of their positions and issues facing their school districts in the new millenium.

The authors of this *2000 Study of the American School Superintendency* would like to acknowledge and thank the following individuals for their contributions and support. Peter Abrams, Professor Emeritus at Northern Illinois University, served as statistical consultant as he did for the 1992 Ten-Year Study. Liz Brookshire and Teri Sloan had the massive responsibility of data processing the very long survey instrument. Blakely Davenport of the University of Memphis worked with the lead researcher in coordinating the development of the survey report. At the University of Kentucky, Marti Fee Quintero assisted Lars Björk in developing chapters three and eight. Meredith Mountford worked with Cryss Brunner at the University of Wisconsin in putting together chapters six and seven.

Also, the researchers would like to express their appreciation for the support from C. J. Reid, AASA Director of State Relations; Joe Schneider, AASA Deputy Executive Director; and, especially, Ginger O'Neil of GRO Communications, who provided important project management.

Ginger wishes to thank Educational Visions for their editing, Eric Stewart of Forte Communications for his layout work, and Sans Serif for the cover design.

Executive Summary

Thomas Glass

In the last 17 years, nearly all national studies of public education have predicted impending disasters. The broad and wide-sweeping reforms called for in these studies have not, to any great extent, come to pass. Certainly, curriculum standards have been imposed, as well as widespread and frequent testing of students, teachers, and administrators. Still, after a "hundred studies," American public schools are little changed.

In 1920 and 1930 the National Education Association's Department of Superintendence sponsored national surveys of the American school superintendency. The purpose of the nationwide superintendent surveys was to compile demographic profiles, opinions on key educational issues, and what constituted "best practices" in the superintendency. After World War II, the American Association of School Administrators continued the surveys, which have become known in the profession as the "Ten-Year Studies."

The 2000 American Association of School Administrators (AASA) Ten-Year Study of the American School Superintendent is not one full of gloom and doom. Superintendents across the nation, in districts of all sizes and types, report the superintendency to be a very viable and rewarding career in public service. They do indicate that a number of problems and troubling challenges exist, but not so many as to seriously impair the educational process in their districts. The overall picture of American school governance the superintendents perceive is one in which superintendents and board members work together to improve the nation's schools.

The 2000 Study results do not dramatically differ from those of the 1982 and 1992 Studies. Both of these studies (for which the original data were collected in 1980 and 1990, respectively), contain many questions comparable to those found in the 2000 Study. These parallels have allowed the authors to analyze the 2000 data with a historical perspective.

The Superintendents

The 2000 sample is the largest of any of the Ten-Year Studies, containing responses from 2,262 superintendents across the nation. The sample is proportional to the differing sizes of districts. Of those reporting their gender, 1,953 were male and 297 were female. One hundred fourteen respondents identified themselves as minorities.

The number of superintendencies is declining in each decade, as districts are consolidated across the nation. The exact number of superintendents in public school districts is not definitely known. The data is presented in percentiles and cross-tabulated by district size categories (**Table 2.5**). The reason for the uncertainty is that many individuals listed as superintendents serve in more than one district, or in a special situation such as an intermediate district. In hundreds of very tiny districts, the superintendent is also a principal, and may or may not be counted as a superintendent. Market Data Retrieval listed the number of superintendents as 13,728 in January 2000. Therefore, the 2000 Study reflects the opinion of about one out of six superintendents (**Table 2.1**). In 1990, there were about 14,000 to 14,500 superintendents, and the Ten-Year Study represented approximately one out of eight practicing superintendents.

The average age of superintendents is 52 (**Table 3.3**). In the 1992 Study, the average age was near 50. In 1923, the average age of superintendents was 43, a time when the national system of schools was very rural and most school districts consisted of one, two, or three schools.

The 2000 Study reveals that superintendents entered the profession a bit later in the 1990s. Most superintendents are married (**Table 3.7**), and grew up in rural areas or small towns. It is curious to note that, in this urban nation, both the superintendency and the organization of school districts still have a rural/small town base.

The Districts

In general, the districts in which the 2000 Study superintendents work are increasing in enrollment. Across the districts, the mean growth in enrollment in the 1990s was 5.87 percent. The very large districts are growing even faster, as urban and minority enrollments climb (**Table 2.3**). Superintendents from nine districts with enrollments over 100,000 responded, as did 251 superintendents of districts with fewer than 300 students (**Table 2.2**). The average size of districts for which a response was received was 4,000 students. Other data sources, including the 1992 Ten-Year Study, describe the average American school district size to be about 3,000 students.

School Board Relationships

Print and electronic media stories often portray boards and superintendents at odds with one other. This view is not supported by data from the 2000 Study, however. Nearly every superintendent is evaluated annually by his or her school board. The study found that 69 percent of those evaluations were in the "excellent" category, and 22 percent in the "good" category (**Table 5.16**).

A corresponding item asked superintendents to rate their personal effectiveness. Ninety-five percent rated their effectiveness to be "excellent or good" (**Table 5.25**). There definitely is a "match" between superintendent board ratings and superintendents' perceptions of personal effectiveness.

When asked to evaluate the adequacy of their school boards, 30 percent found board members "not qualified" to carry out their duties (**Table 5.9**). This is troubling because it indicates that 3 out of 10 school boards are perceived as unqualified by their superintendents. In brief, the superintendents have given school boards lower grades than the superintendents themselves received from those boards.

Career Patterns

Between the 1992 and the 2000 studies there has been a modest shift in career patterns of superintendents. More superintendents are spending a number of years as central office administrators than in the past (**Table 4.9**). In previous decades, a high number of superintendents (usually in smaller districts) jumped directly into the superintendency from the principalship. Today, however, 36 percent have been assistant/associate superintendents and another 32 percent have been district coordinators. This shift may be attributable to the existence of fewer small districts, and the increasing complexity of school district management.

Forty-six percent of superintendents surveyed indicated they have been high school principals. Fifty-nine percent indicated that they have been high school teachers (**Table 4.9**). Historically, the ranks of superintendents have been dominated by former high school teachers and principals. This may have resulted in a disadvantage to women aspiring to be superintendents, since women, who have traditionally dominated elementary teaching, have had fewer opportunities for the type of "entry level" administrative positions available at the secondary level.

Superintendents participating in the 2000 Study indicated that they have spent more years in the classroom than those responding to the 1982 and 1992 studies. Thirty-seven percent reported spending 6 to 10 years in classroom teaching (Table 4.8). Previous studies, including the 1992 Ten-Year Study, have indicated that most superintendents taught about five years; the current group has taught an average of six to seven years.

Seventy-six percent of superintendents gain their first administrative position before they are 35 (**Table 4.1**). This first administrative position is typically assistant principal or principal. In addition, 58 percent of respondents have experience in coaching (**Table 4.10**), but very few are former physical education teachers. As most superintendents are former teachers in secondary or middle schools, where a number of coaching positions are available, it is not surprising that many have had coaching experience.

Most superintendents will spend about 14 to 17 years in the superintendency in about 2 to 3 school districts (**Table 4.14**). Most consider retirement at age 57, as, at that point, they have accrued 35 years in a state teacher retirement system. In recent years, a significant percentage of superintendents have retired early, accepting attractive early retirement options from their states.

Superintendent Tenure

The media typically describe the tenure of superintendents to be 2.5 years. This figure originated about a decade ago in several articles about rapid turnover in the superintendencies of large urban districts. Since that time, the tenure figure has had a life of its own. Unfortunately, it has fostered a negative image of the superintendency.

The 2000 Study was able to look at superintendent tenure from a new perspective. Traditionally, superintendent tenure is assessed by the number of years superintendents have served in their current positions. However, in the 2000 Study, 1,250 superintendents indicated having held only one superintendency. Therefore, instead of calculating the mean number of years in a current position, the tenure data were analyzed by dividing the total number of years in the superintendency by the number of superintendencies held. The outcome was that the mean number of districts served was less than two over a mean period of nearly nine years (**Table 4.16**). By this method, the tenure of superintendents was calculated to be five to six years per district served (**Table 4.14**).

A second AASA-sponsored survey of 2,499 superintendents was conducted in 1999 (Superintendents' Professional Expectations and Advancement Review - SPEAR™; (Cooper, Fusarelli, and Carella, 2000) and included the traditional question: "How many years have you served in your present superintendency?" The finding was that superintendents had held their current jobs 7.25 years. They also indicated holding their previous superintendency 6.43 years. Therefore, the two studies are fairly close in superintendent tenure findings.

Mobility in the superintendency is not substantial, and the only unusual statistic generated by the 2000 Study is that a large number of superintendents are in their first three-year contract in their current districts (**Table 4.15**). A combination of factors contributes to the five to seven year tenure of superintendents. As mentioned before, most superintendents are rated highly by their boards, many have spouses with careers, and the majority are "locked" into state retirement systems.

When superintendents do leave their jobs, the most common reason is an opportunity in a larger (and better paying) district. Only 14 percent said that they left because of conflict with their school boards (**Table 5.28**).

Stress in the Superintendency

Stress is a natural part of any leadership position. Superintendents in the 2000 Study indicated about the same degree of stress as in 1992. Fifty-one percent indicated they feel "very great" or "considerable" stress in their positions. In 1992, 42.3 percent felt "considerable" and 7.8 percent "very great" stress. It is difficult to determine whether the reported stress levels are disabling and interfering with superintendent job performance. This is a topic that needs much further study.

Certainly, threats of school violence, mandated high-stakes testing, tight finances, taxpayer concerns, board turnover, community pressure groups and school reform initiatives all contribute stress to the job of superintendent.

Important Problems Facing Superintendents and Boards

Financial pressure facing school districts and school boards is the most vexing problem reported by superintendents (**Tables 5.22** and **5.24**). This is a historical finding, as each previous Ten-Year Study found exactly the same key problem. Public schools, of course, depend on public tax dollars. These dollars can be at risk in states where school district funding is the only tax that voters can directly approve or disapprove.

Superintendents report that community pressure groups are often a problem for their board members. State mandated high-stakes assessment and testing are significant challenges in their jobs as well. They also see board relations, changing curriculum, and compliance with numerous mandates as formidable challenges.

Satisfaction with the Superintendency

Although superintendents face serious challenges, both from inside and outside their districts, they indicate that they gain a great deal of satisfaction from their jobs. Fifty-six percent feel a "considerable" fulfillment in their current position. This is down five percentage points from 1992, but is still high when taking into account the stress levels of the job. Thirty-four percent feel moderate fulfillment or satisfaction in the superintendency (**Table 5.29**).

When asked whether they would again choose the superintendency as a profession, two-thirds answered in the affirmative (**Table 5.37**). These data are a strong indication of the present state of the superintendency. Superintendents are receiving fulfillment from their jobs, their boards value them highly, and they feel they are getting important tasks accomplished in their districts. The data strongly suggest that the superintendency is not a profession in serious crisis.

Community Pressure/Special Interest Groups

Over half of the superintendents report the existence of "pressure groups" in their communities that attempt to influence board decisions (**Table 5.6**). Superintendents in the large districts almost uniformly report the existence of such pressure groups. Schools are certainly not part of partisan politics, but they definitely are political organizations and participate in the political arena.

The types of pressure groups identified by superintendents were mostly community-based, but religious and political pressure groups were also identified by responding superintendents (**Table 5.7**).

Who Influences the Board?

Only about one in five superintendents believes that their school board is dominated by a distinct faction in the community. Almost two-thirds feel that their boards are aligned with the common interests of the community (**Table 5.10**). Superintendents also report that their boards accept their policy recommendations almost all of the time (**Table 5.19**). Despite the rise of special interest and pressure groups, the superintendent seems to be still very influential in affecting board decisions. Board members themselves feel they are not dominated by community factions and pressure groups.

Expectations of the Superintendent by the Board

In the past decade, education literature has focused on instructional leadership as the key to being an effective principal or superintendent. An accompanying theme has been to demand superintendents and principals be initiators of school reform initiatives, rather than maintainers of the *status quo.*

Superintendents feel that the primary expectations held for them by their boards are that they be educational and managerial leaders. About 3 percent said their boards expect them to be primary leaders of reform. The 40 percent saying their boards expect them to be educational (instructional) leaders. Another 13 percent said that their boards expect them to be political leaders for the district (**Table 5.17**). It appears that superintendents and boards may not feel the urgency for implementation of school reform initiatives to the degree held by some politicians, policy specialists and others engaged in the multi-million dollar school reform industry comprised of reform consultants, commercially sold programs and developers of standardized tests.

Communication with Board Members

A key part of creating an effective working relationship with boards is communication. Superintendents were asked how many hours a week they spend in "direct" communication with board members. Surprisingly, 62 percent reported spending three or fewer hours a week in direct communication. Most superintendents have between five and seven board members. Three hours a week would indicate that many board members have very little contact with board members. Probably, the board president/chair receives a good portion of the direct communication time.

Most boards meet twice a month, usually to work with a complex, and often potentially contentious, agenda. It would seem that superintendents would be well advised to schedule more one-on-one time with board members.

Female Superintendents

The 297 female superintendents who responded to the survey had, as expected, fewer years overall experience in education (**Table 6.5**), but more years as classroom teachers (**Table 6.16**). A majority of them serve smaller districts (**Table 6.13**) and come from an elementary background (**Table 6.17**). Female superintendents typically begin their administrative careers in elementary positions (**Table 6.20**) and few have had coaching experience (**Table 6.18**).

Unlike previous studies, a majority of female superintendents are now in the same career track as most male superintendents: teaching, principal (assistant principal) and central office (**Table 6.23**). Once they make the decision to seek the superintendency, nearly 60 percent gain their first position in less than a year (**Table 6.24**).

Only about half of male superintendents feel an "old boy/girl" network helped them to gain a superintendency position. Three-quarters of female superintendents feel the networking helps in getting a position (**Table 6.26**). Most female superintendents think that gender barriers exist. Most men feel they do, as well, but to a limited extent.

Like male superintendents, female superintendents gain a great deal of satisfaction from their positions, and would choose the superintendency again as a career (**Table 6.32**). Nearly 93 percent were rated by their boards as being "excellent" or "good" and about the same percentage see themselves as being successful (**Tables 6.42** and **6.43**).

A larger percentage of female superintendents are hired to be instructional leaders (**Table 6.40**). They indicated that their boards almost always accept their policy recommendations (**Table 6.52**). Women definitely place a greater degree of importance on interpersonal skills in the superintendency (**Table 6.27**).

Interestingly, the 1950 and 1992 Ten-Year Studies found that women superintendents constituted about 6 percent of the total superintendent group. The 2000 Study, with 13.1 percent, finds a significant difference. Women probably constitute the most important future candidate pool for the superintendency.

Minority Superintendents

A difference exists between minority and non-minority superintendents in that they are selected much more often by their boards to be "change agents" (**Table 7.32**). Four percent of minority respondents, however, were hired to be a "leader of school reform" (**Table 7.33**). This may mean that boards wish to see major changes in districts by doing the same thing as in the past, but by doing it better in the future. Nearly 60 percent were rated by their boards as "excellent" or "good" (**Table 7.35**), and nearly all felt themselves to be "successful" (**Table 7.34**).

Thirty percent of minority respondents indicated they had no minority members on their school boards. Fewer than 20 percent indicated their boards are majority minority (**Table 7.40**). About 38 percent felt their school boards to be "not well qualified" or "incompetent." This was a bit higher than for non-minority superintendents (**Table 7.46**). Minority superintendents tend to serve in smaller districts and are marginally more satisfied with their positions than non-minority superintendents (**Table 7.48**).

Professional Preparation

Forty-five percent of superintendents have doctoral degrees, and nearly all of those degrees are in educational administration (**Table 8.1**). This is a 12 percent increase over the 1992 Study. About a quarter of superintendents rated their graduate programs in educational administration to be "fair" or "poor." Another quarter rated them as "excellent" (**Table 8.16**). Thirty-four percent of study superintendents indicated that they considered the credibility of professors of educational administration to be "fair" or "poor." Fourteen percent responded that professors have "excellent" credibility (**Table 8.20**).

An important aspect of any profession is the preparation of those who will practice that profession in future years. The preparation of school superintendents has never been a high-visibility program in either university educational administration programs, state departments of education, or the profession itself. For the most part, it has been submerged with preparation programs for other educational administrators such as principals, business managers, and central office administrators. Only a handful of university-based preparation programs have focused on the superintendent.

Unlike previous studies, the 2000 Study has been very concerned with the preparation of superintendents. There is very little literature focusing just on superintendent preparation. Most that is published combines superintendents with principals and other types of administrators. The superintendency in the 21st century is changing both in the skills required and the arena in which those skills are practiced. Superintendents in the new century will be spending much more time working with community groups, responding to state-mandated assessment programs, and acting as champions of public education in the face of school choice, vouchers, privatization, and home schooling.

Preparing the superintendents of tomorrow should become a much higher priority for states, higher education institutions and the profession itself. A major finding of the 2000 Study is that superintendent preparation is perceived as adequate by respondents. Their responses, however, are with regard to past and present preparation programs, not those needed for the future.

About three-quarters of the responding superintendents belong to and participate in the American Association of School Administration (AASA). About 40 percent belong to the Association for Supervision and Curriculum Development (ASCD) (**Table 6.11**).

Superintendent Salaries

The salaries of superintendents vary widely. Salaries are greatly affected by district size and location, as well as by the history of the district or surrounding districts. Some states have much higher salary levels than other states, and a superintendent entering a new district sometimes can make considerably more than a predecessor of long tenure.

There are no superintendent salary scales, since the final amount is negotiated between the superintendent and the Board of Education. Several states, such as Minnesota, have placed caps on superintendent salaries to hold them below the salary levels of high elected officials.

The size and wealth of the district seem to be the two primary factors in determining the nature of superintendent compensation packages. A very rough rule of thumb would be that a superintendent might have an initial contract salary level of approximately 20 to 30 percent above district principals and central office administrators. As superintendents do not typically have tenure in school districts, but are often required to live in those districts, boards generally offer compensation which includes a generous benefits package and a salary level permitting a comfortable life in the community. This is especially important, because most superintendents have families and typically purchase houses in their districts.

The financial composition of the superintendent's salary package is often very complex. Sometimes, the fringe benefit package equals half of the stated salary amount. For instance, the yearly salary amount stated in the usual multiyear contract may be $75,000, but the true value of the contract is $120,000 due to such fringe benefits as (1) annuity contribution; (2) paying all the superintendent's state retirement system costs; (3) district leased vehicle; (4) term life insurance; (5) whole life insurance; (6) professional development allowance; (7) social security contributions and other benefits. Possibly, for this reason, it is sometimes difficult for superintendents to know the exact dollar value of their salary/fringe benefit packages. Certainly, all know the dollar amount agreed upon with the board. The media generally report this amount to the public, and it is also sent forward to the state department of education. However, since fringe benefit packages have become so expansive, such data are really not an accurate representation of superintendent salaries. Because of the complexity of superintendent salaries, the 2000 Study did not ask for salary amount. An entirely separate study should be done on superintendent compensation packages.

Conclusion

The superintendency continues to be a very functional position in public education. Superintendents across the nation are the education leaders in their respective districts and communities. They most assuredly are the main link between the district and the community. Survey data definitely indicate they are in the good graces of their boards.

Problems do exist, however; the chief one being the never-ending struggle to acquire adequate financial resources. Other significant problems are a lack of time, high stress, and dealing with various pressure groups with special agendas. But superintendents seem to be doing their jobs in a most creditable manner.

The superintendency is so very different from district to district that making generalizations is hazardous. In fact, there is really no such thing as the *superintendency*; instead, there are many superintendencies. Often they are more unlike than like each other. The diversity is best illustrated when comparing a small 300-student district in Iowa with a 400,000-student urban district.

The future of the superintendency in the 21st century seems to be tied more closely than ever to harmonious working relationships with boards and community groups. Successful superintendents will be those who have excellent communication skills, understand the instructional process, and can work to create functioning coalitions that will ensure the financial and educational survival of the public school system.

Chapter 1

The Superintendency: A Historical Perspective

Thomas Glass

Overview

American public education at the beginning of the 21st century continues in a third decade of reform. Starting in 1983, with the publication of *A Nation at Risk*, America's schools and educators came under fire from the public, media, and politicians to improve student performance. At the start of a new century, nearly every state has developed and implemented academic performance standards programs. High-stakes testing is closely connected to many of these programs. These tests attempt to measure academic gains of students and schools. These "do or die" assessment efforts have, in the 1990s, changed the professional lives of many superintendents and principals.

Previous reform movements, such as "scientific management" in the 1920s, progressive education in the 1930s, and the Sputnik "scare" in the 1950s, were not as far-reaching as the "standards movement" in the 1980s and 1990s. Perhaps the only educational reform that totally permeated schools and classrooms to the degree of the standards movement was the passage and implementation of Public Law 94-142. This federal statute, which guaranteed special education services to eligible students, changed the landscape of American public education. The extent to which today's standards movement is changing practices in classrooms and schools will become clearer in the first decade of the 21st century.

Whenever significant changes are made in how schools are organized and students are taught, the position of the superintendent is affected, and sometimes changed. The women and men who hold these key leadership positions are vitally important to the future success of American public schools. Their leadership will significantly shape and mold the schools of the next century: a century with a focus on high technology, globalization, and challenges to the human and physical condition of the planet.

A Quick Look Back

The position of school superintendent has existed in American public education since the mid-1800s, when many school districts in larger cities appointed an individual to be responsible for the day-to-day operations of a number of schoolhouses. By 1860, 27 cities with school districts had created a position called the *superintendency*. During the next century, the growth of the superintendency closely paralleled the growth of the public schools (Callahan, 1966). The position was closely linked to the evolution of layperson school boards from those dominated by political and religious leaders.

Many early superintendents faced serious challenges, including the survival of the common school movement itself. Those who took on the job of superintendent, in support of the common school, were true educational reformers. They traveled from large cities to villages, spreading the word about a free public education. In some respects, many early superintendents were like secular clergy. They served as moral role models, disseminators of the democratic ethic, and, most importantly, builders of the American dream.

From Schoolmaster to Manager

The American public school superintendency has changed a great deal since its inception in the first half of the 19th century. The original role was that of a schoolmaster, with an appointed or elected lay board of education making almost all decisions of any importance. In fact, the earliest superintendents were head teachers and clerks. By the end of the 19th century, most superintendents in the cities had shed this role of clerical supervisor of students and teachers to become master teachers and educators (Carter and Cunningham, 1997). Superintendents in most states became responsible for all operations in the district, and their day-to-day decisions usually were not subject to examination by the Board of Education (Callahan, 1966). The schools managed by these superintendents reflected the transition in the late 19th and early 20th centuries from an American economy and culture dominated by rural farm concerns, to one in which manufacturing would play an increasing role in shaping society and the emerging public school systems.

Establishing Professionalism

Superintendents did not gain separate operational authority from the board overnight. Ellwood Cubberley, a former superintendent who wrote books and articles on school administration in the early 1900s, called this transition the "struggle to become true professionals" (Cubberley, 1922).

Historically, the partnership between superintendents and school boards has been a subject of discussion and substantial research. The function of the board, and its relationship with the superintendent, has been important in the development of the superintendency.

The "grand old men" of the superintendency — Cubberley, George Strayer, and Frank Spaulding — championed the cause of the common school, and advocated an executive type of leadership. They wrestled with boards of education in large cities such as Chicago, where a political spoils system determined which teachers would be hired, what textbooks would be purchased, and which vendors would be patronized (Callahan, 1966).

In addition to their efforts to reform schools and school boards, the early superintendents also worked diligently to prepare the ground for the future school leaders who would be able to provide civic leadership, scientific management, and established business practices for the schools.

Early superintendents were not unaware of the need for those working in their profession to be current in their knowledge and skills in curriculum and instruction, teacher preparation, and staff training. However, the primary emphasis in the early years was for the superintendent to attend to the *business* of the school (Kowalski, 1999).

The Era of Scientific Management

In his 1966 book, *The School Superintendent*, Daniel Griffiths discusses a second phase in development of the professional superintendency. He describes the "quasi-businessman" attempting to form school districts into industrial models through principles of scientific management. During this period, a significant degree of control over decision making was moved from boards of education into the hands of the superintendent. This period of scientific management, and the resulting bureaucracy, still shape the structure and practices of many school districts, despite the fact that a number of researchers and reformers believe that highly centralized and hierarchical structures are major obstacles to effective school restructuring.

School organizations based on bureaucracy and scientific management were first found in cities, where school districts, hard-pressed to keep up with escalating enrollments, were won over by the promise of management efficiency and increased "production" levels. Scientific management principles were tempting to big city superintendents, who were struggling to "Americanize" immigrants, and deal with migrants from the rural countryside in pre-World War I society. A division of labor and specialization were important aspects of the scientific management principles espoused by Frederick Taylor and others. In the 1930s, this resulted in the creation of such "specialists" in American schools as teachers who only taught one or two subjects. Other specialists, such as social workers, psychologists, and nurses were also brought into school districts to provide services.

In this phase of the American superintendency, a curious anomaly occurred. Although most school districts were still in rural areas, the majority of schoolchildren were beginning to attend city schools. Scientific management principles were generally featured only in the urban and emerging suburban districts. Other scientific management practices were also visible, especially in school district offices. Time management and employee specialization were quickly adopted as a way to improve efficiency at minimum cost to the taxpayer (Norton et. al., 1996).

Toward a Corporate Model

During the first part of the 20th century, larger school boards slowly moved toward a more corporate model of management and governance. The board became more of a policy-making body that met periodically, while day-to-day decisions were made by the superintendent. By the late 1920s, most states had spelled out the legal responsibilities of both parties in statute. In most cases, the superintendent still was responsible to the school board, and lines of authority were more clearly drawn. In some states, there was a dual system of management shared by the superintendent and business manager. Each reported directly and separately to the school board. Interestingly, at the same time scientific management principles were adopted, a substantial emphasis by those preparing administrators and corporate executives was for superintendents to practice the theories and skills advocated by social and behavioral scientists in the human relations movement (Norton et. al., 1996).

Superintendents as "Experts"

As superintendents became more secure in working with school boards, they became more assertive. At the same time, as the country became increasingly urbanized and school districts grew, more efforts were made in school districts to centralize control of all management activity. This move was consistent with scientific management principles, but was seen by many non-superintendent educators as not in the best interests of schools and schoolchildren. Nonetheless, the drive for hierarchical bureaucracy and scientific management continued mostly unabated until the late 1980s, when the role of the superintendent as "expert manager" came under attack by school reformers.

In fact, during the 1980s, and, to some extent earlier in the 1960s and 1970s, minority groups and school reformers who were unhappy with American public schools often zeroed in on the authority and control held by principals and superintendents. Minority parents and school critics claimed that school administrators (educational experts) who would not, or could not, change the educational system (bureaucracy), obstructed equal educational opportunity and reform.

At the beginning of the 21st century, most citizens probably think of the superintendent as the "chief expert on schools in the community." Certainly, school boards look to the superintendents for "expert" knowledge and leadership that will result in peace and harmony in the district. However, as Arthur Blumberg (1985) points out, the modern superintendency, as compared to the same position earlier in the century, must be more politically driven. Many times in the present, traditional views and expectations of the superintendent directly conflict with desires and demands for substantial institutional restructuring (Blumberg, 1985). Even though this may be the case, most school boards expect the superintendent to be a leader of change and a prime influence on establishing a district vision. The role of the superintendent can either be as a leader to manage change, or as a leader of change (Johnson, 1996).

Practice Into Theory: A Revolution in Training

A third phase in the development of the superintendency essentially began in the 1950s, and just now seems to be coming to a close. Daniel Griffiths and Jacob W. Getzels describe this period of "professionalism" as one of great debate about what superintendents should do and how they should be trained.

Most of the early professors of educational administration, such as Strayer, Cubberley, and Spaulding, were former superintendents of large city school districts. They later turned to the college classroom to train and place students in key superintendencies across the nation. These teacher-educators focused on solving what they saw as educational problems. In contrast, more recent training has been based on the development of theory and its application to practice. Many superintendent preparation programs use a problem-solving format in which students solve real-world problems using the theories taught in previous classes (Bridges, 1992).

In the first half of the century, textbooks written by the "founding fathers" of the superintendency were extensive compendia of "best practices" gained from their own experiences, and what they observed in surveys of the best school districts in the country. But as social science theory began to influence preparation programs, growing numbers of professors of educational administration, who had never been practicing superintendents, began to dominate the preparation of administrators (Eaton, 1990).

Today, many "superintendent scientists" now develop or alter theoretical models, test them, and, through training, pass them on to practitioners. This is a subtle, but very critical, change in the way superintendents and principals are trained (Bridges, 1992).

Challenges in the 1960s and 1970s

The 1960s were a time of immense social tension that brought significant changes to American public schools. Issues such as equal educational opportunities for minority groups, community control, compensatory programs, and desegregation resulted in policymakers having a stronger focus on the training and selection of superintendents.

One of the most dynamic changes during the 1960s and 1970s was the dramatic transformation in the role and composition of school boards. In the 1950s, authors such as Charles Reeves held that the role of the board was that of a legal interest group elected by the public. The professional backgrounds of board members often reflected the composition of the local Chamber of Commerce or Rotary Club. In the late 1960s and 1970s, board members became more representative of the total community. Many of the blue-collar workers, homemakers, and others who were elected were intent on changing the system to make it more responsive to their needs (Getzels, 1968). In the 1990s, school board member composition continued to change slowly as more women and minorities were elected to board positions (Kowalski, 1999).

There are few first-person accounts by school leaders of how the role of the superintendent and board changed between 1960 and 1990. Larry Cuban, however, in *The Managerial Imperative and the Practice of Leadership in Schools*, furnishes a candid portrait of the nature of changes in school boards and the superintendency during the 1970s and 1980s. The tension that existed in society during this tumultuous time spilled over to the schools and led to a superintendency much different from the one that existed during the quiet years of the 1950s. Relationships between boards and superintendents began changing; in many districts, boards assumed greater leadership in formulation of policy. There is little doubt that the level of conflict between boards and superintendents increased in the 1990s as both tried to stabilize school districts in a fast-changing time. Community groups, responding to external threats to schools, dramatically changed their expectations of the role of the superintendent. The aftermath of this period of conflict and confusion still exists in many school districts (Kowloski, 1999).

Superintendents Under Fire

Perhaps the greatest challenge to the superintendency during the 1960s Civil Rights era was the greater involvement of school boards and citizens in the job of the school superintendent. At the same time, a wide array of legislative mandates were lessening school system autonomy. The superintendent's traditional role of "expert" was challenged by many parents and board members because the schools were not meeting community expectations (Spring, 1998). As the sole person in charge, the superintendent was the most visible school figure and the target of criticism. The displeasure of parents and citizens during the 1960s and 1970s, combined with growth in the number of unionized teachers, resulted in a superintendency where leaders often found themselves in continuous defensive postures, both personally and on behalf of their districts. This disenchantment with American schools was especially pronounced in large urban systems, where increasing numbers of disadvantaged students dropped out or were chronic underachievers. In such school systems, superintendent firings often were front-page news (Cuban, 1988).

Reform in the 1980s and 1990s

During the 1980s and early 1990s, the policy-making pendulum swung back and forth between the superintendent and school board, reflecting the disagreement between education leaders and theoreticians about what constitutes policymaking and what constitutes management. This fuzzy division between policy and management is a continuing area of concern. Most researchers on the superintendency favor a model of the superintendent as chief executive officer, a model borrowed from the American private sector. In many cases, what has been viewed as policy development in the world of public education is seen as management prerogative in the corporate world. American public school systems in the 1990s were on the receiving end, many times, of the same criticism as corporate America. They were over-managed and under-led (Bolman and Deal, 1997).

The 1980s will likely be remembered as the time in American public education when many players — the private corporate sector, politicians, and citizens of all races and socioeconomic levels — became sufficiently displeased to trigger a nationwide reform movement. With the publication of *A Nation at Risk* in 1983, a diverse group of civil rights and corporate interests led a national educational reform movement. This was inspired by concern over equity issues and the inability of industry to compete successfully in world markets because of the low knowledge and skill levels of high school graduates.

In the 1990s, the reform movement continued unabated, with nearly every state developing assessment programs to monitor and track the learning progress of students and schools. With the advent of the standards movement, the role of the superintendency was shifted even further away from district manager to that of testing expert.

Top-down reform programs, assessment, and testing were initiated in many states in the 1980s. Many of these so-called reforms focused on testing of students and teachers. Legislation created more extensive systems of teacher evaluation and, in some cases, curriculum review.

The effect of these actions often was more bureaucracy, but few changes, since mandates, but not always funding, increased. In states such as Illinois, superintendents concluded that state reform programs initially had no impact, or a negative impact, on their school districts (Glass, 1989). In response, many superintendents and their districts resisted demands made by state legislatures.

The 1980s era of school reform, dominated by state and federal initiatives, created a backseat role for superintendents and school boards, thus putting a damper on successful results. The emergence in 1990 of "choice" movements across the country, as well as advocacy for more control at the local level by principals, parents, teachers, and students themselves, has brought additional challenges to superintendents' authority and policymaking.

The Future of the Superintendency

What will be the role of the superintendent in the 21st century and beyond? Will it be as a facilitator of a number of school buildings located in a certain geographical area, as "choice" and site-based management would indicate? Or will it be as a professional educational executive with a vision for the direction and means by which the district will improve the quality of public education? Or, might it be as a chief executive officer, not necessarily trained or experienced in the public schools?

In 1982, AASA endorsed a series of essential skills for school administrators known as "Guidelines for the Preparation of School Administrators." This publication was later succeeded by the work of the AASA-sponsored National Commission on the Superintendency, which developed a set of professional standards for the superintendency (Hoyle, 1993). A later AASA-sponsored publication, entitled *Skills for Successful 21st Century School Leaders* (Hoyle, English, Steffy, 1998), put those standards into action. These three documents now serve as benchmarks of professional standards for the practice and preparation of future superintendents.

For the superintendency to survive and flourish into the 21st century, superintendents will need to serve as role models, demonstrating the high degree of professionalism necessary to increase their influence in policymaking at the local and state levels. In addition, they will need to attract political support by encouraging needed changes in curriculum and educational technology clearly aligned to a strategic vision. A focus on the future, which involves all the players, both inside and outside the school district, will make the job of the superintendent that of a master juggler in an increasingly complex organization (Carter and Cunningham, 1997).

No definite answers have emerged as to who will develop educational policy and who will control schools in the early 21st century. Every governor claims to be an "education governor" and every president claims to be the "education president." Are these leaders who will seize control of the public schools, or will state legislatures and the courts maintain their strong influence on setting educational policy? Can private sector groups continually whittle away public support and tax dollars and direct them toward private purposes? Most importantly, will parents and other citizens, who believe strongly in public schools, continue to influence legislative policy that funds schools?

In the 21st century, it is likely that American superintendents will revert to the role of their predecessors in the 19th century. They will be the "guardians" of public education, defending and insuring its continued existence. The challenges of 30 years of continuous criticism from the political right; parsimonious legislatures; and emergence of vouchers, charter schools, home schooling, and privatization have all created a climate where strong and knowledgeable education leaders will have to resist efforts to funnel tax dollars away from public schooling. The dream of Horace Mann, and other founders of the concept of a public education, will be seriously challenged in the 21st century.

If school boards and superintendents are to retain their historical leadership positions, they must be open to significant change in areas such as board training and superintendent preparation. They must also examine whether their current roles and activities are consistent with the vision and needs of school systems of the 21st century.

Bibliography

American Association of School Administrators. (1982). *Guidelines for Preparation of School Administrators*. Arlington, VA: Author.

Blumberg, A. (1985). *The Superintendent: Living with Conflict*. New York: Teachers College Press.

Bolman, L.G. and T.E. Deal. (1997). (2nd edition). *Reframing Organizations*. San Francisco: Jossey-Bass.

Bridges, E.M. (1992). *Problem Based Learning for Administrators*. Eugene, OR: ERIC.

Callahan, R.E. (1966). *The Superintendent of Schools*. Eugene, OR: ERIC.

Carter, G.R. and W. G. Cunningham. (1997). *The American School Superintendent: Leading in an Age of Pressure*. San Francisco: Jossey-Bass.

Cuban, L. (1988). *The Managerial Imperative and the Practice of Leadership in Schools*. Chicago: University of Chicago Press.

Cubberly, E.C. (1922). *Public School Administration*. New York: Houghton-Mifflin.

Eaton, W.E. (1992). "The vulnerability of school superintendents: The thesis reconsidered" in *Shaping the Superintendency: a Reexamination of Callahan and the Cult of Efficiency*. W.E. Eaton (Ed.). New York: Teachers College.

Glass, T.E. (1998). *1998 Survey of Illinois Superintendents*. Springfield, IL: Illinois Association of School Administrators.

Glass, T.E. (1997). "The superintendency: yesterday, today, and tomorrow" in Chapman, C.H. (1997) *Becoming a Superintendent:Challenges of School District Leadership*. Saddle River: Prentice-Hall.

Grogan, M.M. (1996). *Voices of Women Aspiring to the Superintendency*. Albany: SUNY Press.

Hoyle, J.R. (1993). *Professional Standards for the Superintendency*. Arlington, VA: American Association of School Administrators.

Hoyle, J.R., F. W. English, and B. E. Steffy. (1998). *Skills for Successful 21st Century School Leaders*. Arlington, VA: American Association of School Administrators.

Johnson, S.M. (1996). *Leading to Change: The Challenge of the New Superintendency*. San Francisco: Jossey-Bass.

Kowalski, T.J. (1999). *The School Superintendent: Theory, Practice and Cases*. Prentice-Hall: Saddle River.

Norton, M.S., L. D. Webb, L. L. Dlugosh, and W. Sybouts. (1996), *The School Superintendency: New Responsibilities, New Leadership*. Needham Heights: Allyn and Bacon.

Shipman, N. and J. Murphy. (1996). *Interstate School Leaders Licensure Consortium: Standards for School Leaders*. Washington, DC: Council of Chief State School Officers.

Spring, J. (1998). (3rd edition). *Conflict of Interests: The Politics of American Education*. Boston: McGraw-Hill.

Chapter 2

The 2000 Study

Thomas Glass

Overview

The 2000 Study of the American School Superintendency follows similar reports issued each decade, beginning in 1923, under the auspices of the Department of Superintendence of the National Education Association. In 1952, the American Association of School Administrators took over the responsibility of the Ten-Year Studies, and has since produced a major survey project each decade. Reports of the previous studies have appeared in various formats, including yearbooks and, most recently, in formal survey project reports. The formal names of each of these studies are, "The Status of the Superintendent in 1923"; "Educational Leadership, 1933"; "The American School Superintendent, 1952"; "Profile of the School Superintendent, 1960"; "The American School Superintendent, 1971"; "The American School Superintendency in 1982" and "The 1990 Study of the American School Superintendency: America's Education Leaders in a Time of Reform." No survey was conducted during the 1940 - 1941 period due to World War II.

The content and the direction of the studies have been varied. So have the sampling techniques, subjects, and issues covered. However, all of the studies have defined the superintendency, who superintendents are, and what they do in their school districts. The 1933 study, conducted during the height of the Depression, looked ahead to the future of the nation, as well as to the role schools would play in the economic and social growth of a rapidly changing world. Special attention has been devoted in some of the studies, such as the one in 1952, to the similarities and differences between urban and rural superintendents. The 1960 Study, in a yearbook format, discussed the preparation of individuals who wanted to become superintendents. During this period, the nation's schools were expanding rapidly, and the preparation of new leaders was of great concern.

The 1971 Study took a different direction. Profiles of urban and rural superintendents were discontinued, and a new format, consisting of about 100 questions, was adopted and subsequently used for the 1982, 1992, and 2000 studies. Some comparisons between the 1971, 1982, 1992 and 2000 survey studies are possible because of similarities in format and question content. The collection of chronological data over nearly a half-century is one of the strengths of the Ten-Year Studies.

Data collection for the 2000 Study was conducted through a survey mailed in 1999 to practicing superintendents across the nation. Additional data used in this report were obtained from previous studies conducted under the sponsorship of AASA.

Survey Objectives

The 2000 Ten-Year Study has four objectives:

- To provide current information on the superintendency to national, state, and local education policymakers, the media, and superintendents themselves.

- To provide trend data that can be compared to studies conducted in 1960, 1971, 1982, and 1992.

- To provide an overview of public education from the perspective of its executive leaders.

- To provide researchers with data and analyses about public education and the superintendent leaders in the 1990s who will lead American public school districts into the 21st century.

Survey Population

The 12,604 superintendents comprising the population of the study are active superintendents in regular public school districts. There are hundreds of "other" superintendents who serve (1) regional districts; (2) intermediate districts; (3) special education districts; (4) county districts; and (5) correctional districts. For instance, Illinois has about 50 regional superintendents and several who serve legally constituted districts in juvenile correctional centers. The likely total number of superintendents of all types is around 13,500.

Content Areas

The content of the 2000 survey partially reflects previous surveys, especially those conducted in 1982 and 1992. Particular attention was paid to maintaining trend data over the past 10 to 20 years.

The 2000 Study includes data on the following:

- Personal profiles of superintendents, including gender, age, family status, education, and area of residence.

- Relationships with board members, including evaluation and terms of employment.

- Characteristics of school districts, including staffing, hiring practices, programming, and size.

- Selected community characteristics, including superintendent involvement and influence in district decision making.

- Superintendents' opinions on key problems and issues confronting public education on the eve of the 21st century.

- The involvement and participation of women and minorities in the superintendency.

- Issues surrounding the preparation of superintendents and professional development of practicing superintendents.

- Career patterns of superintendents.

Instrument Development

The survey instrument used in the 2000 Study was an adjustment of the instrument used in the 1992 Study. The items in the 1992 instrument were largely taken from the 1982 instrument. This was done to provide comparative data. The 2000 instrument development was a joint activity between AASA staff and the researchers. Items were indexed to survey objectives to ensure that data would be available for each objective. In a trial administration of the instrument, respondents took about 25 minutes to complete the questions. They also provided feedback about unclear wording.

Sample Selection

The stratified random sample was obtained from the Common Core of Data Public Education Agency Universe maintained by the U.S. Department of Education, which generates summary information for 12,604 identified school superintendents by type of district and total enrollment.

There are many types of districts, even some without students. The districts identified by the U.S. Department of Education must be said to be "approximate descriptions," as many legally constituted districts do not possess a superintendent, or sometimes share a superintendent with another district. The superintendents comprising the population of the study are active superintendents in regular public school districts. There are hundreds of "other" superintendents such as in special education districts; region districts; and intermediate, county, and correctional districts. The total number of superintendents is about 13,700.

Samples by types of districts and enrollment categories selected were the following:

- **GROUP A:** Districts with enrollments greater than or equal to 25,000 pupils: 222 sampled.

- **GROUP B:** Districts with enrollments greater than or equal to 3,000, but fewer than 25,000 pupils: 1,175 sampled.

- **GROUP C:** Districts with enrollments greater than or equal to 300, but fewer than 3,000 pupils: 3,065 sampled.

- **GROUP D:** Districts with enrollments of fewer than 300 pupils: 874 sampled (see Table 2.1).

An examination of the sample drawn (5,336) of a population of 12,604 was thought to be of an adequate size and proportion to reflect the immense diversity of public school districts and superintendents in the nation. The return rate was 42.4 percent, which is adequate for a mail-out survey with 86 items.

In addition, special attention was paid to ensure that gender and racial diversity in previous studies be reflected to meet the objectives of continuing trend data. The sample reflects the fact that a significant number of American public school districts are still rural, even though over one-third of U.S. students attends school in one of the 10 largest school districts.

TABLE 2.1 2000 SURVEY SAMPLE GROUPS*

PUPIL ENROLLMENT CLASSIFICATION	INCLUDED IN EACH CLASSIFICATION		PUBLIC SCHOOL SUPTS RECEIVING QUESTIONNAIRES		RETURNED QUESTIONNAIRES	
	NUMBER	PERCENT OF TOTAL SUPTS	NUMBER SAMPLED	PERCENT SAMPLED OF EACH GROUP	NUMBER	PERCENT OF THOSE SAMPLED
GROUP A: 25,000 OR MORE	222	1.7	222	100.0	95	42.8
GROUP B: 3,000 TO 24,999	2,648	21.0	1,175	44.3	546	46.4
GROUP C: 300 TO 2,999	7,358	58.3	3,065	41.6	1,346	43.9
GROUP D: FEWER THAN 300	2,376	18.8	874	36.7	251	28.7
TOTALS	12,604	100.0	5,336	42.3	2,262	42.3

* Sample size for each table varies according to number of responses to individual survey items.

TABLE 2.2 SIZE OF DISTRICTS PARTICIPATING IN SAMPLE

PUPILS SERVED	NO. OF DISTRICTS	TOTAL %
MORE THAN 100,000	9	0.3
50,000-99,999	20	1.1
25,000-49,999	66	3.4
10,000-24,999	98	4.4
5,000-9,999	177	7.9
3,000-4,999	271	12.2
1,000-2,999	752	33.2
300-999	594	26.2
LESS THAN 300	251	11.2
TOTAL	2,262	100.0

NOTE: The mean size of districts in the sample group is 4,026

In the smallest districts, those with 300 or fewer students, the individual in charge may be called a superintendent, but in fact, is also principal, business manager and perhaps even a part-time teacher.

Large city superintendents serve many of the minority students in the entire country. Also, the 10 largest districts in the nation are majority minority, as are most of the other 25 largest. A majority of these superintendencies are held by minority superintendents

Survey Implementation and Return Rate

The 5,336 survey instruments were mailed to superintendents in April 1999. There were few requests for additional information or assistance in filling out the instrument. As has been mentioned earlier, a trial test indicated that a superintendent would need about 25 minutes to complete the instrument. All district information requested on the instrument is normally found in the office of a superintendent.

TABLE 2.3 HOW DOES YOUR PRESENT ENROLLMENT COMPARE WITH THAT OF JANUARY 1992?

	GROUP A 25,000 OR MORE PUPILS		GROUP B 3,000-24,999 PUPILS		GROUP C 300-2,999 PUPILS		GROUP D FEWER THAN 300 PUPILS		NATIONAL UNWEIGHTED PROFILE	
	No.	%	No.	%	No.	%	No.	%	No.	%
INCREASE OF 25% OR MORE	22	23.4	119	21.9	185	13.9	21	8.5	347	15.7
INCREASE OF 20 TO 24%	13	13.8	48	8.8	78	5.9	6	2.4	145	6.6
INCREASE OF 15 TO 19%	11	11.7	49	9.0	88	6.6	7	2.8	155	7.0
INCREASE OF 10 TO 14%	6	6.4	76	14.0	131	9.9	22	8.9	235	10.6
INCREASE OF 5 TO 9%	13	13.8	62	11.4	151	11.4	21	8.5	247	11.2
INCREASE OF LESS THAN 5%	13	13.8	77	14.2	248	18.7	38	15.4	376	17.0
DECREASE OF 25% OR MORE	1	1.1	5	.9	36	2.7	33	13.4	75	3.4
DECREASE OF 20 TO 24%	1	1.1	1	.2	22	1.7	11	4.5	35	1.6
DECREASE OF 15 TO 19%	1	1.1	11	2.0	38	2.9	10	4.1	60	2.9
DECREASE OF 10 TO 14%	2	2.1	22	4.1	80	6.0	25	10.2	129	5.8
DECREASE OF 5 TO 9%	3	3.2	28	5.2	115	8.7	25	10.2	171	7.7
DECREASE OF LESS THAN 5%	8	8.5	45	8.3	156	11.7	27	11.0	236	10.7
TOTAL	94	100.0	543	100.0	1328	100.0	246	100.0	2211	100.0

• The mean enrollment increase for sample districts was +5.87

TABLE 2.4 IN WHICH GEOGRAPHICAL REGION IS YOUR SCHOOL DISTRICT LOCATED?

	GROUP A 25,000 OR MORE PUPILS		GROUP B 3,000-24,999 PUPILS		GROUP C 300-2,999 PUPILS		GROUP D FEWER THAN 300 PUPILS		NATIONAL UNWEIGHTED PROFILE	
	No.	%	No.	%	No.	%	No.	%	No.	%
NEW ENGLAND	2	2.1	33	6.0	75	5.6	3	1.2	113	5.1
ROCKY MOUNTAINS	5	5.3	18	3.3	49	3.6	24	9.6	96	4.3
SOUTHEAST	26	27.7	106	19.4	127	9.5	6	2.4	265	11.9
GREAT LAKES	8	8.5	111	20.3	350	26.1	42	16.8	511	22.9
MIDEAST	12	12.8	97	17.8	206	15.3	19	7.6	334	15.0
SOUTHWEST	16	17.0	65	11.9	145	10.8	37	14.8	263	11.8
PLAINS	3	3.2	53	9.7	299	22.3	92	36.8	447	20.0
FAR WEST	19	20.2	61	11.2	80	6.0	25	10.0	185	8.3
ALASKA	1	1.1	1	.2	4	.3	1	.4	7	.3
HAWAII	1	1.1	0	0.0	0	0.0	0	0.0	1	.0
OTHER	1	1.1	1	.2	8	.6	1	.4	11	.5
TOTAL	94	100.0	546	100.0	1343	100.0	250	100.0	2233	100.0

By June 1999, all completed surveys were forwarded by AASA to the principal researcher for tabulation and analysis. The number of usable surveys returned was 2,262, for a return rate of 42.4 percent, or 18 percent of all identified superintendents. Table 2.1 describes the sample and return rate in more detail.

Data Analysis

Data contained in the 2,262 usable surveys were coded and processed by Peter Abrams, Professor Emeritus at Northern Illinois University in July/August 1999. The statistical analysis was performed using Social Science Statistical Package software. Data were analyzed for the total response group, as well as enrollment strata, gender, and minority categories. Simple percentage and cross-tabulations are used in this text because of the wide variety of readers it aims to serve, both inside and outside the field of education. Additional statistical test and measurement data generated by the study can be obtained by contacting the study's lead researcher, Thomas Glass, at tglass@memphis.edu.

TABLE 2.5 SELECTED CHARACTERISTICS OF SAMPLE SUPERINTENDENTS

	GROUP A: 25,000 OR MORE PUPILS	GROUP B: 3,000-24,999 PUPILS	GROUP C: 300-2,999 PUPILS	GROUP D: FEWER THAN 300 PUPILS	ALL GROUPS
MALE	79	469	1191	199	1938
FEMALE	16	77	149	52	294
MINORITY	21	36	50	7	114
NON-MINORITY	73	508	1289	242	2112
YEARS AS SUPERINTENDENT	8.59	8.78	6.82	8.35	8.35
YEARS AS CLASSROOM TEACHER	5.4	6.79	8.1	10.6	7.9
APPOINTED FROM INSIDE DISTRICT	40	200	407	60	707
APPOINTED FROM OUTSIDE DISTRICT	55	341	933	191	1520

NOTE: Three female superintendents and three minority superintendents did not indicate the size of their district.

TABLE 2.6 ARE YOU SUPERINTENDENT OF MORE THAN ONE DISTRICT?

	GROUP A: 25,000 OR MORE PUPILS		GROUP B: 3,000-24,999 PUPILS		GROUP C: 300-2,999 PUPILS		GROUP D: FEWER THAN 300 PUPILS		ALL GROUPS	
	No.	%	No.	%	No.	%	No.	%	No.	%
YES	5	5.5	8	1.5	44	3.4	11	4.5	68	3.2
NO	86	94.5	515	98.5	1243	96.6	233	95.5	2077	96.8
TOTAL	91	100.0	523	100.0	1287	100.0	244	100.0	2145	100.0

TABLE 2.7 IF YES, HOW MANY?

	GROUP A: 25,000 OR MORE PUPILS		GROUP B: 3,000-24,999 PUPILS		GROUP C: 300-2,999 PUPILS		GROUP D: FEWER THAN 300 PUPILS		NATIONAL UNWEIGHTED PROFILE	
	No.	%	No.	%	No.	%	No.	%	No.	%
1	0	0.0	0	0.0	1	2.1	1	8.3	2	2.9
2	0	0.0	3	60.0	38	79.2	9	75.0	50	72.5
3	1	25.0	2	40.0	5	10.4	2	16.7	10	14.5
4	2	50.0	0	0.0	3	6.3	0	0.0	5	7.2
5	1	25.0	0	0.0	1	2.1	0	0.0	2	2.9
TOTAL	4	100.0	5	100.0	48	100.0	12	100.0	69	100.0

District Size of the Sample Group

While the return rate was low for superintendents of districts enrolling fewer than 300 students, this should not be a concern to policymakers who seek to influence schooling of large numbers of students. This is because the smallest districts, even when counted as a whole, serve a comparatively small number of students.

The excellent return rates for the other three groups, especially superintendents from districts with more than 25,000 students, further strengthens the validity of the data. In Table 2.3, the decline of enrollment in many small districts can be seen between 1990 and 2000.

The shifts in the national population illustrated in this table, as well as in the number of children in families, suggest district demographics be considered in policies addressing reform or restructuring. Some large districts are getting much larger, and small rural districts are in decline. The composition of the sample groups in terms of demography and personal characteristics is discussed elsewhere in the report.

The *baby boomlet* is clearly evident when looking at the two-digit percentage increases in the larger district size types. Thirty-five districts with over 25,000 students grew more than 20 percent in a 10-year period. This means that a student increase of at least 5,000 must be housed and provided with teachers. This is tremendous growth. Even more difficult to visualize is that three of the districts of 100,000 students reported growing more than 20 percent in the 10-year period.

Very few of the very small districts reported significant growth during the 10-year period, perhaps indicating consolidation of districts and population movement to more urban areas.

Geographical Dispersion of the Sample Group

The greatest number of returns was from the Great Lakes and Plains states. This is also where the greatest number of school districts exist. It is interesting that only 185 superintendents responded from the Far West; California has over 1,000 districts, and Oregon and Washington together have about 400.

Selected Characteristics of the Sample Group

The sample group of 2,262 appears to reflect the general characteristics of the nation's superintendents. The percentages of women and minorities are very close to national figures.

The superintendents in this study have been superintendents for about eight years and served as classroom teachers for about seven to eight years. In previous Ten-Year Studies, superintendents had served as teachers about five to six years. About twice as many superintendents were appointed from outside the district as inside the district.

Superintendents Serving More than One District

The organization of school districts is sometimes surprising. It is not uncommon for one superintendent to serve more than one school district. In the 2000 Study sample, there are 68 superintendents serving more than one district. Forty-four of those served at least one district of 300 to 2,999 students. Therefore, the number of districts represented in the sample is greater than the number of superintendents represented.

Chapter 3

Personal Characteristics

Lars Björk

Overview

Widespread concern for the quality of schooling during the last two decades of the 20th century launched what is arguably the most intense, comprehensive, and sustained effort to improve education in American history. As the nature of educational reform shifted in form and texture (Murphy, 1990), it was accompanied by growing national debate on conditions of the superintendency and superintendents' roles in school reform. Compelling arguments for improving classroom instruction, and fundamentally altering the manner in which schools are structured, managed, and governed, not only challenged conventional assumptions about the nature of schooling, but also called for redefining superintendents' work. Speculation about the ways the superintendency is changing and may change (see Crowson, 1988) underscores a need for understanding not only the complex organizational and political issues facing superintendents, but also the personal characteristics of those who serve in these positions. Questions posed to the sample of superintendents elicited information that delineates who they are, where they come from, their ages, political inclinations, and other dimensions of their personal lives. This delineation may provide a framework for developing a composite picture of the typical superintendent based on district enrollment size.

Gender and Race

The characteristics of superintendents reported by scholars during recent years (Hodgkinson and Montenegro, 1999; Johnson, 1996; Kowalski, 1995) are generally consistent with findings in this study. Most superintendents are married, white, male, of middle age, come from small towns, have advanced degrees in educational administration, and, for the most part, share common values and opinions.

This study, like those released in 1982 and 1992, found that the vast majority (94.9 percent) of American superintendents are white, and 86.6 percent are male. However, the number of female and minority superintendents has increased since 1992. The number of female superintendents increased from 6.6 percent in 1992, to 13.2 percent in 2,000. Superintendencies held by minorities moved from 3.9 percent to 5.1 percent during the same period. Although these data indicate progress, they also confirm a dramatic underrepresentation of these two groups in relation to white males. The extraordinary disparity between men and women in the superintendency is paradoxical in the field of education, an enterprise dominated by women serving as teachers, principals, and central office staff. Of the more than four million professional educators in the nation (Blount, 1998) only a few women (fewer than 2,000) serve in executive leadership positions.

Data suggest the near absence of women in the superintendency may have less to do with their lack of training, availability, or presence in the administrator "pipeline" than other factors related to search and selection processes. During the past decade, the number of women eclipsed men in professional preparation programs. In 1993, over half of education-related master's and doctoral degree students were women, and one fifth were minorities (Milstein and Associates, 1993; Murphy, 1993).

Male and female superintendents have remarkably different perceptions of barriers faced by women entering the profession. Men do not view the following factors as hindrances to women entering the superintendency: lack of recruiting by boards of education; opportunities to gain professional experience; professional networks; or likelihood of a glass ceiling to career advancement. Female superintendents, on the other hand, see these as important. There is also a large discrepancy in perceptions of hiring and promotional practice between white superintendents and minority superintendents. Close to 50 percent of minority superintendents see these issues as major problems, while only 10 percent of white superintendents view them in the same way. Understanding significant gender- and racially-related differences between superintendents' hiring and promotional experiences and perceptions may help boards of education, professional associations, search consultants, state education agencies, practicing superintendents, and professional preparation programs to address these barriers.

As the proportion of minorities in the nation's population increases in the 21st century, they will have a significant impact on the nature of schooling, how schools are governed, and who leads them. Demographic projections indicate that, by the year 2020, one-third of the nation will be non-white, and the proportion of minority students in American schools will increase to 38 percent (Hodgkinson, 1985, 1991). Additional estimates indicate that, in the 21st century, a larger proportion of the nation's youth will have to be more highly educated, and that minority students, those historically least well served by schools, will constitute a significant segment of the nation's future workforce (Björk, 1996a). Since the early 1980s, the nation's business leaders have, in their quest for economic self-preservation, become acutely aware of the strategic importance of public schools in preparing this future workforce. In this context, access and excellence, issues once considered by policymakers as being mutually exclusive, are now viewed as intrinsically related. Liberals and conservatives became natural allies in promoting the education of all children, particularly those at risk. Together, they have contributed to efforts directed towards increasing the number of minorities in school administration to serve both as advocates and as role models. Growth in the number of minority superintendents during the past decade is promising, but remains unacceptably low.

Gender

The American school superintendency, like many other high-profile executive leadership positions in the public and private sector, is dominated by white males. Historically, the percentage of women in the superintendency varied considerably. Blount (1998) reported that in 1910, 8.9 percent of school superintendents were women, increasing to 10.98 percent in 1930, then declining to 9.07 percent in 1950. In 1952, 6.7 percent of sampled superintendents were women, but many were located in small rural districts. During this period, consolidation of small school districts in which many women served as chief executive officers probably reduced their numbers (Glass, 1992). Consequently, the number of women serving in the superintendency precipitously declined to 1.3 percent in 1971, and stayed low well into the next decade (1.2 percent in 1982).

In 1992, 6.6 percent of superintendents surveyed were women, climbing to 14 percent in 2000, the highest level achieved during the 20th century. The greatest gains for women in the superintendency over the past decade were in suburban/urban districts serving 3,000 - 24,999 students. The number of female superintendents in these districts nearly tripled, moving from 5 percent in 1992, to 14.1 percent in 2000. In addition, 71 percent of female superintendents responded that they were working under their first contract. More than one-third of the 297 female superintendents had been superintendents for fewer than 3 years and 58 percent had served fewer than 5 years. This suggests that the gains for women as superintendents are rather recent. Sixty-eight percent of female respondents were in rural/suburban districts with fewer than 2,999 students (See **Table 3.1** and **Chapter 6**). The increased number of female superintendents is a laudable achievement; however, women continue to be significantly underrepresented in the superintendency. The United States Census Bureau has characterized the superintendency as being the most male-dominated executive position of any profession in the United States.

A growing body of research on women in school administration suggests that the characteristics of female school administrators, while different from those of men, are highly desirable qualities for leaders in educational reform initiatives. Although these findings may not apply to every individual in every school setting, they nonetheless support the notion that women bring considerable professional capital to the superintendency.

In general, women tend to be more concerned with teachers and marginal students, are more motivational, and value working with parents and the community. Consequently, school staffs rate female superintendents more highly than male superintendents. These staff members also tend to be more productive, and to have higher morale than those led by male superintendents. Students in these districts also have higher morale than students in districts with male superintendents, and parents view schools and districts headed by women more favorably. Women also tend to have greater knowledge of instructional methods, spend more time assisting new teachers, tend to supervise teachers directly, and create school climates more conducive to learning. In addition, female superintendents encourage participation, use democratic leadership styles, achieve higher levels of participation, maintain more closely knit organizations, and produce higher levels of job satisfaction than do their male counterparts (Frascher and Frascher, 1979; Hemphil, Griffiths, and Fredericksen, 1962; Shakeshaft, 1987).

Women need to become a part of the discourse of professional preparation programs so that they may assume their place in the superintendency (Grogan, 1996, 2000). Women bring to practice many of the characteristics currently missing and thought necessary for reform. These characteristics are extremely pertinent to all superintendents as they consider changing their practices. While

TABLE 3.1 GENDER OF RESPONDENTS

GENDER	GROUP A: 25,000 OR MORE PUPILS		GROUP B: 3,000-24,999 PUPILS		GROUP C: 300-2,999 PUPILS		GROUP D: FEWER THAN 300 PUPILS		NATIONAL UNWEIGHTED PROFILE	
	No.	%	No.	%	No.	%	No.	%	No.	%
MALE	79	83.2	469	85.9	1191	88.9	199	79.3	1938	86.8
FEMALE	16	16.8	77	14.1	149	11.1	52	20.7	294	13.2
TOTAL	95	4.2	546	24.4	1340	60.0	251	11.2	2232	100.0

TABLE 3.2 RACE OF RESPONDENTS

RACE	GROUP A: 25,000 OR MORE PUPILS		GROUP B: 3,000-24,999 PUPILS		GROUP C: 300-2,999 PUPILS		GROUP D: FEWER THAN 300 PUPILS		NATIONAL UNWEIGHTED PROFILE	
	No.	%	No.	%	No.	%	No.	%	No.	%
WHITE	73	76.8	508	93.4	1289	96.4	242	97.2	2112	94.9
BLACK	14	14.7	22	3.9	14	1.0	0	0.0	50	2.2
HISPANIC	7	7.4	9	1.7	13	.9	2	.8	31	1.4
ASIAN	0	0.0	3	0.6	2	0.1	0	0.0	5	0.2
NATIVE AMERICAN	0	0.0	2	0.4	12	0.9	4	1.6	18	0.8
OTHER	1	1.1	0	0.0	9	0.7	1	0.4	11	0.5
TOTAL	95	100.0	544	100.0	1339	100.0	249	100.0	2227	100.0

the women's movement and equity legislation may have positively influenced the attitudes of some individuals, it has not dramatically altered the norms and values that perpetuate the "glass ceiling" that limits career advancement for women in the superintendency.

Growth in the percentage of women in the superintendency over the past several decades may result from changes in individuals' perceptions and an increasing will to ensure equitable treatment in search and selection processes. In her discussion of issues related to women and minorities gaining access to the superintendency, Tallerico (1999b) identifies a number of factors that have previously helped, as well as those that may thwart future efforts. Kamler and Shakeshaft (1989) support the notion that some search consultants are proactive in recruiting women, help to educate boards of education about the strengths of women in executive leadership positions, and advocate for more equitable search and selection processes. Aspiring women who are linked to university professors, superintendent networks, and board of education networks are more likely to learn about superintendent vacancies and district circumstances. Chase and Bell (1990) found that search firms (headhunters) and boards of education serve as gatekeepers of the superintendency and can be "positively disposed toward women as education leaders," "supportive of women in leadership positions," and "helpful to individual women" (p.174). They apparently fail to see the contradiction of providing support "even while simultaneously reinforcing systems and ideologies that perpetuate males' predominance in the superintendency" (Tallerico, 1999b). Although encouragement and support of women may be increasing, these individual acts have neither altered organizational practices nor enhanced the social responsibility essential to changing a system dominated by white males (Chase and Bell, 1990; Tallerico, 1999a, b; Young, 1999). [For a more complete discussion of gaining access to the superintendency see Tallerico, M. (1999a, b).]

Race

Although most historical data on minority superintendents tend to focus on African Americans, recent studies of Hispanics in school administration (Ortiz, 1998) have expanded our understanding of the diverse characteristics of those who serve as chief executive officers. Early reports on minorities in the superintendency between the 1930s -1950s indicate their numbers were sparse, and they were predominantly employed in black districts in southern states (AASA, 1983). The American Association of School Administrators, in their report, *Women and Racial Minority Representation In School Administration* (1993), found that superintendents of different racial backgrounds tend to serve in areas where persons of the same race live in significant numbers. In 1980, only 2.1 percent of superintendents were minorities (Cunningham and Hentges, 1982), increasing to 3.2 percent a decade later (Jones and Montenegro, 1990). In 1993, minorities accounted for 3.9 percent of superintendents in the nation; however, nearly half (46 percent) were employed in urban districts with

TABLE 3.3 AGES OF SUPERINTENDENTS

AGE	GROUP A: 25,000 OR MORE PUPILS		GROUP B: 3,000-24,999 PUPILS		GROUP C: 300-2,999 PUPILS		GROUP D: FEWER THAN 300 PUPILS		NATIONAL UNWEIGHTED PROFILE	
	No.	%	No.	%	No.	%	No.	%	No.	%
30-35	0	0.0	0	0.0	10	0.7	7	2.8	17	0.8
36-40	0	0.0	4	0.7	27	2.0	9	3.6	40	1.8
41-45	4	4.2	25	4.6	95	7.1	27	10.9	151	6.8
46-50	15	15.8	130	24.0	344	25.7	75	30.2	564	25.3
51-55	29	30.5	227	41.9	505	37.7	61	24.6	822	36.9
56-60	32	33.7	111	20.5	263	19.9	47	19.0	453	20.4
61-65	12	12.6	40	7.4	87	6.5	18	7.3	157	7.1
66+	3	3.2	5	0.9	9	0.7	4	1.6	21	0.9

more than 50,000 students (Glass, 1992). In several of the nation's large cities, demographic changes in several racial groups have made minority groups majority populations. There are, however, comparatively few majority minority medium size districts with minority superintendents (Rist, 1991).

According to the current national profile, 5.1 percent of the nation's superintendents are minorities. Most serve in large/urban or small town/rural districts. More than 50 percent of minority superintendents serve in districts with 3,000 or more students. Of the 95 superintendents in this study who serve in districts with enrollments of more than 25,000 students, 23 percent were minorities (see **Table 3.2**).

Although the number of minority superintendents serving as school superintendents increased by 31 percent over the past decade, concerns are being raised that the number may plateau or precipitously decline as their presence in the administrator "pipeline" declines (Björk, 1996b). Increasing the number of minorities in the superintendency in the future is dependent on a number of factors, including increasing the number of minority teachers, principals, and central office staff in the "pipeline" (Hodgkinson and Montenegro, 1999). This will prove difficult as opportunities for minorities expand in better paying fields, thus decreasing interest in pursuing a career in education. This situation may be corrected through state and federal initiatives or grants from philanthropic organizations to support the identification and training of minorities in all professional levels of education. Other important factors include initiatives that support efforts by search consultants and boards of education to remove barriers to career advancement (Tallerico, 2000) (See **Chapter 7**).

Age

It appears that the superintendency is an aging profession. The 1923 AASA study found a median age of 43.1, the youngest age registered in eight consecutive studies. Between 1950 and 1992, the median age of superintendents hovered around 48 to 50. Since 1992, however, the median age of superintendents increased to 52.5; the oldest recorded median age during the 20th century (see **Figure 3.1** and **Table 3.4**). In districts with enrollments of greater than 25,000 students, nearly 40 percent of superintendents were under age 50 in 1992, declining to 20 percent in 2000. In 1992, a slim majority of superintendents, 59.3 percent, from districts with fewer than 300 students, were less than 50 years old. In 2000, however, only 47.5 percent of the sample fell into this category. In 1992, 29 percent of superintendents over the age of 55 are serving in urban districts with enrollments of more than 25,000 students, whereas, in 2000, 49.5 percent were above that age (See **Table 3.4**). Although there are generally very few superintendents over the age of 60, it is evident that their presence has increased in very large districts with 25,000 or more students, and very small districts with fewer than 300 students. In 1992, 10.4 percent of superintendents over 60 were serving in large, urban districts, whereas in 2000, 15.8 percent held similar chief executive positions. In districts with fewer that 300 students, those over 60 increased from 4.8 to 8.9 percent during the

TABLE 3.4 AGES OF SUPERINTENDENTS: 1971, 1982, 1992, AND 2000 COMPARISONS

AGE GROUP	GROUP A 25,000 OR MORE PUPILS				GROUP B 3,000-24,999 PUPILS				GROUP C 300-2,999 PUPILS				GROUP D FEWER THAN 300 PUPILS			
	1971	1982	1992	2000	1971	1982	1992	2000	1971	1982	1992	2000	1971	1982	1992	2000
UNDER 40	3.6	4.5	1.4	0.0	7.1	6.3	3.3	0.7	21.5	14.8	8.1	2.7	46.5	35.3	17.0	6.4
40-44	13.9	13.4	10.4	4.2	22.2	13.8	15.3	4.6	23.5	18.2	21.6	7.1	11.3	16.1	24.5	10.9
45-49	19.0	21.4	28.5	15.8	20.9	22.1	28.9	24.0	15.6	21.6	28.1	25.7	14.1	14.7	17.8	30.2
50-54	19.0	25.0	26.4	30.5	21.8	30.3	27.1	41.9	15.2	22.3	22.2	37.7	2.8	19.2	21.7	24.6
55-59	10.7	27.7	18.7	33.7	16.7	20.8	18.7	20.5	15.9	18.1	15.5	19.0	8.5	8.5	14.2	19.0
60+	24.8	7.2	10.4	15.8	11.3	6.8	6.8	8.3	8.3	4.9	4.5	7.0	16.9	6.2	4.8	8.9

same period. However, 66 percent of the women were between the ages of 46 - 55, slightly younger than the national average. (See **Table 3.3, Figure 3.2** and **Chapters 4, 5,** and 7).

Career Path

The overall median age of superintendents of about 50, recorded during the 1950 - 2000 period, is not surprising considering the time involved in "moving through the ranks" characteristic of the typical career path. Recent studies claim that fewer young professional educators are aspiring to the superintendency (Daresh and Playko, 1992), making issues related to career paths of great interest to boards of education, professional associations, and policymakers (Kowalski, 1995). In retrospect, the typical career track of superintendents has not changed appreciably over the past decade. Even though few individuals who begin their careers as teachers plan to become superintendents, current data point to two career paths. The most common (48.5 percent) is from teacher to assistant principal or principal to central office administrator to superintendent. The second most prevalent path (31.2 percent) is from teacher to assistant principal or principal to superintendent. In 1992, 36.4 percent of superintendents in the sample took the first career track, and 37.7 percent took the second route. The first career path appears to be most common among superintendents serving in large urban districts with more than 25,000 students and urban/suburban districts with 3,000-24,999 students. The second pattern (teacher to principal to superintendent) appears to be most common in very small districts with fewer than 300 students and suburban/rural districts with fewer than 2,999 students. That trend is understandable given that these districts tend to have fewer professional central office positions that may serve as stepping-stones to the superintendency (see **Table 3.5).**

It appears that during the past decade aspiring superintendents are spending more time in the "ranks" before becoming CEOs. Each of these career steps requires additional years of graduate study and professional experience. Most students across educational administration programs are characterized as part-time students who pursue their graduate degrees or certification on a part-time basis during evenings and in summer school (McCarthy, 1999). The typical career path, a professional rite of passage, significantly increases the average age of superintendents. Most individuals do not aspire to become a school administrator until mid-career, usually when serving as an assistant principal or principal. Superintendents typically spend an average of six to seven years as a classroom teacher before obtaining their first administrative position. A large majority (84 percent) become an assistant principal or principal between the ages of 25 – 35. Superintendents obtained their first superintendency an average of 1.4 years after being certified and actively seeking a position, and 56 percent indicated they had served in only one district.

TABLE 3.5 CAREER PATHS OF RESPONDENTS

CAREER PATH	GROUP A: 25,000 OR MORE PUPILS No.	%	GROUP B: 3,000-24,999 PUPILS No.	%	GROUP C: 300-2,999 PUPILS No.	%	GROUP D: FEWER THAN 300 PUPILS No.	%	NATIONAL UNWEIGHTED PROFILE No.	%
TEACHER, PRINCIPAL & CENTRAL OFFICE	65	68.4	322	59.0	624	46.4	74	29.5	1085	48.5
PRINCIPAL & CENTRAL OFFICE	3	3.2	11	2.0	20	1.5	2	0.8	36	1.6
TEACHER & CENTRAL OFFICE	11	11.6	84	15.4	89	6.6	13	5.2	197	8.8
TEACHER & PRINCIPAL	6	6.3	83	15.2	488	36.3	121	48.2	698	31.2
CENTRAL OFFICE ONLY	1	1.1	11	2.0	8	0.6	6	2.4	26	1.2
PRINCIPAL ONLY	0	0.0	4	0.7	24	1.8	4	1.6	32	1.4
TEACHER ONLY	1	1.1	3	0.5	27	2.0	18	7.2	49	2.2
OTHER	8	8.4	28	5.1	65	4.8	13	5.2	114	5.1
TOTAL	95	100.0	546	100.0	1345	100.0	251	100.0	2237	100.0

ndents indicated they were hired from outside the district in
strative positions, confirming earlier observations of the imper-
, 87.5 percent spent their professional careers in one state. The
achers at 23, before obtaining an assistant principalship or
30s; securing a central office staff position in their late 30s. They
arly to mid-40s and serve in this position between 15 -18 years,
nce 1992. Most superintendents (69.4 percent) hold contracts
e often given several three-year contracts in the same district.

young superintendents before they move to larger, better
changing. In the 1970s and 1980s, more superintendents under
all districts. In 1971, for instance, 46.5 percent of all superinten-
rollments of fewer than 300 students were under the age of 40.
t, and in 2000, only 6.4 percent. The same trend is seen in
e 21.5 percent of superintendents were under 40 in 1971,
92, and 2.1 percent in 2000.

rly Retirement

for early retirement at age 55. With a median age of 52.5, this
er of superintendents may retire in the middle of the coming
st this is not highly probable. The study finds that current
e of 8.5 years in the superintendency and are at midpoints in
s, it is anticipated that nearly 8,000 new superintendents will
ars, with nearly half of those needed in districts serving
rural areas and small towns.

A number of factors tend to hasten or delay early retirement. The study finds that 60.4 percent of
superintendents intend to serve in the superintendency until they are eligible for retirement,
whereas only 14.3 percent express their intent to continue until minimum retirement age. Several
studies (Glass, 1989) have found that many superintendents who announce their intentions to retire
early often hang on for "just one more year." The increasing median age, however, may suggest that
rather than taking early retirement, many superintendents are remaining in their positions until
they retire in their early 60s.

TABLE 3.6 CAREER PATTERN PRIOR TO SUPERINTENDENCY—2000-1992 COMPARISONS

CAREER PATTERNS	GROUP A: 25,000 OR MORE PUPILS		GROUP B: 3,000-24,999 PUPILS		GROUP C: 300-2,999 PUPILS		GROUP D: FEWER THAN 300 PUPILS		NATIONAL UNWEIGHTED PROFILE	
	2000	1992	2000	1992	2000	1992	2000	1992	2000	1992
TEACHER ONLY	1.1	.7	.5	2.7	2.0	5.4	7.2	17.7	2.2	5.9
PRINCIPAL ONLY	-	.7	.7	2.7	1.8	5.7	1.6	4.6	1.4	4.0
CENTRAL OFFICE ONLY	1.1	5.2	2.0	2.8	.6	1.0	2.4	.8	1.2	2.0
TEACHER & PRINCIPAL	6.3	17.2	15.2	18.2	36.3	49.7	48.2	53.2	31.2	36.4
TEACHER & CENTRAL OFFICE	11.6	17.2	15.4	13.6	6.6	8.1	5.2	5.1	8.8	10.3
PRINCIPAL & CENTRAL OFFICE	3.2	5.2	2.0	5.7	1.5	2.5	.8	1.3	1.6	3.7
TEACHER, PRINCIPAL, & CENTRAL OFFICE	68.4	53.7	59.0	54.3	46.4	27.6	29.5	17.3	48.5	37.7
OTHER/NOT SURE	8.4	7.3	5.1	5.5	4.8	6.0	5.2	-	5.1	-
TOTAL	100.0	100.0	100.0	100.0	100.0	100.0	100.0	100.0	100.0	100.0

Attrition

The issue of superintendent attrition and supply emerged as a significant issue among boards of education, practitioners, and policymakers during the latter part of the 1990s. Heightened concern for the lack of adequate financing, accountability for student learning outcomes on standardized tests, administrator-board relations, recruitment and selection of teachers, as well as demands for new ways of teaching and "doing administration" have changed the nature of superintendents' work and increased stress. These circumstances have also helped to create perceptions that superintendents are leaving the profession faster than they could be replaced (Brockett, 1996). However, national attrition levels have not changed appreciably over the past several decades. In fact, data suggest the median age of superintendents has increased since 1992, suggesting that they are entering the superintendency later in their professional careers, and, projections indicate, staying longer.

Current estimates of the attrition rate for superintendents are based upon a number of assumptions. Given that the median age of superintendents has increased from 48.5 to 52.5 over the past decade, and the average length of time served in the position is 8.5 years, most superintendents enter the profession later in their careers than during previous decades. Most begin their careers in their mid-40s and serve in 2 to 3 different districts during careers lasting approximately 15 to 18 years. In 2000, most superintendents are mid-career and may retire in their early to mid-60s. The predicted massive exodus of superintendents in the coming decade will probably not occur. What we most likely will experience is a modest attrition rate of 5 to 6 percent per year for the coming decade (2000 - 2010), a rate not unlike that experienced during the 1990s. The rate of attrition, however, may be increased by state education policy decisions. For example, demands for systemic reform placed on superintendents by the 1990 Kentucky Education Reform Act (KERA) dramatically increased superintendent resignations and retirements during the first 5 years of this legislative initiative to a level approaching 20 percent per year. Despite a robust economy in Colorado during the 1990s, legislative reform initiatives severely limited growth of educational expenditures and restricted superintendents to one-year contracts. During this same period, Colorado's superintendent attrition equaled that of Kentucky. It is difficult to track the number of superintendents actually leaving the profession, as many individuals may resign and move to another district in state, move to a district out of state, retire, or retire from one school district and obtain superintendency in another state to get additional pension benefits.

A prudent estimate is that during the coming decade half of the nation's superintendents will be replaced. Boards probably will not be so vulnerable to high attrition rates if the nation continues to enjoy a sound economy, modest inflation, and better health of its chief executive officers. Any or all of these assumptions, however, could change without warning.

Marital Status

The superintendency is a highly visible public position. Traditionally, many male superintendents' wives have been teachers or homemakers who generally believed their roles required participation in school affairs (akin to that of the clergy). In the past, the superintendents' visibility in the community altered their lives as well as the lives of their spouses and children. Brinson (1997) observes that "much of the ability to be successful as a superintendent may be attributed to the help and support of the superintendent's spouse and family" (p. 29). How a superintendent's wife enacts her supportive role is highly individualistic. Phyllis Blumberg (1985) characterized the role as being a "helpmate wife," emphasizing that it was "a necessity of life in the superintendent's family" (p.185). This situation, however, may be changing, as the number of women in the workplace increases and the male spouses of female superintendents pursue their own careers.

In 1992, the overwhelming majority of superintendents (92.3 percent) were married. In 2000, 92.4 percent are married. In 1992, of the 7.7 percent indicating they were not married: two percent were single, 5.6 percent were divorced/separated, and 0.8 percent were widowed. In 2000, the survey eliminated two categories, divorced/separated and widowed, forcing non-married respondents (7.6 percent) to select "single" (See **Table 3.7**). Only 5.3 percent of men were single in comparison to 23 percent of female superintendents.

Spouses often play a big role in superintendents' decisions to accept new jobs. Typically, men are less accustomed to the idea of disrupting their professional lives for a spouse (*The School Administrator*, October 1990). In some cases, the prospect of relocating might create a hardship for female superintendents in their 40s or 50s who have husbands employed in local communities and children in school who are not willing to relocate. The increasing number of women in the superintendency, however, may indicate a greater willingness among men to support career moves by their spouses. In this regard, the notion of a superintendent's spouse being a "helpmate wife" may be in the process of being redefined.

Politics and Political Party Preference

Politics. The notion of politics in education has long been a troublesome issue that carries negative connotations. It frequently is portrayed as the antithesis of professional behavior (Kowalski, 1999), and many educators persist in the belief that politics has no place in the schoolhouse. Arthur Blumberg (1985) explains that educators tend to view teaching and learning as an important societal function; a sacred trust that should not be tainted by partisan politics, manipulation by community interest groups, or power struggles among board of education members. They conceive of politics in a narrow sense of the term, and envision shady deals being made by old cronies in smoke-filled back rooms. Although superintendents may encounter the negative side of politics in the form of corrupt patronage practices, discrimination, nepotism, and political pressure, they may also experience the best traditions of democracy. These can include the direct involvement of citizens, parents, teachers, and legislators in resolving differences and making decisions about the distribution of educational values and resources.

During the past three decades, politics in education has moved from being a spectator sport to active participation of citizens, all in the same districts. Even though the culture of education mitigates against viewing the superintendency as political, superintendents are drawn almost daily into contact with elected public officials, special interest groups, and elected or appointed members of boards of education, and are asked to orchestrate efforts to obtain voter support for school bond issues (Blumberg, 1985). They not only are in the fray (Johnson, 1996) but also are expected to have "extraordinarily good political acuity — including knowing how to apply power and effectively communicate with diverse groups" (Carter & Cunningham, 1997, p. 44). Research on the superintendent as political leader suggests that this work extends well beyond local communities and boards of education; frequently involving superintendents in regulatory and policy issues deliberated by education agencies, state legislatures, and professional associations. Researchers and practi-

TABLE 3.7 MARITAL STATUS OF SUPERINTENDENTS

MARITAL STATUS	GROUP A: 25,000 OR MORE PUPILS		GROUP B: 3,000-24,999 PUPILS		GROUP C: 300-2,999 PUPILS		GROUP D: FEWER THAN 300 PUPILS		NATIONAL UNWEIGHTED PROFILE	
	No.	%	No.	%	No.	%	No.	%	No.	%
SINGLE	11	11.7	37	6.8	92	6.9	26	10.4	166	7.5
MARRIED	83	88.3	506	93.2	1234	93.1	223	89.6	2046	92.5
TOTAL	94	100.0	543	100.0	1326	100.0	249	100.0	2212	100.0

tioners concur that school boards are composed of political factions or are aligned with special interest groups, which often makes superintendents' work uncommonly difficult. Their ability to work with individual board members and influence key education policy decisions not only may determine the success of the district, but also the length of their tenure (Kowalski, 1999).

Questions about superintendents/board of education relations (McCarty & Ramsey, 1971) and democratic responsiveness of school boards to their local community (Zeigler & Jennings, 1974) have a long history. Fundamentally, these questions are concerned with the exercise of power. McCarty and Ramsey (1971), in *School Managers,* approach understanding superintendent-board relations through an analysis of community political structures. They assert that four types of community power structures exist (dominated, factional, pluralistic, and inert) and that the character of the school board reflects the nature of the community power structure. Thus, there are four kinds of school boards (dominated, factional, status congruent, and sanctioning). In addition, the role of the superintendent is determined by the character of the board vis-a-vis the community (functionary, political strategist, professional advisor, and decision maker). Their research findings generally supported the notion of a positive correlation between similar types of communities, and school boards, and superintendents' roles. McCarty and Ramsey (1971) anticipated that superintendents would be more adept at changing their ways to fit changing community interests and positions of boards of education. However, they found that superintendents tend not to see the need to work in a fashion congruent with political power structures in the community or factions on boards of education, preferring to act as professional advisors and decision makers. McCarty and Ramsey (1971) were also highly critical of educational administration programs for stressing the importance of superintendents' roles as managers, professional advisors, and decision makers to the near exclusion of their roles as political leaders or development of their political analytical skills and suitable leadership strategies.

A sizable majority of superintendents in the 2000 survey, 66 percent, characterized boards of education as being active and aligned with community interests. A modest number of superintendents, 19 percent, characterized board members as representing distinct factions in the community, and 12.5 percent characterized boards as not being active in communities, preferring to accept recommendations made by the superintendent and other district professional staff. Very few superintendents characterized boards of education as being dominated by elitists (2.5 percent). In districts with more than 25,000 students, however, 32 percent of superintendents characterized school boards as representing distinct factions in the community. In very small districts with fewer than 300 students, only 14 percent of superintendents characterized board members in this fashion. (See **Table 3.8**) Six percent of minority superintendents tended to characterize board members as representing elitists in the community, and 27 percent thought of board members as representing factions. In comparison, 2.5 percent of white superintendents characterized board members as representing elitists, and 19 percent as representing factions. Fewer female superintendents (3.4 percent) view boards as dominated by elitists, and 24 percent think of board members as representing factions. Minority superintendents also view boards as being more active and less willing to accept recommendations made by the superintendent and district professional staff than whites. Female superintendents share this view.

Superintendents indicated that board of education members give very great weight or considerable weight to superintendents, central office staff, and principals rather than power structures or special interest groups in local communities. In a similar fashion, superintendents indicated they give very great weight or considerable weight to board of education members, principals, central office staff, and fellow superintendents, rather than community group sources of information for decision making.

Forty-eight percent of superintendents characterized the way in which they work with boards of education as serving as a professional advisor, presenting alternatives and consequences in an objective fashion Fifty percent characterized their work as initiating action to maintain district effectiveness. Nearly half (42.5 percent) of superintendents view themselves as being primarily responsible for developing policy and policy options, while more than one-third (36.4 percent) share that role with boards of education. They indicated that central office staff had a greater role in formulating policy than boards of education. In large districts with more than 25,000 students, only 20 percent of superintendents viewed themselves as being primarily responsible for developing policy. In these districts, often marked by fractious politics, 43 percent of superintendents view formulating policy as a shared responsibility. In very small districts, the opposite appears to be the case. Fifty-three percent of superintendents in districts with fewer than 300 students tend to view themselves as being primarily responsible for formulating district education policy (see **Table 3.9**). In addition, 89 percent of superintendents indicate that boards of education accept their policy recommendations 90 - 100 percent of the time. Domination of the nature and direction of policy formation in school districts by superintendents (management), rather than boards of education (community representatives), directly opposes the normative policy-making process in democratic societies.

Even though research suggests that the politics in education have intensified over the past 30 years, this study confirms that superintendents recognize that board of education members are aligned with factions and community interests. However, they continue to imperil themselves by disregarding the need to behave in a political fashion by adopting different leadership styles to fit changing circumstances. In 2000, superintendents generally regard boards of education as being active and aligned with community interests, rather than representing factions or elitists. Community interests, however, not only are diverse but also inconstant. These characteristics underscore the importance of understanding the political dynamics of communities and learning to work effectively in these contexts. Unfortunately, superintendents prefer to enact roles as professional advisors to boards of education, initiating action (i.e., "doing administration" and developing district policy) (see **Table 3.10**). While they appear to be highly successful in getting their recommendations adopted, 39 percent indicated that the administrator-board relationship is one of the most signifi-

TABLE 3.8 PERCEPTIONS OF SCHOOL BOARD MEMBERS

PERCEPTIONS	GROUP A: 25,000 OR MORE PUPILS		GROUP B: 3,000-24,999 PUPILS		GROUP C: 300-2,999 PUPILS		GROUP D: FEWER THAN 300 PUPILS		NATIONAL UNWEIGHTED PROFILE	
	No.	%	No.	%	No.	%	No.	%	No.	%
DOMINATED BY ELITE	1	131	17	3.1	36	2.7	5	2.0	59	2.6
REPRESENTS DISTINCT FACTIONS	30	32.3	107	19.6	251	18.7	35	13.9	423	19.0
ALIGNED COMMUNITY INTERESTS	59	63.4	374	68.6	868	64.6	170	67.7	1471	65.9
NOT ACTIVE	3	3.2	47	8.6	188	14.0	41	16.3	279	12.5
TOTAL	93	100.0	545	100.0	1343	100.0	251	100.0	2232	100.0

TABLE 3.9 WAYS IN WHICH SUPERINTENDENTS WORK WITH SCHOOL BOARDS

PERCEPTIONS	GROUP A: 25,000 OR MORE PUPILS		GROUP B: 3,000-24,999 PUPILS		GROUP C: 300-2,999 PUPILS		GROUP D: FEWER THAN 300 PUPILS		NATIONAL UNWEIGHTED PROFILE	
	No.	%	No.	%	No.	%	No.	%	No.	%
CUES FROM DOMINANT GROUP	2	2.1	8	1.5	11	0.8	5	2.0	26	1.2
RELATIONS WITH ALL FACTIONS	1	1.1	9	1.7	23	1.7	4	1.6	37	1.6
PROFESSIONAL ADVISOR	31	33.0	245	45.0	644	48.0	143	57.4	1063	47.7
INITIATE ACTION	60	63.8	282	51.8	665	49.5	97	39.0	1104	49.5
TOTAL	94	100.0	544	100.0	1343	100.0	249	100.0	2230	100.0

cant issues challenging superintendents now and in the future. This finding should not be surprising, given the disconnection between the political nature of the job and superintendents' preference for serving as professional advisors and managers.

Superintendents' roles are learned through informal and formal professional socialization as they progress in their careers as teachers, principals, and central office staff, as well as in the position of chief executive officer. They successfully advance their careers, not only because of their mastery of administrative skills, but also because of their perceived congruence with the norms, beliefs, attitudes, and values of schools. The notion of politics is absent from the culture of education. Thus, it is understandable that superintendents enact their roles of professional advisors and managers; those prescribed, learned, and reinforced by the culture of schools.

In addition, the problem identified by McCarty and Ramsey in 1971, that educational administration programs emphasize managerial and professional dimensions of superintendents' work, while neglecting political aspects of their jobs, remains the case in 2000. Changing superintendents' preference for "doing administration" presents a particularly difficult challenge to the field. There are, however, indications that the preparation of aspiring superintendents may be changing. The reform era provided a valuable crucible to test thinking about how the next generation of school leaders are identified and prepared. Since 1988, we "have witnessed the most intense effort to redefine educational leadership that we have seen in the short history of the profession" (Murphy and Louis, 1999, p. 475). The challenge of rethinking professional preparation has been taken up by a wide variety of stakeholders, including the American Association of School Administrators, the University Council for Educational Administration, the National Policy Board for Educational Administration, the Danforth Foundation, and others who are proposing a broad range of options. There is solid consensus that professional preparation programs must be reconfigured to confront the problems that face school administrators.

An important outcome of discussions about leadership and superintendent preparation is a recognition of the heightened political nature of the work of school leaders, and acknowledgement that they need to acquire political skills to work effectively in emerging contexts of schools and communities. Acknowledging that "politics can be both professional and valuable" (Murphy and Louis,

TABLE 3.10 COMPARISON OF THE SUPERINTENDENTS' VIEWS OF SCHOOL BOARDS

SCHOOL BOARD	GROUP A: 25,000 OR MORE PUPILS		GROUP B: 3,000-24,999 PUPILS		GROUP C: 300-2,999 PUPILS		GROUP D: FEWER THAN 300 PUPILS		NATIONAL UNWEIGHTED PROFILE	
	No.	%	No.	%	No.	%	No.	%	No.	%
DOMINATED BY ELITE IN COMMUNITY	1	1.7	1	1.7	32	53.3	26	43.3	60	100.0
REPRESENT FACTIONS IN COMMUNITY	13	3.0	17	3.9	224	52.0	177	41.1	431	100.0
ACTIVE, ALIGNED WITH INTERESTS	10	0.7	11	0.7	722	48.9	732	49.6	1475	100.0
NOT ACTIVE, ACCEPT RECOMMENDATIONS OF PROFESSIONAL STAFF	2	0.7	8	2.8	92	32.7	179	63.7	281	100.0
TOTALS	26	100.0	37	100.0	1070	100.0	1114	100.0	2247	100.0

TABLE 3.11 POLITICAL PARTY PREFERENCES OF SUPERINTENDENTS

POLITICAL PARTY PREFERENCE	GROUP A: 25,000 OR MORE PUPILS		GROUP B: 3,000-24,999 PUPILS		GROUP C: 300-2,999 PUPILS		GROUP D: FEWER THAN 300 PUPILS		NATIONAL UNWEIGHTED PROFILE	
	No.	%	No.	%	No.	%	No.	%	No.	%
DEMOCRAT	46	49.5	180	33.8	449	34.0	91	37.6	766	35.0
INDEPENDENT	21	22.6	189	35.5	420	31.8	58	24.0	688	31.5
REPUBLICAN	26	28.0	164	30.8	450	34.1	93	38.4	733	33.5
TOTAL	93	100.0	533	100.0	1319	100.0	242	100.0	2187	100.0

1999, p. xxvi) for superintendents in carrying out managerial, instructional, and institutional leadership tasks, may present an opportunity to temper the field's long-standing aversion to "playing politics." As the complexity of school organizations increases, and participation in governance and decision making expands, administrators will need to learn new ways of working. Although changing administrator attitudes, and expanding the scope of professional preparation programs to include micro-politics may be uncommonly difficult; continuance of an apolitical stance may be inappropriate and counterproductive. Some educational administration programs have moved beyond a traditional emphasis on management, and have incorporated notions of instructional and political leadership (Björk, 1993; Johnson, 1996). However, few have the time or resources needed for intensive training in these areas. To work successfully in uncertain and often turbulent political environments, superintendents must be adept at analyzing the political dynamics of communities and boards of education and proficient in using a wide variety of leadership styles appropriate to changing circumstances.

Political parties. Very few superintendents in the nation obtain their offices through partisan political elections or through appointment by mayors or city councils. Beyond this fact, superintendents respond that they do have political party preferences. The level of activity of superintendents in supporting the political party of their choice is not known, nor is the political affiliation of their spouses. Data indicate that there is appreciably little difference in the percentage of superintendents indicating preference for Democratic (35 percent) or Republican (33.5 percent) or independent party affiliation (31.5 percent). Large city superintendents favor the Democratic Party (49.5 percent), which coincides with the traditional political voting pattern of their communities. Superintendents serving in rural/suburban districts with 300 - 2,999 students were more evenly divided between Democrats, Republicans, and Independents (see **Table 3.11**). There is little difference in political party preference according to superintendents' age (see **Tables 3.12 and 3.13**) or gender. Fifty-nine percent of minority superintendents are Democrat.

TABLE 3.12 POLITICAL PARTY PREFERENCE OF SUPERINTENDENTS, ANALYZED BY AGE

	INDEPENDENT		DEMOCRATIC		REPUBLICAN	
AGE	No.	%	No.	%	No.	%
30-35	3	0.4	5	0.7	7	1.0
36-40	11	1.6	14	1.8	12	1.6
41-45	39	5.7	51	6.7	58	7.9
46-50	189	27.5	201	26.2	168	23.0
51-55	275	40.0	263	34.3	273	37.1
56-60	124	18.1	169	22.0	158	21.4
61-65	42	6.1	58	7.4	50	6.7
66+	4	0.6	6	0.8	10	1.3

TABLE 3.13 POLITICAL PARTY PREFERENCE OF SUPERINTENDENTS, ANALYZED BY AGE: 1982, 1992, AND 2000 COMPARISONS

	INDEPENDENT			DEMOCRATIC			REPUBLICAN		
	1982	1992	2000	1982	1992	2000	1982	1992	2000
AGE*	%	%	%	%	%	%	%	%	%
30-34	43.5	35.3	20.0	30.4	17.6	33.3	23.9	47.1	46.7
35-39	35.8	35.2	29.7	26.5	35.2	37.8	37.7	29.5	32.5
40-44	35.5	31.1	26.4	29.5	32.9	34.4	34.6	36.0	39.2
45-49	32.2	26.1	33.9	31.9	34.8	36.0	35.5	39.1	30.1
50-54	33.9	29.4	33.9	32.4	35.2	32.4	33.6	35.4	33.7
55-59	33.8	27.0	27.5	31.3	35.8	37.5	33.8	37.2	35.0
60+	25.0	17.2	27.1	33.8	38.4	37.6	41.2	44.4	35.3

* NOTE: The age groupings presented here were used in 1982 and 1992. The age groupings for the 2000 data are shown in Table 3.12.

In addition, when asked whether they considered themselves liberal, conservative, or moderate, 57 percent of superintendents, regardless of whether they are Democrat or Republican, perceive themselves as moderates (see **Table 3.14**). Only a small minority, 11 percent, see themselves as liberal, and about one-third view themselves as conservative. The political postures of superintendents are fairly typical of the majority of middle class, college-educated Americans. Sixty-seven percent of minority superintendents view themselves as moderates, compared to 56 percent of whites. A majority of female superintendents, 62 percent, also view themselves as moderates. Superintendents serving in rural and suburban districts, with fewer than 2,999 students, however, tend to view themselves as conservative.

Community Background

Survey data indicate that superintendents continue to reflect the contemporary composition of American society in terms of community size origins. Traditionally, superintendents have reflected the rural or small town origins of most Americans. Considering that superintendents' median age was close to 50 in 1971, most of them were born shortly after World War I or just before the Great Depression. At that time, America was in the early stages of urbanization. Vocational and professional opportunities were limited in rural and small towns, and graduates often attended "normal" schools (later state colleges), usually located in small towns. These "colleges" were much less expensive to attend than universities, and were more convenient for aspiring educators from rural communities (Tyack and Hansot, 1982).

In the 2000 Study, most superintendents responding were born in the mid-1940s. The parents of these "baby boomers" benefited greatly from the GI Bill. Enrollments in colleges and universities increased to a level unprecedented in the history of American higher education. The expansion of state-supported institutions and, later, regional campuses that served rural areas and small towns, enabled many returning veterans to complete their college degrees. The remarkable increase in the birth rate in the mid-1940s created an unparalleled demand for teachers, which provided opportunities for many new college graduates. Despite the nation's urbanization over the past 60 years, 75 percent of superintendents in 2000 had rural/small town origins and only 25 percent of superintendents came from suburban upbringings. This finding is similar to those reported in 1982. It appears that, in 1992, a temporary shift in superintendent origins occurred, with fewer superintendents having rural/small town origins (56 percent) and suburban/urban upbringings (44 percent) (see **Table 3.15**).

TABLE 3.14 POLITICAL POSTURE OF SUPERINTENDENTS

POLITICAL POSTURE/VIEWS	GROUP A: 25,000 OR MORE PUPILS		GROUP B: 3,000-24,999 PUPILS		GROUP C: 300-2,999 PUPILS		GROUP D: FEWER THAN 300 PUPILS		NATIONAL UNWEIGHTED PROFILE	
	No.	%	No.	%	No.	%	No.	%	No.	%
LIBERAL	15	16.5	65	12.1	136	10.2	27	11.0	243	11.0
MODERATE	60	65.9	362	67.4	709	53.4	114	46.5	1245	56.6
CONSERVATIVE	16	17.6	110	20.5	483	36.4	104	42.4	713	32.4
TOTAL	91	100.0	537	100.0	1328	100.0	245	100.0	2201	100.0

TABLE 3.15 TYPE OF COMMUNITY IN WHICH SUPERINTENDENTS SPENT PRECOLLEGE YEARS: 1971, 1982, 1992, AND 2000

COMMUNITY TYPE	1971	1982	1992	2000
RURAL/SMALL TOWN	86.0	78.0	56.0	74.9
SUBURBAN/URBAN	14.0	22.0	44.0	25.1

After completing study at normal schools or state colleges, the most common career path for superintendents of the 1930s and 1940s was a teaching position in a small school; then a principalship in a small district; and, finally, a superintendency. However, after World War II, men graduating from college under the auspices of the GI Bill began to obtain teaching jobs in larger districts in more urban and suburban communities. The growth of the suburbs after World War II provided many of these educators their first superintendency. In 1992, the number of suburban/urban superintendents sampled doubled from 22 to 44 percent, but declined to 25 percent in 2000. In 2000, 71.4 percent of superintendents served in rural and small town districts with fewer than 2,999 students.

Superintendents serving in rural and small town districts tend to come from communities of similar size. In this study, 63 percent of superintendents were raised in communities with fewer than ten thousand people. In a similar fashion, 59 percent of superintendents serving in districts with fewer than 300 students were raised in communities with fewer than 2,500 people, and 63 percent serving in districts with less than 2,999 students, grew up in communities with fewer than 10,000 people. Surprisingly, 39 percent of superintendents in districts with more than 25,000 students still claim rural or small town origins. More than half of these come from a community of fewer than 2,500 people (See **Table 3.16**). Large city superintendents typically come from medium and large communities. Nearly 38 percent of superintendents serving in districts with more than 25,000 grew up in large cities. In districts with student enrollments of between 3,000 to 25,000 students, superintendents are also predominantly from small town and rural backgrounds (see **Table 3.17**). The influences of small town and rural origins on the attitudes and behaviors of superintendents have not been thoroughly studied. But survey responses in 1992 and 2000 suggest superintendents, as a group, are moderately conservative in their social values and lifestyles. This profile matches that of the teaching ranks from which they come (Lortie, 1975).

TABLE 3.16 TYPE OF COMMUNITY LIVED IN BEFORE COLLEGE (ANALYZED BY AGE)

COMMUNITY TYPE	AGE 45 OR YOUNGER		AGE 46-50		AGE 51-55		AGE 56-60		AGE 61 OR OLDER		NATIONAL UNWEIGHTED	
	No.	%	No.	%	No.	%	No.	%	No.	%	No.	%
RURAL	104	50.2	202	35.6	262	31.7	168	36.7	57	32.0	793	35.5
SMALL TOWN	56	27.1	193	34.0	293	35.4	149	32.5	66	37.1	757	33.8
SUBURBAN	30	14.5	108	19.1	141	17.0	74	16.2	24	13.5	377	16.8
LARGE CITY	17	8.2	64	11.3	132	15.9	67	14.6	31	17.4	311	13.9
TOTAL	207	100.0	567	100.0	828	100.0	458	100.0	178	100.0	2238	100.0

TABLE 3.17 TYPE OF COMMUNITY IN WHICH SUPERINTENDENT SPENT PRECOLLEGE YEARS

COMMUNITY TYPE	GROUP A: 25,000 OR MORE PUPILS		GROUP B: 3,000-24,999 PUPILS		GROUP C: 300-2,999 PUPILS		GROUP D: FEWER THAN 300 PUPILS		NATIONAL UNWEIGHTED PROFILE	
	No.	%	No.	%	No.	%	No.	%	No.	%
RURAL	18	18.9	128	23.6	518	38.6	122	48.8	786	35.3
SMALL TOWN	19	20.0	185	34.1	467	34.8	85	34.0	756	33.9
SUBURBAN	22	23.2	129	23.8	197	14.7	27	10.8	375	16.8
LARGE CITY	36	37.9	100	18.5	159	11.9	16	6.4	311	14.0
TOTAL	95	100.0	542	100.0	1341	100.0	250	100.0	2228	100.0

Bibliography

American Association of School Administrators. (1983). *Perspectives on Racial Minority Women School Administrators.* Alexandria, VA: Author.

American Association of School Administrators. (1993). *Women and Racial Minority Representation in School Administration.* Alexandria, VA: Author.

Bell, C. (1995). '"If I weren't involved with schools, I might be radical": Gender consciousness in context.' In D. Dunlap and P. Schmuck (Eds.), *Women Leading in Education.* Albany, NY: State University of New York Press.

Björk, L. (1993). "Effective schools ;effective superintendents: The emerging instructional leadership role." *Journal of School Leadership* 3: 246-259.

Björk, L. (1996a). "The revisionists' critique of the education reform reports." *Journal of School Leadership* 6: 290-315.

Björk, L. (1996b). "Educational reform in changing contexts of families and communities: Leading school-interagency collaboration." In Lane, K. and M. Richardson (Eds.). *The School Safety Handbook: Taking Action for Student and Staff Protection* (253-275). Lancaster, PA: Technomic Publishing Company.

Blount, J. M. (1998). *Destined to Rule the Schools: Women and the Superintendency, 1873-1995.* Albany, NY: State University of New York Press.

Blumberg, A. (1985). *The School Superintendent: Living with Conflict.* New York: Teachers College Press.

Blumberg, P. (1985). "Being a superintendent's wife." In Blumberg, A. *The School Superintendent: Living with Conflict,* (172-185). New York: Teachers College Press.

Brinson, K.H. (1997). "The impact of the superintendency on the spouses and families of retired public school superintendents." Unpublished dissertation, The Pennsylvania State University.

Brockett, D. (1996). "Boards find fewer superintendent candidates." *School Board News* 16, 10: 1.

Carter, G. and W. Cunningham. (1997). *The American School Superintendent: Leading in the Age of Pressure.* San Francisco: Jossey-Bass.

Chapman, C. H. (1997). *Becoming a Superintendent: Challenges of School District Leadership.* Upper Saddle River, NJ: Merrill.

Chase, S. (1988). *Ambiguous Empowerment: The Work Narratives of Women School Superintendents.* Amherst, MA: University of Massachusetts Press.

Chase, S. and C. Bell. (1990). "Ideology, discourse, and gender: How gatekeepers talk about women school superintendents." *Social Problems* 37: 163-177.

Crowson, R. L. (1988). Editors introduction. *Peabody Journal of Education* 65, 4: 18.

Cunningham, L. and J. Hentges. (1982). *The American School Superintendency 1982: A Summary Report.* Arlington, VA: American Association of School Administrators.

Daresh, J.C. and M. A. Playko. (1992, April). "Aspiring administrators' perceptions of the superintendency as a viable career choice." Paper presented at the Annual meeting of the American Educational Research Association. San Francisco, CA.

Frascher, J. and R. Frascher. (1979). "Educational administration: A feminine profession." *Educational Administration Quarterly* 15: 1-15.

Glass, T.E. (1992). *The Study of the American School Superintendency: America's Education Leaders in a Time of Reform.* Arlington, VA: American Association of School Administrators.

Glass, T.E. (1989). *Survey of Illinois Superintendents.* Springfield, IL: Illinois Association of School Administrators.

Grogan, M. (1996). *Voices of Women Aspiring to the Superintendency.* Albany, NY: SUNY Press.

Grogan, M. (2000). "A reconception of the superintendency from feminist/postmodern perspectives." *Educational Administration Quarterly.*

Hemphil, J., D. Griffiths and N. Fredericksen (Eds.) (1962). *Administrative Performance and Personality.* New York: Teachers College Press.

Hodgkinson, H. (1985). *All one system: Demographics of Education, Kindergarten through Graduate School.* Washington, DC: Institute for Educational Leadership.

Hodgkinson, H. (1991). "Reform vs. reality." *Phi Delta Kappan* 73, 1:8-16.

Hodgkinson, H. and X. Montenegro. (1999). *The U.S. School Superintendent: The Invisible CEO.* Washington, DC: Institute for Educational Leadership.

Johnson, S. M. (1996). *Leading to Change: The Challenge of the New Superintendency.* San Francisco: Jossey-Bass.

Jones, E. and X. Montenegro. (1990). *Women and Minorities in School Administration.* Arlington, VA: American Association of School Administrators.

Kamler, E. and C. Shakeshaft. (1999). "The role of search consultants in the career path of women superintendents." In C.C. Brunner (Ed.) *Sacred Dreams: Women and the Superintendency* (51-62). Albany, NY: SUNY Press

Kantor, R. (1987). *Men and Women of the Corporation.* New York: Basic Books, Inc.

Kowalski, T. J. (1995). *Keeper of the Flame: Contemporary Urban Superintendents.* Thousand Oaks, CA: Corwin.

Kowalski, T.J. (1999). *The School Superintendent: Theory, Practice, and Cases.* Upper Saddle River, NJ: Prentice-Hall.

Lortie, D. (1975). *Teacher.* Chicago: University of Chicago Press.

McCarthy, M. (1999). "The evolution of educational leadership preparation programs." In Murphy, L. and K. S. Louis. *Handbook of Research on Educational Administration, 2nd edition.* (119-139). San Francisco: Jossey-Bass.

McCarty, D. and C. Ramsey. (1971). *The School Managers.* Westport, CN: Greenwood.

Milstein, M. (1990). "Rethinking the clinical aspects in administrative preparation: From theory to practice." In S. L. Jacobson and J. Conway (Eds.), *Educational Leadership in an Age of Reform.* New York: Longman.

Milstein and Associates. (1993). *Changing the Way We Prepare Educational Leaders: The Danforth Experience.* Newbury Park, CA: Corwin.

Moody, C. (1985, August). "The black superintendent." *National Scene* (Magazine Supplement). 22: 9-14.

Murphy, J. (1990). "The educational reform movement of the 1980s: A comprehensive analysis." In J. Murphy (Ed.) *The Reform of American Public Education in the 1980s: Perspectives and Cases.* Berkeley, CA: McCutchan.

Murphy, J. (Ed.). (1993). *Preparing Tomorrow's School Leaders: Alternative Designs.* University Park, PA: UCEA.

Murphy, J. and K. S. Louis. (1999). "*Handbook* editors' introduction: Notes from the *Handbook.*" *Educational Administration Quarterly* 35: 472-476.

Ortiz, F. (1998, April). "Who controls succession in the superintendency? A minority perspective." Paper presented at the Annual meeting of the American Educational Research Association. San Diego, CA.

Pitner, N. J. and R. Ogawa, R. (1981). "Organizational leadership: The case of the school superintendent." *Educational Administration Quarterly* 17, 2: 45-65.

Rist, M.C. (December 1991). "Race and Politics Rip Into the Urban Superintendency." *Executive Educator* 12, 12: 12-14.

Shakeshaft, C. (1987). *Women in Administration.* Newbury Park, CA: Sage Publications.

Shakeshaft, C. (1989). "The gender gap in research in educational administration." *Educational Administration Quarterly* 25: 324-337.

Shein, E. H. (1992). *Organizational Culture and Leadership (2nd ed.).* San Francisco: Jossey-Bass.

Tallerico, M. (1999a). *Accessing the Superintendency: The Unwritten Rules.* Thousand Oaks, CA: Corwin.

Tallerico, M. (1999b). "Gaining access to the superintendency: Headhunting, gender, and color." *Educational Administration Quarterly.*

Tyack, D.B. and E.E. Hansot. (1982). *Managers of Virtue: Public School Leadership in America, 1820-1980.* New York: Basic Books.

Young, M. (1999, April). "The leadership crisis in Iowa." Paper presented at the annual meeting on the American Educational Research Association. Montreal.

Zeigler, L. and K. Jennings. (1974). *Governing America's Schools.* N. Scitutate, MA: Doxbury Press.

Chapter 4

Professional Experience

Thomas Glass

Overview

During the past half century, professional training for the superintendency has evolved along somewhat the same lines as the professions of law and medicine. Most superintendents must take undergraduate and graduate training and gain experiences in teaching and administration. Very few superintendents deviate from this set of pre-superintendency experiences. The superintendency as a profession, however, is still very much in a developmental state.

The current wave of school reform has created a great deal of discussion and some state legislation aimed at improving the training of superintendents by use of performance standards. Additionally, organizations that accredit superintendent training in conjunction with state departments of education are beginning to mandate extensive internships for superintendents. Some states that test teachers for competence now also test administrators who want to be certified superintendents.

In some states, early in the 21st century, prospective superintendents and principals will be required to pass a nationally standardized examination developed recently by the Educational Testing Service (ETS).

The objective of these "standardizing agencies" (such as the Interstate School Leaders Licensure Consortium sponsored by the Council of Chief State School Officers) is not only to create uniformity in administrator preparation, but also to increase the competence of school leaders across the nation. Another advantage to national standardization of supervisors would be reciprocity of licenses and credentials between states.

In the 1990s, serious efforts were made to "professionalize" the superintendency. The American Association of School Administrators created a national commission on the superintendency to develop a set of performance standards for superintendents. This commission, chaired by John Hoyle, produced a set of standards and indicators in 1993 (Hoyle, 1993). These standards have been field tested for validity through doctoral dissertation studies conducted in Illinois and Texas.

Currently, greater emphasis is being given by state agencies and professional groups to improve the instructional leadership of principals. Much research in the 1990s reinforced that of the 1980s, which strongly declared instructional leadership to be the most important part of quality schools (districts). Because there are fewer aspiring superintendents than principals, higher education preparation programs generally focus on the principalship. This seems to be especially true in states that have opened the superintendency to non-educators, or have extensive testing for the superintendency.

Entry into Administration

Nearly half of the superintendents (48.5 percent) obtained their first administrative position in a school district before age 30. This finding also was true in the AASA studies conducted in 1992, 1982, and 1971. This is more typical in larger districts than in smaller districts. In districts with enrollments of more than 3,000, nearly 60 percent of current superintendents obtained their first administrative jobs before age 30. In the very small districts, those with enrollments of fewer than 300 students, only 31.5 percent of current superintendents obtained their first administrative position by age 30. In some cases, that position was a superintendency. In the large urban districts, only 9.6 percent entered administration after the age of 36 (see **Table 4.1**).

It is interesting to reflect on why so many superintendents made a relatively early career decision to seek administrative positions. Were the strongest factors salary, a desire to "make a difference," a need to lead, a desire for status, or something else? Perhaps many aspiring superintendents wish to be "heroes" in their profession by making a difference for children, the community, and their colleagues (Chapman, 1997). No matter what the driving forces were (or are), individuals' motivations for selecting a career in educational administration need much more research.

The Dominance of Former Secondary Teachers

The superintendency has been historically dominated by former secondary level teachers. Only 28.5 percent of respondents indicated that they had first taught in the elementary grades in the 1992 study. The popular belief that superintendents are former physical education teachers and coaches is not supported by the 2000, 1992, nor 1982 surveys. Many were social studies teachers, and others were science, mathematics, or English teachers. The percentages are small enough in each of these teaching fields to preclude predicting which kinds of teachers are most likely to become superintendents.

Conventional wisdom might predict that, in very small districts, more elementary teachers might become superintendents, since some of these districts do not have a secondary school. That, however, proved not to be the case in the 1982 or 1992 studies. The 2000 study shows only 24 percent of the very small districts have superintendents with an elementary background. Apparently, teachers of older students in a departmentalized type of instructional environment not only are more familiar with the greater degree of bureaucracy in secondary schools, but also may find administration more alluring than elementary school teachers.

Nearly 50 percent of superintendents indicated they had their first administrative position in a junior or senior high school. This would mean they were likely to have been secondary-certified. Many secondary teachers find their first position in smaller districts. Only 26 percent of the superintendents indicated that their first teaching assignment was in the elementary grades. Thirty-three percent of superintendents did indicate they had at least one full year experience teaching in the

TABLE 4.1 AGE AT ENTERING FIRST FULL-TIME ADMINISTRATIVE POSITION OTHER THAN SUPERINTENDENT

AGE GROUP	GROUP A: 25,000 OR MORE PUPILS		GROUP B: 3,000-24,999 PUPILS		GROUP C: 300-2,999 PUPILS		GROUP D: FEWER THAN 300 PUPILS		NATIONAL UNWEIGHTED PROFILE	
	NO.	%	NO.	%	NO.	%	NO.	%	NO.	%
25-30	60	63.8	314	57.7	627	46.9	79	31.5	1080	48.5
31-35	25	26.6	153	28.1	381	28.5	52	20.7	611	27.5
36-40	7	7.4	59	10.8	193	14.4	60	23.9	319	14.3
41-45	1	1.1	17	3.1	103	7.7	31	12.4	152	6.8
46 OR MORE	1	1.1	1	.2	32	2.4	29	11.6	63	2.8
TOTALS	94	100.0	544	100.0	1326	100.0	251	100.0	2225	100.0

elementary level. Interestingly, 44.2 percent indicated a year of experience at the junior high or middle school level, but 59 percent said they had at least a year at the secondary level.

Secondary teachers were more represented in the larger-sized districts. It is very apparent from the data that a large majority of superintendents begin their careers in the secondary, junior high, or middle school level. It is most likely in many districts to be easier to gain the first administrative position at the middle or junior level as an assistant principal. Many times, secondary assistant principals are more senior and are in the position for a career. This may be the basis for criticism that superintendents are not particularly instructionally-oriented.

What's in a Name?

The title of the first administrative position held by respondents depends, for the most part, on the size of school and district. For example, for superintendents of large districts, the first administrative position usually was assistant principal. The principalship was the first position for most superintendents of small districts, where it is less likely that the position of assistant principal exists. This is especially true for districts without a secondary school. In 1982, 18.9 percent of super-intendents had served as assistant principals, compared to 30.3 percent in 1992, and 34.6 percent in 2000 (see **Table 4.4**).

A less common entry-level position is that of coordinator or director of a special program. After the emergence of categorical programs in the 1960s, many teachers were able to leave the classroom and become coordinators in remedial or special education. These programs, in particular, provided entry-level positions for female administrators. In some cases, however, they created a disadvantage for prospective administrators because these positions generally do not provide "line" or

TABLE 4.2 SUBJECTS TAUGHT BY SUPERINTENDENT IN FIRST FULL-TIME POSITION IN EDUCATION

SUBJECTS	GROUP A: 25,000 OR MORE PUPILS		GROUP B: 3,000-24,999 PUPILS		GROUP C: 300-2,999 PUPILS		GROUP D: FEWER THAN 300 PUPILS		NATIONAL UNWEIGHTED PROFILE	
	NO.	%	NO.	%	NO.	%	NO.	%	NO.	%
ELEMENTARY	21	22.1	119	21.8	261	19.4	60	24.0	461	20.6
COUNSELING	-	-	3	.5	8	.6	-	-	11	.5
FOREIGN LANGUAGE	3	3.2	16	2.9	14	1.0	-	-	33	1.5
SOCIAL STUDIES	23	24.2	123	22.5	284	21.1	38	15.2	468	20.9
SPECIAL EDUCATION	2	2.1	24	4.4	56	4.2	10	4.0	92	4.1
P.E./HEALTH	5	5.3	26	4.8	104	7.7	12	4.8	147	6.6
BUSINESS EDUCATION	3	3.2	10	1.8	55	4.1	19	7.6	87	3.9
INDUSTRIAL ARTS	2	2.1	5	.9	32	2.4	7	2.8	46	2.1
COMPUTER EDUCATION	0	-	0	-	3	.2	0	-	3	.1
ART	-	-	2	.4	9	.7	4	1.6	15	.7
MATH	10	10.5	62	11.4	131	9.7	28	11.2	231	10.3
MUSIC	-	-	12	2.2	27	2.0	6	2.4	45	2.0
ENGLISH	10	10.5	65	11.9	124	9.2	17	6.8	216	9.7
SCIENCE	13	13.7	57	10.4	168	12.5	25	10.0	263	11.8
DRIVER EDUCATION	1	1.1	1	.2	14	1.0	3	1.2	19	.8
VOCATIONAL EDUCATION	1	1.1	3	.5	12	.9	2	.8	18	.8
HOME ECONOMICS	-	-	1	.2	1	.1	1	.4	3	.1
VOCATIONAL AGRICULTURE	-	-	4	.7	19	1.4	5	2.0	28	1.3
OTHER	1	1.1	11	2.0	23	1.7	10	4.0	45	2.0
NO TEACHING EXPERIENCE	-	-	2	.4	1	.1	3	1.2	6	.3
TOTAL	95	100.0	546	100.0	1346	100.0	250	100.0	2237	100.0

employee supervision experience, or direct supervision and evaluation of instructional staff. In 2000, only 13.7 percent of superintendents indicated this to be their first administrative role. Currently, many large urban districts have created a role, which is neither coordinator nor assistant principal. This new role is that of a non-evaluating supervisor of reform initiatives.

Years Superintendents Spend in the Classroom

Superintendents, on average, have spent five to seven years as classroom teachers before becoming administrators (see **Table 4.7**). In the largest districts, this is true of 60 percent of superintendents. The years spent in the classroom reinforce the survey data and indicate that most administrators take their first job in administration around the age of 30.

Superintendents in smaller districts typically have more years of experience in the classroom (see **Table 4.7**). This situation might be attributable to the fact that fewer administrative positions are available in small districts. Only about one-third of the superintendents in the 1992 study indicated they had taught in the classroom for six to eight years. In 2000, nearly 38 percent indicated they have 6 to 10 years teaching experience. Most studies indicate that female superintendents spend more years as classroom teachers than their male counterparts.

The data indicate early administrative career choices by respondents who aspired to a principalship or superintendency. Because so many superintendents are former secondary teachers, the position of department chair may be considered a "quasi" administrative role (in some districts, it is classified as a management role), and is often the first stepping stone to the superintendency. Department chair positions are typically available to tenured teachers with four or five years of experience. In some districts, department chairs evaluate teachers, administer budgets, and develop schedules.

TABLE 4.3 SUBJECTS TAUGHT BY SUPERINTENDENT IN FIRST FULL-TIME POSITION IN EDUCATION COMPARISON 2000-1992

SUBJECTS	GROUP A: 25,000 OR MORE PUPILS		GROUP B: 3,000-24,999 PUPILS		GROUP C: 300-2,999 PUPILS		GROUP D: FEWER THAN 300 PUPILS		NATIONAL UNWEIGHTED PROFILE	
	2000	1992	2000	1992	2000	1992	2000	1992	2000	1992
ELEMENTARY	22.1	28.7	21.8	30.6	19.4	26.4	24.0	29.7	20.6	28.5
COUNSELING	0.0	0.0	0.5	0.0	0.6	0.5	0.0	0.0	0.5	0.2
FOREIGN LANGUAGE	3.2	0.8	2.9	1.2	1.0	0.7	0.0	1.0	1.5	0.9
SOCIAL STUDIES	24.2	27.9	22.5	19.1	21.1	19.9	15.2	12.0	20.9	19.1
SPECIAL EDUCATION	2.1	0.8	4.4	3.2	4.2	0.8	4.0	8.1	4.1	2.7
P.E./HEALTH	5.3	4.1	4.8	2.8	7.7	6.3	4.8	5.3	6.6	4.7
BUSINESS EDUCATION	3.2	5.7	1.8	2.2	4.1	4.4	7.6	6.2	3.9	4.0
INDUSTRIAL ARTS	2.1	3.3	0.9	3.0	2.4	2.0	2.8	3.8	2.1	2.7
COMPUTER EDUCATION	0.0	0.0	0.0	0.0	0.2	0.0	0.0	0.5	0.1	0.1
ART	0.0	0.8	0.4	0.2	0.7	0.5	1.6	0.5	0.7	0.4
MATH	10.5	9.0	11.4	9.1	9.7	9.6	11.2	8.6	10.3	9.3
MUSIC	0.0	1.6	2.2	2.2	2.0	1.5	2.4	4.3	2.0	2.2
ENGLISH	10.5	7.4	11.9	12.1	9.2	7.9	6.8	6.7	9.7	9.2
SCIENCE	13.7	5.7	10.4	10.7	12.5	12.8	10.0	9.6	11.8	11.0
DRIVER EDUCATION	1.1	0.0	0.2	0.6	1.0	0.2	1.2	0.0	0.8	0.3
VOCATIONAL EDUCATION	1.1	2.5	0.5	0.2	0.9	1.7	0.8	0.0	0.8	1.0
HOME ECONOMICS	0.0	0.0	0.2	0.2	0.1	0.0	0.4	1.4	0.1	0.3
VOCATIONAL AGRICULTURE	0.0	0.0	0.7	0.8	1.4	2.7	2.0	1.9	1.3	1.7
OTHER	1.1	0.8	2.0	1.2	1.7	1.4	4.0	0.5	2.0	1.1
NO TEACHING EXPERIENCE	0.0	0.8	0.4	0.6	0.1	0.7	1.2	0.0	0.3	0.6

Beginning in the 1990s, there was particular interest in the educational media about instructional leadership for principals, central office administrators, and superintendents (Henry, 1997). Many articles criticized administrators for being paper pusher managers, rather taking an active role in improving instruction in the classrooms. Questions were asked as to how principals and superintendents could be instructional leaders with so few years of actual classroom teaching experience.

Most states require at least two full years of teaching experience for initial administrative certification. An additional two or three years are required for the superintendency credential. These certification requirements perhaps may provide the reason for the number of years that superintendents spend in a classroom teaching position. Most superintendents probably believe that five to seven years of classroom teaching is sufficient for entry into administration. Critics often indicate that administrators need more classroom experience. Perhaps the most important question is: How good were these future administrators as teachers? Were they evaluated as being exemplary teachers? This type of data does not seem to be available.

Extracurricular Activities

Because so many superintendents are former secondary and junior high school teachers, their involvement in extracurricular activities is an important future career indicator. Many extracurricular assignments have responsibilities and experiences that relate directly to administrative leadership.

TABLE 4.4 NATURE OF FIRST ADMINISTRATIVE/SUPERVISORY POSITION

ADMINISTRATIVE SUPERVISORY POSITION	GROUP A: 25,000 OR MORE PUPILS		GROUP B: 3,000-24,999 PUPILS		GROUP C: 300-2,999 PUPILS		GROUP D: FEWER THAN 300 PUPILS		NATIONAL UNWEIGHTED PROFILE	
	NO.	%	NO.	%	NO.	%	NO.	%	NO.	%
ASSISTANT PRINCIPAL	48	50.5	240	44.1	436	32.6	45	18.3	769	34.6
DEAN OF STUDENTS	5	5.3	13	2.4	33	2.5	5	2.0	56	2.5
PRINCIPAL	13	13.7	143	26.3	600	44.9	149	60.6	905	40.7
DIRECTOR-COORDINATOR	17	17.9	98	18.0	169	12.6	21	8.5	305	13.7
ASSISTANT SUPERINTENDENT	3	3.2	9	1.7	19	1.4	2	.8	33	1.5
STATE AGENCY	-	-	4	.7	11	.8	2	.8	33	1.5
BUSINESS OFFICE	-	-	6	1.1	5	.4	2	.8	13	.6
OTHER	9	9.5	31	5.7	64	4.8	20	8.1	124	5.6
TOTAL	95	100.0	544	100.0	1337	100.0	246	100.0	2222	100.0

TABLE 4.5 NATURE OF FIRST ADMINISTRATIVE/SUPERVISORY POSITION COMPARISON 2000-1992

ADMINISTRATIVE SUPERVISORY POSITION	GROUP A: 25,000 OR MORE PUPILS		GROUP B: 3,000-24,999 PUPILS		GROUP C: 300-2,999 PUPILS		GROUP D: FEWER THAN 300 PUPILS		NATIONAL UNWEIGHTED PROFILE	
	2000	1992	2000	1992	2000	1992	2000	1992	2000	1992
ASSISTANT PRINCIPAL	50.5	43.4	44.1	37.3	32.6	26.7	18.3	16.0	34.6	30.3
DEAN OF STUDENTS	5.3	2.8	2.4	1.8	2.5	1.7	2.0	2.0	2.5	1.9
PRINCIPAL	13.7	21.4	26.3	32.0	44.9	49.2	60.6	56.1	40.7	41.7
DIRECTOR-COORDINATOR	17.9	17.9	18.0	15.9	12.6	10.8	8.5	9.0	13.7	13.0
ASSISTANT SUPERINTENDENT	3.2	2.1	1.7	1.7	1.4	2.6	0.8	1.6	1.5	2.1
STATE AGENCY	0.0	2.1	0.7	1.2	0.8	0.3	0.8	1.2	1.5	0.9
BUSINESS OFFICE	0.0	0.7	1.1	1.3	0.4	0.9	0.8	0.4	0.6	0.9
OTHER	9.5	9.7	5.7	8.9	4.8	7.9	8.1	13.5	5.6	9.2
TOTALS	100.0	100.0	100.0	100.0	100.0	100.0	100.0	100.0	100.0	100.0

One example is interaction between coaches, parents, and community members. In many secondary schools, where athletic offerings have been enlarged since the implementation of Title IX, coaching is almost mandatory as a precursor to the superintendency. **Table 4.10** shows that over half of the 2000 study respondents (58.9 percent) have coaching experience, with an even greater percentage in smaller school districts. In 1992, this number was 48 percent.

Other extracurricular assignments, such as newspaper advisor, music director, or club advisor are not widely represented in the backgrounds of superintendents. It is likely that many superintendents, during their secondary teaching experiences, found interaction with the community and student athletes satisfying. That may have helped them in making the decision to seek the secondary or junior high school principalship, and later, the superintendency.

TABLE 4.6 TYPE OF SCHOOL WHERE SUPERINTENDENT HELD FIRST FULL-TIME POSITION IN EDUCATION: 2000-1992 SUPERINTENDENT COMPARISONS

	GROUP A: 25,000 OR MORE PUPILS		GROUP B: 3,000-24,999 PUPILS		GROUP C: 300-2,999 PUPILS		GROUP D: FEWER THAN 300 PUPILS		NATIONAL UNWEIGHTED PROFILE	
TYPE OF SCHOOL	2000	1992	2000	1992	2000	1992	2000	1992	2000	1992
ELEMENTARY	24.2	19.4	23.8	25.3	24.8	26.5	32.3	31.2	25.3	26.1
JUNIOR HIGH	17.9	22.2	11.0	16.9	8.5	13.5	6.0	9.2	9.2	14.9
MIDDLE SCHOOL	5.3	22.2	6.4	16.9	7.6	13.5	3.6	9.2	6.8	14.9
HIGH SCHOOL	33.7	33.3	34.6	33.6	40.3	37.3	35.5	32.4	38.1	34.9
COLLEGE/UNIVERSITY	·	1.4	.7	1.3	.5	.9	·	0.0	.5	1.1
VOCATIONAL/TECHNICAL	1.1	0.0	.7	1.3	1.3	1.8	1.2	.8	1.2	1.2
PAROCHIAL	·	.7	.2	.1	.8	.3	1.6	·	.7	·
DISTRICT OFFICE	15.8	18.1	17.4	11.7	8.8	12.6	6.4	·	10.9	·
OTHER	2.1	4.9	5.1	6.6	7.4	8.3	13.5	19.2	10.9	9.0
TOTAL	100.0	100.0	100.0	100.0	100.0	100.0	100.0	100.0	100.0	100.1

TABLE 4.7 LENGTH OF SERVICE AS CLASSROOM TEACHER PRIOR TO ENTERING ADMINISTRATION OR SUPERVISION

	GROUP A: 25,000 OR MORE PUPILS		GROUP B: 3,000-24,999 PUPILS		GROUP C: 300-2,999 PUPILS		GROUP D: FEWER THAN 300 PUPILS		NATIONAL UNWEIGHTED PROFILE	
YEARS AS A TEACHER	No.	%	No.	%	No.	%	No.	%	No.	%
0-5	57	60.0	242	44.6	487	36.2	55	22.2	841	37.7
6-10	32	33.7	212	39.0	523	38.9	80	32.3	847	37.9
11-15	4	4.2	71	13.1	226	16.8	61	24.6	362	16.2
16-20	2	2.1	15	2.8	73	5.4	34	13.7	124	5.6
21-25	·	·	2	.4	30	2.2	15	6.0	47	2.1
26+	·	·	1	.2	7	.5	3	1.2	11	.5
TOTAL	95	100.0	543	100.0	1346	100.0	248	100.0	2232	100.0

TABLE 4.8 LENGTH OF SERVICE AS CLASSROOM TEACHER PRIOR TO ENTERING ADMINISTRATION OR SUPERVISION COMPARISON 2000-1992

	GROUP A: 25,000 OR MORE PUPILS		GROUP B: 3,000-24,999 PUPILS		GROUP C: 300-2,999 PUPILS		GROUP D: FEWER THAN 300 PUPILS		NATIONAL UNWEIGHTED PROFILE	
YEARS AS A TEACHER	No.	%	No.	%	No.	%	No.	%	No.	%
0-5	60	63.4	44.6	57.7	36.2	42.9	22.2	29.8	37.7	47.9
6-10	33.7	30.3	39.0	31.3	38.9	40.9	32.3	37.3	37.9	36.1
11-15	4.2	4.1	13.1	9.8	16.8	12.3	24.6	21.8	16.2	12.1
16-20	2.1	2.1	2.8	1.0	5.4	2.9	13.7	7.1	5.6	2.8
21-25	0.0	0.0	0.4	0.2	2.2	0.8	6.0	2.0	2.1	0.7
26+	0.0	0.0	0.2	0.0	0.5	0.1	1.2	2.0	0.5	0.3

A common stereotype is that of the former coach who becomes a high school principal and superintendent. This stereotype may be true today in a few regions of the country, but, for the most part, no longer exists. The emphasis on instructional leadership in the past two decades has shifted the preparation and backgrounds of teachers entering the principalship. This does not mean that superintendents are not former coaches. In the world of public schools today, nearly all male (and many female) teachers coach. In a typical secondary school of 1,200 students, there will be between six and eight competitive sports for both boys and girls. This results in perhaps 30 to 40 coaching contracts in a school with fewer than 60 teachers. Many of these teachers may be older and tired of coaching. The result is that younger teachers are almost forced into coaching sports. It is surprising the survey data only indicate that 58.9 percent of superintendents are former coaches. An argument can be made that perhaps teachers focusing on the superintendency and the principalship try not to coach athletics as much as their colleagues. The many evenings they have to attend graduate classes at nearby colleges and universities may force them to reduce coaching activities.

Gaining the First Superintendency

As stated earlier, a majority of superintendents achieve their first full-time position in educational administration in a secondary school. This finding is consistent for superintendents of districts of all sizes and types. Only about 26 percent of current superintendents gained their first administrative position in an elementary school (see **Table 4.6**). There is little doubt that the principalship, and, especially the superintendency, appeals to secondary teachers. This is true in all sizes of districts, and is probably the result of a majority of secondary teachers being men (Tyack and Hansot, 1982). Until recently, most board members and even educators considered the superintendency the province of males. This is changing, but, as indicated in data discussed elsewhere in this study, not to a significant degree.

Most administrators seeking a first superintendency indicated they were able to obtain a position in one year or less (58.6 percent). Whether their first superintendency was the size, type, and location of district they most preferred, was not asked. The mean time for finding the first superintendency for the entire group was 1.3 years.

TABLE 4.9 HAD ONE FULL YEAR OR MORE OF EXPERIENCE IN THE FOLLOWING POSITIONS

	GROUP A: 25,000 OR MORE PUPILS		GROUP B: 3,000-24,999 PUPILS		GROUP C: 300-2,999 PUPILS		GROUP D: FEWER THAN 300 PUPILS		NATIONAL UNWEIGHTED PROFILE	
	No.	%	No.	%	No.	%	No.	%	No.	%
ELEMENTARY TEACHER	32	33.7	182	33.3	427	31.7	101	40.2	742	33.2
ELEMENTARY ASSISTANT PRINCIPAL	11	11.6	36	6.6	89	6.6	21	8.4	157	7.0
ELEMENTARY PRINCIPAL	28	29.5	178	32.6	516	38.3	129	51.4	851	38.0
JUNIOR HIGH/MIDDLE TEACHER	43	45.3	216	39.6	614	45.6	117	46.6	990	44.2
JUNIOR HIGH/MIDDLE ASSIST. PRINCIPAL	22	23.2	84	15.4	204	15.2	24	9.6	334	14.9
JUNIOR HIGH/ MIDDLE PRINCIPAL	30	31.6	125	22.9	399	29.6	77	30.7	631	28.2
HIGH SCHOOL TEACHER	50	52.6	295	54.0	828	61.5	153	61.0	1326	59.2
HIGH SCHOOL ASSIST. PRINCIPAL	36	37.9	172	31.5	347	25.8	34	13.5	589	26.3
HIGH SCHOOL PRINCIPAL	36	37.9	207	37.9	680	50.5	123	49.0	1046	46.7
DIRECTOR/COORDINATOR	50	52.6	242	44.3	381	28.3	50	19.9	723	32.3
ASSISTANT/ASSOCIATE SUPERINTENDENT	65	68.4	345	63.2	378	28.1	24	9.6	812	36.3
COLLEGE/UNIVERSITY PROFESSOR	15	15.8	70	12.8	117	8.7	25	10.0	227	10.1
COUNSELOR	9	9.5	39	7.1	122	9.1	30	12.0	200	8.9
SUPERVISOR/CONSULTANT	19	20.0	83	15.2	124	9.2	19	7.6	245	10.9
OTHER	6	6.3	48	8.8	84	6.2	26	10.4	164	7.3

Thirty-eight percent of the superintendents indicated they had received their terminal degree less than 10 years prior to seeking their first superintendency. The success of women and minorities in obtaining their first superintendency is discussed in a later chapter in this study. In general, female superintendent applicants find their first superintendency more quickly than males. This was also true in the 1992 study (p. 23).

In past decades, for an average size school district vacancy, there might be between 20 and 30 applicants. In recent years, the number of applicants for desirable districts with high salaries has remained high and competitive. However, for rural and less desirable districts, the number of applicants has become alarmingly low. The number of well-qualified applicants for these jobs has been described in many popular and educational articles as being very low. This "perceived" lack of quality candidates is also seen by many writers to exist in the principalship. Teacher shortages exist across the nation and eventually will affect the principalship and the superintendency. A dearth of high-quality board candidates is also constantly mentioned in the literature.

The 1992 Study asked whether new superintendents were hired from the "inside," meaning that they were already working within the district. About a third (64 percent) of the sample indicated they had been promoted from inside the district (see **Table 4.13**). In the 2000 Study, 68.3 percent of the superintendents indicated they were hired from outside. The lack of candidates in many super-intendent searches might be an advantage to internal candidates.

In the larger districts, promotions to the superintendency were more common in 1992 and 2000 than in 1982. Overall, however, the 1982 Study indicated 38 percent were promotions; in 1992, 36 percent were promotions. In 2000, 42.1 percent of the largest district superintendents indicated they had been hired from within. This may be attributable to a board's thinking that it is best to hire a super-intendent it knows, and who knows the complexities of the large district. Richard Carlson, in a 1972 study, advanced the reasons for insider selection: district financial problems; elimination of another

TABLE 4.10 EXTRACURRICULAR ACTIVITY AS A TEACHER

ACTIVITY/PARTICIPATION	GROUP A: 25,000 OR MORE PUPILS		GROUP B: 3,000-24,999 PUPILS		GROUP C: 300-2,999 PUPILS		GROUP D: FEWER THAN 300 PUPILS		NATIONAL UNWEIGHTED PROFILE	
	No.	%	No.	%	No.	%	No.	%	No.	%
COACHING ATHLETICS	43	47.3	281	54.8	785	61.0	146	61.1	1255	58.9
CLUB ADVISOR	19	20.9	117	22.8	220	17.1	33	13.8	389	18.3
CLASS ADVISOR	9	9.9	34	6.6	92	7.2	17	7.1	152	7.1
NEWSPAPER/ANNUAL	2	2.2	20	3.9	38	3.0	8	3.3	68	3.2
MUSIC GROUPS	3	3.3	21	4.1	47	3.7	7	2.9	78	3.7
OTHER	15	16.5	40	7.8	104	8.1	28	11.7	187	8.8
TOTAL	91	100.0	513	100.0	1286	100.0	239	100.0	2129	100.0

TABLE 4.11 LENGTH IT TOOK TO OBTAIN FIRST SUPERINTENDENCY ONCE CERTIFIED/ACTIVELY SOUGHT

YEARS	GROUP A: 25,000 OR MORE PUPILS		GROUP B: 3,000-24,999 PUPILS		GROUP C: 300-2,999 PUPILS		GROUP D: FEWER THAN 300 PUPILS		NATIONAL UNWEIGHTED PROFILE	
	No.	%	No.	%	No.	%	No.	%	No.	%
LESS THAN 1 YEAR	40	43.0	272	50.0	789	58.7	160	64.5	1261	56.6
1 YEAR	10	10.8	83	15.3	213	15.9	37	14.9	343	15.4
2 YEARS	5	5.4	19	3.5	30	2.2	6	2.4	60	2.7
3 YEARS	10	10.8	30	5.5	66	4.9	12	4.8	118	5.3
4 YEARS	5	5.4	19	3.5	30	2.2	6	2.4	60	2.7
5+ YEARS	14	15.1	63	11.6	93	6.9	14	5.6	184	8.3
TOTAL	93	100.0	544	100.0	1343	100.0	248	100.0	2228	100.0

position; and the fact that superintendents appointed from the inside will sometimes work for less money. However, they never enjoy a period of grace in their new positions. It is likely that boards not interested in dramatic changes might lean toward a known candidate who is content maintaining the status quo. The lack of a quantity of highly-qualified outside applicants might also play a part in selecting an inside candidate in a large district.

Number of Superintendencies

The superintendency often is perceived as a position with rapid turnover and mobility. This is not the case, however, since most superintendents indicate they have spent over half of their superintendency career in only one district. As **Table 4.14** indicates, about one-fourth (24.5 percent) have had two superintendencies, and 11.8 percent have held three. Superintendents in the 2000 Study had served as superintendents for an average of 8.75 years.

It is a matter of judgment whether this level of mobility is excessive for an executive position. The 1982 and 1992 study data reported that most superintendents had held about two superintendencies. In 2000, the average number of superintendencies held was 1.75. Taking into account the number of new superintendents filling the positions vacated by retirees, it would be expected that in another 10 years the average would be about 2 to 3 years. There is not much variance in these data in relation to district size.

Even among the oldest age groups, 75 percent of respondents had held fewer than three superintendencies (see **Table 4.14**).

Years in the Superintendency

A common theme in the popular media is that of a board and superintendent falling into conflict, resulting in the superintendent being dismissed. Stories of a superintendent moving on to a new district may imply that these educators are a highly transitory professional group.

However, data concerning tenure of the survey sample of superintendents show a much different picture. The average length of tenure for superintendents was 6.47 years in the 1992 study. Keeping in mind that the typical employment contract for a superintendent is three years, this implies that the average superintendent was in his/her second or third full contract in the 1992 study. However,

TABLE 4.12 NUMBER OF YEARS AGO YOU RECEIVED HIGHEST ACADEMIC DEGREE

YEARS	GROUP A: 25,000 OR MORE PUPILS		GROUP B: 3,000-24,999 PUPILS		GROUP C: 300-2,999 PUPILS		GROUP D: FEWER THAN 300 PUPILS		NATIONAL UNWEIGHTED PROFILE	
	No.	%	No.	%	No.	%	No.	%	No.	%
0-5	2	2.1	56	10.3	207	15.4	67	26.7	332	14.8
6-10	16	17.0	115	21.1	329	24.4	67	26.7	527	23.6
11-15	18	19.1	133	24.4	291	21.6	37	14.7	479	21.4
15+	58	61.7	242	44.3	519	38.6	80	31.9	899	40.2

TABLE 4.13 WERE YOU HIRED FROM WITHIN YOUR SCHOOL DISTRICT?

SUCCESSOR TYPE	GROUP A: 25,000 OR MORE PUPILS		GROUP B: 3,000-24,999 PUPILS		GROUP C: 300-2,999 PUPILS		GROUP D: FEWER THAN 300 PUPILS		NATIONAL UNWEIGHTED PROFILE	
	No.	%	No.	%	No.	%	No.	%	No.	%
INSIDE CANDIDATE	40	42.1	200	37.0	407	30.4	60	23.9	707	31.7
OUTSIDE CANDIDATE	55	57.9	341	63.0	933	69.6	191	76.1	1520	68.3
TOTAL	95	100.0	541	100.0	1340	100.0	251	100.0	2227	100.0

the practice in many states is that of "rollover," which means that each year the board of education may extend the contract of the superintendent for an additional year, thus maintaining the contract at three years.

In 2000, with superintendents serving on the average of 1.75 districts in 8.75 years average time in the superintendency, an approximate tenure of 5 years can be estimated. The decline of nearly a year and half tenure from the 1992 Study is attributable to the abnormal number of superintendents just entering the profession during the 1990s.

Twenty-one percent of the superintendents have been superintendents between 14 and 15 years. Interestingly, 23.7 percent of the largest district superintendents have been in the profession for 14 or 15 years (see **Table 4.16**). It is an important finding that 41.3 percent of the superintendents have been in the position for 10 or more years. Only eight percent of superintendents have held four or more superintendencies.

Superintendent Tenure

The 2000 Study did not contain a question asking superintendents the length of tenure in their current position. The reason for this was that prior data were available for examination that indicated that, due to normal and early retirements, a very large number of superintendents were in their first contract in their present district. This turned out to be the case when the sample was analyzed. Nearly 50 percent of the sample were in their first contract in their present district. A question about length of tenure would have resulted in a national average of perhaps two to three years, creating the impression the superintendency to be more transient than it actually is. Other recent superintendent data (Cooper, Fusarelli and Carella, 2000) of a sample of larger district superintendents show their tenure in current positions to be 7.25 years.

TABLE 4.14 NUMBER OF PUBLIC SCHOOL SUPERINTENDENCIES HELD INCLUDING CURRENT ONE

NUMBER HELD	GROUP A: 25,000 OR MORE PUPILS		GROUP B: 3,000-24,999 PUPILS		GROUP C: 300-2,999 PUPILS		GROUP D: FEWER THAN 300 PUPILS		NATIONAL UNWEIGHTED PROFILE	
	No.	%	No.	%	No.	%	No.	%	No.	%
1	45	47.4	297	54.5	755	56.1	153	61.0	1250	55.9
2	17	17.9	131	24.0	337	25.0	60	23.9	545	24.4
3	18	18.9	80	14.7	150	11.1	16	6.4	264	11.8
4	10	10.5	25	4.6	67	5.0	16	6.4	118	5.3
5	5	5.3	10	1.8	26	1.9	5	2.0	46	2.1
6	-	-	2	.4	8	.6	-	-	10	.4
MORE	-	-	-	-	3	.2	1	.4	4	.2
TOTAL	95	100.0	545	100.0	1346	100.0	251	100.0	2237	100.0

TABLE 4.15 LENGTH OF CURRENT CONTRACT

LENGTH IN YEARS	GROUP A: 25,000 OR MORE PUPILS		GROUP B: 3,000-24,999 PUPILS		GROUP C: 300-2,999 PUPILS		GROUP D: FEWER THAN 300 PUPILS		NATIONAL UNWEIGHTED PROFILE	
	No.	%	No.	%	No.	%	No.	%	No.	%
ONE	7	7.4	22	4.0	154	11.5	96	38.4	279	12.5
TWO	7	7.4	61	11.2	268	20.0	65	26.0	401	18.0
THREE	30	31.6	270	49.5	611	45.5	70	28.0	981	44.8
MORE THAN FOUR	51	53.7	192	35.2	309	23.0	19	7.6	571	25.6
TOTAL	95	100.0	545	100.0	1342	100.0	250	100.0	2232	100.0

The 2000 Study of the American School Superintendency

Again, due to the presence of early retirement incentives, and normal retirement dates at age 57, many superintendents either entered the field or moved up all at the same time. The 1992 Study data indicated that a large number of superintendents would be retiring in the later part of the decade due to reaching retirement age (57).

The Urban Superintendency Tenure Problem

In December 1990, 14 large urban school district superintendencies were vacant (Bradley, 1990). In 1997, Carter and Cunningham reported essentially the same type of data. This is not to minimize the effectiveness of short-term superintendencies, wherever they occur. However, instability in leadership in urban districts, which serve large proportions of at-risk students, surely does nothing to advance reform and excellence.

In 1990, Allan Ornstein found, in a survey of 86 of the largest district superintendents, that 41 had been in their current positions 2 to 5 years, 22 less than one year, and 23 had more than 5 years of tenure (Ornstein, 1990). In appraising the tenure of large urban districts, the evaluator might ask the question, "How long would big-city mayors last if the city councils appointed them?" In fact, during the 1990s, through state legislation, several big-city mayors are now appointing superintendents.

Summary of Tenure

If anything, tenure for most superintendents has stayed the same during the past decade. The *1992 Study of the American School Superintendency* found tenure to be 6.4 years. In the 1982 Study, the average length of superintendent tenure was 5.6 years. In the 1971 Study, the tenure length was six years. The current estimate of 5 - 6 years in the 2000 Study data is not a substantial departure from previous decades.

TABLE 4.16 HOW MANY YEARS TOTAL HAVE YOU SERVED AS A SUPERINTENDENT?

Years	GROUP A: 25,000 OR MORE PUPILS		GROUP B: 3,000-24,999 PUPILS		GROUP C: 300-2,999 PUPILS		GROUP D: FEWER THAN 300 PUPILS		NATIONAL UNWEIGHTED PROFILE	
	No.	%	No.	%	No.	%	No.	%	No.	%
1	4	4.3	24	4.4	86	6.4	39	15.5	153	6.9
2-3	15	16.1	50	9.2	193	14.4	44	17.5	302	13.5
4-5	13	14.0	80	14.7	158	11.8	38	15.1	289	13.0
6-7	11	11.8	81	14.9	179	13.3	28	11.2	299	13.4
8-9	9	9.7	71	13.1	156	11.6	26	10.4	262	11.7
10-11	9	9.7	68	12.5	151	11.2	24	9.6	252	11.3
12-13	7	7.5	38	7.0	85	6.3	10	4.0	140	6.3
14-15	22	23.7	116	21.3	303	22.6	41	16.3	482	21.6
16+	3	3.2	16	2.9	32	2.4	1	.4	52	2.3
TOTAL	93	100.0	544	100.0	1343	100.0	251	100.0	2231	100.0

TABLE 4.17 IS THERE AN OLD BOY/GIRL NETWORK IN YOUR STATE THAT HELPS INDIVIDUALS GET POSITIONS AS SUPERINTENDENTS?

	GROUP A: 25,000 OR MORE PUPILS		GROUP B: 3,000-24,999 PUPILS		GROUP C: 300-2,999 PUPILS		GROUP D: FEWER THAN 300 PUPILS		NATIONAL UNWEIGHTED PROFILE	
	No.	%	No.	%	No.	%	No.	%	No.	%
YES	47	51.1	256	48.9	677	52.6	145	60.7	1125	52.5
NO	33	35.9	195	37.3	418	32.5	54	22.6	700	32.7
DON'T KNOW	12	13.0	72	13.8	193	15.0	40	16.7	317	14.8
TOTAL	92	100.0	523	100.0	1288	100.0	239	100.0	2142	100.0

The probable reason for the increased superintendent tenure in the 1980s and its stabilization in the 1990s was that most districts already had been through the most severe enrollment declines and politically divisive activities such as reductions-in-force and school closings. Contributing factors to reduction to five years in 2000, besides early retirement packages, might be stress and the robust economy, which made earlier retirement feasible.

In summary, when considering that half of superintendents are over age 50, that most states have early retirement programs beginning at age 55, and that most superintendents retire between the ages of 57 and 60, it would not be uncommon to see about 8 to 10 percent retiring early, and another 20 percent looking for new districts with larger enrollments, greater wealth, and higher administrator salaries in the first decade of the new century.

Other Superintendent Studies' Data on Tenure

In a study titled *Career Crisis in the School Superintendency?* conducted by Bruce Cooper, Lance Fusarelli and Vincent Carella in 1999 for AASA, superintendent tenure was found to be 7.25 years. This was the length of time the superintendents had been in their current positions. For the largest districts, 4.71 years was the mean. On the average, the sample of superintendents indicated that they had been in their previous superintendency a little over six years. Additionally, the SPEAR™ study showed 62 percent of current superintendents in the 50-59-age range. About half (51 percent) indicated they would take a better position if the opportunity arose. The SPEAR™ study sample was skewed toward larger districts. Larger districts typically have older superintendents with longer tenure.

Mentoring, Discrimination, Hiring

Old Boy/Old Girl Network

Researchers such as Grogran (1996) believe that the superintendency has been dominated by an "old boy" network of mentors and sponsors. This contention was supported by the 1992 Study, which found that an old boy network did exist according to 56.5 percent of superintendents (see **Table 4.17**).

TABLE 4.18 SCHOOL BOARD DOES NOT ACTIVELY RECRUIT WOMEN

SEVERITY OF PROBLEM	GROUP A: 25,000 OR MORE PUPILS		GROUP B: 3,000-24,999 PUPILS		GROUP C: 300-2,999 PUPILS		GROUP D: FEWER THAN 300 PUPILS		NATIONAL UNWEIGHTED PROFILE	
	No.	%	No.	%	No.	%	No.	%	No.	%
IMPORTANT FACTOR	13	13.7	49	9.1	129	9.7	28	11.2	219	9.9
SOMEWHAT IMPORTANT FACTOR	34	35.8	181	33.7	414	31.1	81	32.4	710	32.1
NOT A FACTOR	38	40.0	269	50.1	642	48.3	111	44.4	1060	47.9
DO NOT KNOW	10	10.5	38	7.1	145	10.9	30	12.0	223	10.1
TOTAL	95	100.0	537	100.0	1330	100.0	250	100.0	2212	100.0

TABLE 4.19 SEVERITY OF PROBLEM OF DISCRIMINATORY HIRING PRACTICES FOR MINORITIES

SEVERITY OF PROBLEM	GROUP A: 25,000 OR MORE PUPILS		GROUP B: 3,000-24,999 PUPILS		GROUP C: 300-2,999 PUPILS		GROUP D: FEWER THAN 300 PUPILS		NATIONAL UNWEIGHTED PROFILE	
	No.	%	No.	%	No.	%	No.	%	No.	%
MAJOR PROBLEM	18	19.1	83	15.6	129	9.8	32	13.0	262	12.0
MINOR PROBLEM	35	37.2	184	34.5	474	36.2	84	34.1	777	36.6
LITTLE PROBLEM	25	26.6	181	34.0	448	34.2	86	35.0	740	33.9
NO PROBLEM	16	17.0	85	15.9	259	19.8	44	17.9	404	18.5
TOTAL	94	100.0	533	100.0	1310	100.0	246	100.0	2183	100.0

The 2000 Study data find that only 52.5 percent of superintendents feel this network exists. This does indicate an "opening" of the superintendency for more women and minorities. These networks are reported to exist in many other professions, as well. Many respondents undoubtedly think that individuals working for superintendent search firms or state school boards associations are part of an informal network.

Gender Discrimination

Considering the small numbers of minority and female superintendents (about 14.6 percent), job discrimination should be a national concern. In 1982, 14 percent of the superintendents said hiring discrimination seriously affected prospective female superintendents. In the 1992 Study, 13.7 percent called it a major problem (see **Table 4.18**). In 2000, about the same percentage (12.0) felt gender discrimination to be a serious problem. The number of women in the 2000 Study (13 percent) is significantly larger than in previous studies. About half of the respondents in 1982 and 1992 thought discrimination against women posed little or no problem. In 2000, this figure had grown to about 70 percent.

The question then arises: What deters large numbers of women from becoming superintendents? Is the position not alluring to women? Are preparation program entryways blocked? Are school board members not inclined to hire women? Are search firms not bringing women into their pools? These and other questions are in need of substantial research.

Discrimination Against Minorities

In general, superintendents today think that women have a more difficult time being hired than do minorities. Fewer superintendents think that hiring discrimination against minorities is a major problem. The 2000 Study found only 12 percent of superintendents think that significant discrimination exists in hiring minorities. Sixteen percent thought it was a major problem in 1982, while 18.4 percent expressed the same view in 1992. Large-district superintendents believed discriminatory hiring is more of a problem than did superintendents in smaller districts (see **Table 4.19**).

Recruitment of Women and Minorities

Whether or not discrimination in hiring women and minorities exists, the presence of so few women and minority superintendents presents a major challenge to the profession. The compositions of student bodies and teaching staffs, along with community makeup, challenge the profession to improve its record in preparing and placing women and minority administrators as superintendents. Most minority administrators currently work in majority minority school districts, often under less than ideal conditions for professional development. It appears minority superintendents may be locked into minority populated districts.

TABLE 4.20 HAVE YOU SPENT YOUR ENTIRE EDUCATIONAL CAREER IN ONE SCHOOL DISTRICT?

	GROUP A: 25,000 OR MORE PUPILS		GROUP B: 3,000-24,999 PUPILS		GROUP C: 300-2,999 PUPILS		GROUP D: FEWER THAN 300 PUPILS		NATIONAL UNWEIGHTED PROFILE	
	No.	%	No.	%	No.	%	No.	%	No.	%
YES	14	14.7	62	11.4	94	7.0	26	10.4	196	8.8
NO	81	85.3	484	88.6	1252	93.0	225	89.6	2042	91.2
TOTAL	95	100.0	546	100.0	1346	100.0	251	100.0	2238	100.0

Superintendents Spending a Career in One District

Very few superintendents (8.8 percent) have spent their entire careers in one school district. A few more of the larger district superintendents have been in one district for their entire careers. This means that, from becoming a teacher and moving through the ranks to the superintendency, a superintendent is likely to move several times. This is very comparable to what happens in other professions (see **Table 4.20**).

Number of States in Which Superintendents Served

Due to the existence of state-sponsored retirement systems, relatively few superintendents cross state lines for employment. Only 11 percent indicated they had worked in more than one state. Many articles portray superintendents as wandering from state to state. This simply is not true. It is slightly true for superintendents in the very largest districts. The state retirement programs often end up being a problem for large urban districts, as qualified candidates do not want to leave the years they have built up in other state programs (see **Table 4.21**).

Selection to the Superintendency

Search Committees

Superintendents are selected for their positions in several ways. The first, and most prevalent, is that the school board forms its own search committee (54 percent). One or two members are then designated to work with school staff to draw up a job description, which is sent to universities, state associations, professional publications, and newspapers. The board meets and decides which of the applicants it will interview. The smaller the school district, the more likely it is to use this method of superintendent selection. In the very small districts, the board acts as its own search agent 76 percent of the time. In the very large districts, a private search firm or an agency, such as the state school boards association, conducts the search 46 percent of the time (see **Table 4.23**).

TABLE 4.21 NUMBER OF STATES SERVED AS A PUBLIC SCHOOL SUPERINTENDENT

NUMBER OF STATES	GROUP A: 25,000 OR MORE PUPILS		GROUP B: 3,000-24,999 PUPILS		GROUP C: 300-2,999 PUPILS		GROUP D: FEWER THAN 300 PUPILS		NATIONAL UNWEIGHTED PROFILE	
	No.	%	No.	%	No.	%	No.	%	No.	%
1	61	64.9	459	84.2	1204	89.5	229	91.2	1953	87.3
2	19	20.2	63	11.6	118	8.8	19	7.6	219	9.8
3	10	10.6	17	3.1	14	1.0	2	.8	43	1.9
4+	4	4.3	6	1.1	10	.7	1	.4	21	.9
TOTAL	94	100.0	545	100.0	1346	100.0	251	100.0	2236	100.0

TABLE 4.22 REASONS GIVEN BY SUPERINTENDENTS FOR THEIR SELECTION TO CURRENT POSITION

REASON FOR SELECTION	GROUP A: 25,000 OR MORE PUPILS		GROUP B: 3,000-24,999 PUPILS		GROUP C: 300-2,999 PUPILS		GROUP D: FEWER THAN 300 PUPILS		NATIONAL UNWEIGHTED PROFILE	
	No.	%	No.	%	No.	%	No.	%	No.	%
PERSONAL CHARACTERISTICS	30	31.9	204	37.5	554	41.3	105	42.0	893	40.1
CHANGE AGENT	27	28.7	157	28.9	341	25.4	62	24.8	587	26.3
MAINTAIN STATUS QUO	1	1.1	4	.7	22	1.6	6	2.4	33	1.5
INSTRUCTIONAL LEADER	30	31.9	157	28.9	330	24.6	57	22.8	574	25.8
NO PARTICULAR REASON	1	1.1	9	1.7	39	2.9	13	5.2	62	2.8
NOT SURE	5	5.3	13	2.4	55	4.1	7	2.8	80	3.6
TOTAL	94	100.0	544	100.0	1341	100.0	250	100.0	2229	100.0

The fees charged by private search firms usually are dictated by the size of the district, the number of services the board wishes, and whether the search is restricted to local candidates. Some search firms are owned and staffed by retired superintendents who have established a reputation for competence and knowledge of the profession. Sometimes, professors of educational administrations also work as consultants for private search firms or the state school boards associations (Tallerico, 1999a).

Most state school boards associations provide some in-service training for board members in superintendent selection. The process is complex, however, and laypersons may be at a disadvantage in assessing whether candidates are fully qualified for the position.

Reasons Why a Superintendent is Selected

The 2000 Study indicates that 40.1 percent of the superintendents attributed their hiring to personal characteristics. In the 1982 Study, two-thirds of the superintendents declared they were hired for their positions because of "personal characteristics." These qualities might include the image of role model they presented during the interview process, as well as information the board learned from community members from their last district. The decrease of personal characteristics as a basis for selection may reflect a "maturing" of the profession and, perhaps, the use of more stringent selection criteria by local school boards. Superintendents in the very small districts still are more likely to cite personal characteristics as the reason they were hired, perhaps because of the position's higher visibility in those communities.

Movers, Shakers, and Peacekeepers

Three roles are typical in the general mission of the superintendency:

Change agent. First, boards may be looking for a change agent, a superintendent who will initiate changes in the district that the board thinks are necessary. School districts sometimes are change-resistant, and superintendents in the role of change agent can start enough conflict and pressure that the board (or a new board) has little choice but to make significant changes. School boards that are newly elected, or that believe the district is not operating very well, often seek the change agent role. Superintendents in these roles typically are hired from the outside.

Only 26.3 percent of superintendents in the 2000 Study felt that they were hired by their boards to be agents of change. This was true for all district sizes.

Instructional leader. A second role is that of instructional leader. In the past decade, the literature, as well as the inservice thrust by professional associations, has been on instructional leadership. Interestingly, the largest district superintendents felt this to be truer than those in smaller districts. About a third (31.9 percent) indicated they thought this was the primary reason they were hired.

TABLE 4.23 WHAT GROUP/INDIVIDUALS MANAGED THE SEARCH PROCESS FOR YOUR CURRENT SUPERINTENDENCY?

GROUP	GROUP A: 25,000 OR MORE PUPILS		GROUP B: 3,000-24,999 PUPILS		GROUP C: 300-2,999 PUPILS		GROUP D: FEWER THAN 300 PUPILS		NATIONAL UNWEIGHTED PROFILE	
	No.	%	No.	%	No.	%	No.	%	No.	%
PROFESSIONAL SEARCH FIRM	44	46.8	140	25.7	194	14.5	16	6.4	394	17.7
STATE SCHOOL BOARDS ASSOC.	14	14.9	118	21.7	275	20.6	20	8.0	427	19.2
LOCAL SCHOOL BOARD ASSOC.	28	29.8	240	44.0	745	55.7	190	76.0	1203	54.0
OTHER	8	8.5	47	8.6	124	9.3	24	9.6	203	9.1
TOTAL	94	100.0	545	100.0	1338	100.0	250	100.0	2227	100.0

Maintaining the status quo. The third role is as maintainer of the status quo. This role is often found in school districts where things have been going well for a number of years. Perhaps an admired superintendent is retiring, and the board is looking for someone of similar personality and program philosophy. Many times, these types of superintendent vacancies are filled from within the district (Carlson, 1972). Only 1.5 percent of the superintendents felt this was the reason they were hired. This might indicate that most boards are actively looking to improve the district through new programs and initiatives.

Summary of Reasons for Selection

In **Table 4.23**, 28.7 percent of the superintendents in large school districts indicated that they had been hired to be change agents. The urban superintendency is a difficult position, and boards typically are pressured for improvement in test scores and responsiveness to the community. In the urban setting, new superintendents are sought who will correct the ills of their urban school districts. Still, 28.9 percent of the superintendents of districts with enrollments of 3,000 to 24,999 indicated they were hired for the change agent role. This, in a general way, may account for some controversy in many of their districts. Often change agent roles are assigned to new superintendents moving to districts in turmoil.

In the 1990s, the role of instructional leader was emphasized in myriad school reform reports. Since the back-to-basics movement of the 1970s, instructional leadership by superintendents and principals has been proposed as a remedy for improving the nation's schools. To a lesser extent, about 22 percent of superintendents in 1992, and 25.8 percent in 2000 said their skills and abilities in instructional leadership were what convinced their present boards to hire them. Certainly, superintendents are concerned about improving instruction, and carry that concern into interviews with prospective board employers. A slightly lower number of smaller district superintendents (enrollments of 300 - 2,999) indicated they were hired because of their instructional leadership capabilities.

The emphasis on instructional leadership is likely to continue. Laws in states such as Illinois require principals to spend at least 51 percent of their time in instructional leadership. Such reform legislation has helped create a nationwide emphasis on instruction that has carried over into the superintendency. In addition, the high-stakes assessment systems in place in many states create a situation where principals (and superintendents) will be more concerned with test scores.

TABLE 4.24 MEMBERSHIPS IN PROFESSIONAL ORGANIZATIONS

ORGANIZATIONAL MEMBERSHIPS	GROUP A: 25,000 OR MORE PUPILS		GROUP B: 3,000-24,999 PUPILS		GROUP C: 300-2,999 PUPILS		GROUP D: FEWER THAN 300 PUPILS		NATIONAL UNWEIGHTED PROFILE	
	No.	%	No.	%	No.	%	No.	%	No.	%
AASA	85	89.5	490	89.7	997	74.1	127	50.6	1699	75.9
ASBO	5	5.3	26	4.8	143	10.6	16	6.4	190	8.5
NASSP	16	16.8	41	7.5	129	9.6	33	13.1	219	9.8
NABSE	9	9.5	9	1.6	6	.4	3	1.2	27	1.2
NSBA	34	35.8	148	27.1	192	14.3	21	8.4	395	17.6
ASCD	53	55.8	286	52.4	530	39.4	56	22.3	925	41.3
NAESP	7	7.4	13	2.4	39	2.9	17	6.8	76	3.4
NEA	4	4.2	18	3.3	52	3.9	13	5.2	87	3.9
STATE AASA	63	66.3	372	68.1	847	62.9	132	52.6	1414	63.2
PHI DELTA KAPPAN	52	54.7	278	50.9	495	36.8	355	21.9	880	36.3
OTHER	13	13.7	86	15.8	231	17.2	59	23.5	389	17.4

Participation in Professional Organizations

Membership and participation in professional organizations is common in the superintendency, and has increased since 1982. For instance, the 1982 sample of superintendents indicated that 66 percent belonged to AASA, which is considered the flagship professional organization for superintendents. In the 1992 Study, 76.6 percent of sampled superintendents belonged to AASA. In the 2000 Study, this number has stayed very consistent at 75.9 percent. In addition, 66.1 percent belonged to their state professional associations in 1992, and 63.2 percent in 2000. Also, the 1982 Study found that 19.7 percent of respondents belonged to the Association for Supervision and Curriculum Development (ASCD). In the 1992 survey, 45.3 percent held ASCD membership (see **Table 4.24**), which is slightly more than in 2000. Superintendents from larger districts are much likely to belong to ASCD than those from smaller districts.

Participation of superintendents in professional associations provides opportunities for information sharing and inservice training, as well as the chance to meet with fellow superintendents. The superintendency is often a lonely position, and the opportunity to interact with others in the same role is a welcome change of pace. One of the most important opportunities provided by professional association membership is networking.

Professional Journals Read by Superintendents

The most read professional journal is *The School Administrator* (see **Table 7.10**). More than half (53.7%) of study superintendents indicated they frequently read this publication of AASA. Most (88.8%) either frequently or occasionally read it. The second most read professional journal was

TABLE 4.25 MEMBERSHIPS IN PROFESSIONAL ORGANIZATIONS COMPARISON 2000-1992

ORGANIZATIONAL MEMBERSHIPS	GROUP A: 25,000 OR MORE PUPILS 2000	1992	GROUP B: 3,000-24,999 PUPILS 2000	1992	GROUP C: 300-2,999 PUPILS 2000	1992	GROUP D: FEWER THAN 300 PUPILS 2000	1992	NATIONAL UNWEIGHTED PROFILE 2000	1992
AASA	89.5	93.1	89.7	85.1	74.1	75.0	50.6	51.4	75.9	76.6
ASBO	5.3	12.4	4.8	6.1	10.6	8.2	6.4	4.0	8.5	7.2
NASSP	16.8	13.1	7.5	10.2	9.6	7.1	13.1	11.5	9.8	9.3
NABSE	9.5	.	1.6	.	.4	.	1.2	.	1.2	.
NSBA	35.8	.	27.1	.	14.3	.	8.4	.	17.6	.
ASCD	55.8	60.7	52.4	48.2	39.4	45.3	22.3	29.6	41.3	45.3
NAESP	7.4	2.8	2.4	3.4	2.9	3.5	6.8	8.3	3.4	4.1
NEA	4.2	6.2	3.3	7.2	3.9	2.8	5.2	6.3	3.9	5.2
STATE AASA	66.3	70.3	68.1	70.7	62.9	64.2	52.6	58.1	63.2	66.1
PHI DELTA KAPPAN	54.7	.	50.9	.	36.8	.	21.9	.	39.3	.
OTHER	13.7	15.2	15.8	19.8	17.2	20.3	23.5	21.7	17.4	19.9

TABLE 4.26 SUPERINTENDENTS BEING MENTORS FOR SOMEONE ASPIRING TO BE AN ADMINISTRATOR OR SUPERINTENDENT

	GROUP A: 25,000 OR MORE PUPILS No.	%	GROUP B: 3,000-24,999 PUPILS No.	%	GROUP C: 300-2,999 PUPILS No.	%	GROUP D: FEWER THAN 300 PUPILS No.	%	NATIONAL UNWEIGHTED PROFILE No.	%
YES	86	90.5	477	87.4	1034	76.9	145	58.0	1742	77.9
NO	6	6.3	59	10.8	268	19.9	93	37.2	426	19.1
DON'T KNOW	3	3.2	10	1.8	43	3.2	12	4.8	68	3.0
TOTAL	95	100.0	546	100.0	1345	100.0	250	100.0	2236	100.0

Educational Leadership, read frequently by 49.4 percent of superintendents. It is the primary publication of the Association for Supervision and Curriculum Development (ASCD). Forty-six percent of superintendents also frequently read *American School Board Journal*, published by the National School Boards Association. These three journals are forwarded to superintendents as part of their membership in the respective organization. However, the third most read publication is *Education Week*, which 46.6 percent of superintendents said they frequently read and is not part of a professional organization. The role of *Education Week* has become very important in the past decade, as it provides its readers with important news about education each week. Sixty-nine percent of responding superintendents indicated they frequently read some other professional journal.

The importance of professional journals should not be underestimated as they frequently print articles that inspire superintendents and districts to investigate the possible adoption of new programs and policies. Also, they serve as a connecting link between members of the profession and keep them abreast of what is new in practice. Interestingly, few superintendents frequently read journals directly related to the principalship even though most were principals for a number of years.

Mentoring and Being a Mentor

School superintendents are leaders in their school districts, and many also serve in that capacity in their peer groups. This is reflected by the fact that 77.9 percent consider themselves mentors to others interested in the superintendency as a career. Some 58.5 percent indicated that they were assisted by a mentor in their own career development. Also, 90.5 percent of superintendents in larger districts said they have served as mentors, in contrast to 58 to 76 percent of those from very small to small districts (see **Table 4.27**).

Mentors and mentoring are important aspects of any profession. A great deal of professional knowledge is best transferred in a mentoring relationship, rather than in a university classroom or in an

TABLE 4.27 SUPERINTENDENTS HAVING MENTORS FOR THE SUPERINTENDENCY

	GROUP A: 25,000 OR MORE PUPILS		GROUP B: 3,000-24,999 PUPILS		GROUP C: 300-2,999 PUPILS		GROUP D: FEWER THAN 300 PUPILS		NATIONAL UNWEIGHTED PROFILE	
	No.	%	No.	%	No.	%	No.	%	No.	%
YES	62	65.3	343	62.8	769	57.2	135	54.0	1309	58.5
NO	31	32.6	198	36.3	567	42.2	115	46.0	911	40.7
DON'T KNOW	2	2.1	5	.9	9	.7	0	0.0	16	.7
TOTAL	95	100.0	546	100.0	1345	100.0	250	100.0	2236	100.0

TABLE 4.28 WHERE YOU SEE YOURSELF IN 5 YEARS

	GROUP A: 25,000 OR MORE PUPILS		GROUP B: 3,000-24,999 PUPILS		GROUP C: 300-2,999 PUPILS		GROUP D: FEWER THAN 300 PUPILS		NATIONAL UNWEIGHTED PROFILE	
	No.	%	No.	%	No.	%	No.	%	No.	%
WILL CONTINUE TIL RETIREMENT	61	66.3	330	60.8	825	61.5	130	52.0	1346	60.4
WILL CONTINUE TIL MINIMUM RETIREMENT	5	5.4	64	11.8	209	15.6	41	16.4	319	14.3
LEAVE FOR DESIRABLE POSITION IN UNIVERSITY	3	3.3	25	4.6	41	3.1	9	3.6	78	3.5
LEAVE FOR DESIRABLE POSITION OUTSIDE OF EDUCATION	3	3.3	30	5.5	48	3.6	12	4.8	93	4.2
LEAVE SUPERINTENDENCY	0	0.0	4	.7	13	1.0	1	.4	18	.8
OTHER	20	21.7	90	16.6	206	15.4	57	22.8	373	16.7
TOTAL	92	100.0	543	100.0	1342	100.0	250	100.0	2227	100.0

inservice workshop. Also, the opportunity for constructive feedback is present in most mentor relationships, which often are outside the supervisor/employee situation (Healy and Welchert, 1990). Because the superintendency is a self-selected profession in which principals and central office administrators enroll in a graduate program to earn the superintendency credential, mentorships are an important link between the academic and the practical preparation for the job (see **Table 4.28**.)

Future Plans of Superintendents

Even though a significant percentage of superintendents will be eligible for retirement in the first decade of the 21st century, only 14.3 percent indicated they would seek early retirement, which is available in many states at the age of 55. This number was 15.6 percent in 1992. Sixty percent indicate they plan to continue in the superintendency well into the first decade of the 21st century. Two-thirds (67.7 percent) indicated in 1992 they would "soldier on" through the 1990s. A few (3.5 percent) indicated an interest in a professorial position in educational administration, and 4.2 percent indicated preference for a position outside the field of education. These data seem to complement the strong indication by superintendents that they receive a good deal of satisfaction from the superintendency, and would choose the career over again if given the chance. It seems reasonable to say that superintendents nationwide will not be retiring in large numbers in the next 5 to 10 years (**Table 4.28**).

Bibliography

Bradley, A. (December 12, 1990). "Rapid Turnover in Urban Superintendents Prompts Calls for Reform in Governance." *Education Week*, pp. 1-2.

Carlson, R.O. (1972). *School Superintendents: Careers and Performance*. Columbus, OH: Charles Merrill.

Carter, G. R. and W. F. Cunningham. 1997. *The American School Superintendent: Leading in an Age of Pressure*. Jossey-Bass, p. 103.

Chapman, C. H. (1997). *Becoming a Superintendent: Challenges of School District Leadership*. Upper Saddle River, NJ: Merrill.

Cooper, B., L. Fusarelli, V. Carella. (2000). *Career Crisis in the Superintendency?* Arlington, VA: AASA.

Grogan, M. (1996). *Voices of Women Aspiring to the Superintendency*. Albany, NY: SUNY Press.

Healy, C. and A. Welchert. (December 1990). "Mentoring Relations: A Definition to Advance Research and Practice." *Educational Researcher*, 19, 9: 17-21.

Henry, D. A. "The Road to Superintendency," In Becoming a Superintendent. 1997. Chapman, C. (Ed.) Prentice-Hall: Englewood, CA.

Hoyle, J. (1993). *Professional Standards for the Superintendency*. Arlington, VA: AASA.

Ornstein, A. (November 14, 1990). "Dimensions: Tenure of Superintendents." *Education Week*, pp. 3-4.

Tallerico, M. (1999a). *Accessing the Superintendency*. Thousand Oaks, CA: Corwin Press.

Chapter 5

Superintendent/School Board Relations

Thomas Glass

Overview

Early in the history of the superintendency, school boards interacted very directly with school employees such as teachers and principals. The superintendent was often little more than a supervisor whose position was generally tenuous. During the 19th century, many school boards considered themselves the administrative body of the nation's small and highly localized school districts. Many school boards were quite large, and operated on the premise of direct participatory democracy (Griffiths, 1988). This often resulted in the board members attending to the most mundane of tasks such as buying the coal for the school stove. The hiring of teachers was also usually a direct action upon the part of school board members.

The working relationship and lines of authority between school boards and superintendents have evolved over the last hundred years in several stages. Before 1900, superintendents, for the most part, were general supervisors, and board members were the primary policy and decision makers. After the turn of the century, many superintendents became advocates of business ideology, which dictated that executives (superintendents) should be highly trained professionals. The role of the executive was to make decisions requiring technical expertise. In each of these stages, the superintendents' relationships with school board members changed (Callahan, 1966).

During the era of scientific management and efficiency (1900-1930), superintendents in large districts coaxed board members into adopting a quasi-corporate board model of governance. In a later period, through the 1940s, superintendents changed their self-perceptions to that of "professional educators." This change of identity was accompanied by superintendents viewing their boards as interest groups, primarily involved in setting general policy (Tyack and Hansot, 1982).

This general trend continued in most school districts into the 1990s, with the exception of districts in which board members began to be more intrusive into what had been the traditional domain of the superintendency. Often, these efforts on the part of the boards brought about conflict and instability (Carter and Cunningham, 1997).

The future role of boards and superintendents seems to be one of continuing partnership, with the superintendent managing the business of the district and serving as the primary initiator of policy. The possibility of boards allowing superintendents to adopt the role of chief executive, akin to that in a private sector corporation, seems unlikely except in the large urban districts where non-educators have been hired as chief executives.

As most school districts have between 3,000 and 4,000 students, it is unlikely that most school boards would feel comfortable hiring a highly paid executive without school experience.

Power Struggles

The literature on the relationships between the superintendency and school boards contains many studies of conflicts between the two groups. Many authors cite the differing job expectations held by boards and superintendents as the root cause of most conflicts. Researchers such as Nancy Pitner and Rodney Ogawa (1981) illustrate this theme in their research on the sociocultural context, in which superintendents work and make decisions about which priorities to address. They also suggest that successful superintendents are perceptive, and react appropriately to external forces. Other researchers reinforce the contention that superintendents, as well as boards, generally react to external forces (Norton et. al., 1996).

Many textbooks used to prepare administrators in the first half of the century espoused the theory that schools were apolitical. These texts actually meant that schools were not players in partisan politics. Schools today engage in political power struggles at a level similar to other public institutions. However, today, and certainly in the future, power struggles between boards and superintendents will become more visible to the lay community as media sources become more widespread in even the smallest communities. An excellent example is that many school boards now broadcast public board meetings on cable television.

It is likely that a majority of power struggles between boards and superintendents occur when some outside group pressures the board for an action that violates the best interest of the district as perceived by the superintendent. When this occurs, board factions emerge and the superintendent must take the side of the one acting in the best interest of the district and its educational programs (McCurdy, 1992).

Overlapping Roles

Without clear demarcation between the roles of superintendents and school boards, tensions in many districts are part of daily life. In thousands of school districts, these tensions are minimal and do not seriously interrupt district operations. But role conflict is often the reason superintendents get into trouble with their school boards and move on to other positions. Very few superintendents actually get fired or have their contracts bought out. When this does occur, however, there is usually more than ample media coverage, which creates an illusion that boards and superintendents in most districts are constantly in conflict (McCurdy, 1992).

A 1986 study of boards and board members by the Institute for Educational Leadership (IEL) argued that school boards, as an institution, are in trouble. The IEL study found a great deal of support for the traditional role of the school board as a grass-roots community institution. But, at

TABLE 5.1 WHO TAKES THE LEAD IN DEVELOPING POLICY?

	GROUP A: 25,000 OR MORE PUPILS		GROUP B: 3,000-24,999 PUPILS		GROUP C: 300-2,999 PUPILS		GROUP D: FEWER THAN 300 PUPILS		NATIONAL UNWEIGHTED PROFILE	
	No.	%	No.	%	No.	%	No.	%	No.	%
PRINCIPAL	1	1.1	9	1.7	20	1.5	3	1.2	33	1.5
CENTRAL OFFICE STAFF	21	22.1	140	25.8	58	4.3	4	1.6	223	10.0
SUPERINTENDENT	19	20.0	151	27.8	647	48.4	133	53.4	950	42.7
SCHOOL BOARD	10	10.5	35	6.4	105	7.9	27	10.9	177	7.9
SCHOOL BOARD CHAIR	0	0.0	3	.6	3	.2	0	0.0	6	.3
SHARED RESPONSIBILITY	43	45.3	202	37.3	493	36.9	77	30.9	815	36.7
OTHER	1	1.0	2	.4	11	.8	5	2.0	19	.9
TOTAL	95	100.0	542	100.0	1337	100.0	249	100.0	2223	100.0

the same time, it found apathy and ignorance in the community about what school board members do and the challenges they face in the future (IEL, 1986).

In 1992, IEL published another follow-up study declaring that school board governance needed drastic reforms that were not likely to occur internally, but through outside agents. They suggested that better board performance could be obtained through more thoughtful participation in the political sector, and especially in the community. A more collaborative relationship with the superintendent was also recommended (IEL, 1992).

This theme was also suggested in a study conducted by Educational Research Service within the context of developing a governance team to improve student achievement (Goodman, Fulbright, and Zimmerman, 1997).

Who Initiates Policy?

Table 5.1 shows that initiation of new policy and direction for school districts usually is considered a function of the superintendent. Two-thirds of the superintendents (66.9 percent) in 1992 said they were the primary initiators of new policy in their school districts. This is not the case in 2000, as only 42.9 percent indicated they originate most policy initiatives. The superintendents indicated that while board members act on policy, the members actually initiate policy decisions less than 8 percent of the time.

Shared Responsibility

In the 1992 Study, 28.5 percent of superintendents said they considered policy initiation a shared responsibility with the board. In 2000, 36.7 percent of superintendents indicated policy initiation to be a shared activity. This is a marked increase from 1992, and might signify a change in board governance in many districts. Shared responsibility is greatest in the larger districts, possibly because many large districts have more board members on standing committees that study issues and recommend new policies to the whole board. In smaller districts with fewer board members, the whole board often makes decisions as one body.

TABLE 5.2 WHO PROVIDES BOARD MEMBER ORIENTATION?

	GROUP A: 25,000 OR MORE PUPILS		GROUP B: 3,000-24,999 PUPILS		GROUP C: 300-2,999 PUPILS		GROUP D: FEWER THAN 300 PUPILS		NATIONAL UNWEIGHTED PROFILE	
	No.	%	No.	%	No.	%	No.	%	No.	%
SUPERINTENDENT	58	62.3	315	58.4	727	54.7	106	42.7	1206	54.6
EXPERIENCED BOARD MEMBERS	10	10.8	43	8.0	111	8.4	20	8.1	184	8.3
SCHOOL BOARDS ASSOCIATION	13	14.0	136	25.3	353	26.6	78	31.5	580	26.3
NEW BOARD MEMBER	4	4.3	12	2.2	76	5.7	31	12.5	123	5.6
OTHER	8	8.6	33	6.1	61	4.6	13	5.2	115	5.2
TOTAL	93	100.0	539	100.0	1328	100.0	248	100.0	2208	100.0

TABLE 5.3 HOW WILLING ARE PARENTS AND THE COMMUNITY TO PARTICIPATE IN DECISION MAKING?

	GROUP A: 25,000 OR MORE PUPILS		GROUP B: 3,000-24,999 PUPILS		GROUP C: 300-2,999 PUPILS		GROUP D: FEWER THAN 300 PUPILS		NATIONAL UNWEIGHTED PROFILE	
WILLINGNESS	No.	%	No.	%	No.	%	No.	%	No.	%
MORE WILLING TO PARTICIPATE	65	68.4	284	52.2	503	37.6	70	28.1	922	41.4
ABOUT THE SAME	25	26.3	200	36.8	640	47.8	133	53.4	998	44.8
LESS WILLING TO PARTICIPATE	1	1.1	6	1.1	21	1.6	4	1.6	32	1.4
DO NOT KNOW	4	4.2	54	9.9	174	13.0	42	16.9	274	12.4
TOTAL	95	100.0	544	100.0	1338	100.0	249	100.0	2226	100.0

Superintendents in smaller districts say they initiate policy more often than superintendents in larger districts. For instance, 20 percent of large-district superintendents took the lead in policymaking, compared to about 50 percent of superintendents in districts with 3,000 or fewer students.

How Are Board Members Oriented?

As district management and policymaking has become more complex, expectations for board members have become more technical and time consuming. The current interest in school reform and restructuring has put many board members on the "hot seat." Though some are well informed, board members may be inexperienced or uninformed in areas such as technology, facility development, curriculum evaluation/assessment, affirmative action requirements, teacher evaluation statutes, purchasing and bids, collective bargaining, and other technical and legal concerns. For this reason, many school board associations conduct orientation sessions for new board members and provide ongoing inservice training. Often, though, the task of initiating new board members is left to the superintendent and/or other local board members.

Overall, however, 46.2 percent of superintendents indicated they provide board members their primary orientation. State school board associations provide primary orientation only 15.6 percent of the time. In addition, 27.4 percent of responding superintendents said primary board member orientation is a shared responsibility between the superintendent and the school board association. Superintendents apparently believe it is important to provide the primary orientation for new board members, since developing good personal and working relationships with the board is a key factor in superintendent employment and success. In the 1992 Study, as in 1982, about 8 of every 10 superintendents provided the initial orientation of new board members. The 2000 Study shows this

TABLE 5.4 DO YOU ACTIVELY SEEK COMMUNITY PARTICIPATION?

HOW OFTEN	GROUP A: 25,000 OR MORE PUPILS		GROUP B: 3,000-24,999 PUPILS		GROUP C: 300-2,999 PUPILS		GROUP D: FEWER THAN 300 PUPILS		NATIONAL UNWEIGHTED PROFILE	
	No.	%	No.	%	No.	%	No.	%	No.	%
ALL THE TIME	25	26.3	94	17.3	151	11.3	30	12.0	300	13.5
FREQUENTLY	61	64.2	343	63.1	713	53.4	125	50.2	1242	55.9
SELDOM	0	0.0	6	1.1	75	5.6	13	5.2	94	4.2
WHEN REQUIRED	9	9.5	101	18.5	396	29.6	80	32.2	586	26.3
NEVER	0	0.0	0	0.0	2	.1	1	.4	3	.1
TOTAL	95	100.0	544	100.0	1337	100.0	249	100.0	2225	100.0

TABLE 5.5 AREAS IN WHICH SUPERINTENDENTS INVOLVE COMMUNITY IN PLANNING/ADVISORY CAPACITY

AREAS OF INVOLVEMENT	GROUP A: 25,000 OR MORE PUPILS		GROUP B: 3,000-24,999 PUPILS		GROUP C: 300-2,999 PUPILS		GROUP D: FEWER THAN 300 PUPILS		NATIONAL UNWEIGHTED PROFILE	
	No.	%	No.	%	No.	%	No.	%	No.	%
OBJECTIVES/PRIORITIES	82	86.3	409	74.9	910	67.6	137	54.6	1538	68.7
PROGRAM/CURRICULUM	67	70.5	356	65.2	772	57.4	134	53.4	1329	59.4
STUDENT ACTIVITIES	38	40.0	249	45.6	615	45.7	123	49.0	1025	45.8
STUDENT BEHAVIOR/RIGHTS	53	55.8	236	43.2	588	43.7	102	40.6	979	43.7
FINANCE AND BUDGET	48	50.5	219	40.1	298	22.1	41	16.3	606	27.1
EVALUATION OF PROGRAMS	41	43.2	187	34.2	363	27.0	68	27.1	659	29.4
SCHOOL-BASED DECISION MAKING	79	83.2	357	65.4	619	46.0	83	33.1	1138	50.8
FUNDRAISING	46	48.4	338	61.9	806	59.9	152	60.6	1342	60.0
STRATEGIC PLANNING	66	69.5	392	71.8	806	59.9	92	36.7	1356	60.6
OTHER	5	5.3	40	7.3	79	5.9	9	3.6	133	5.9

has become less common, as only 54.6 percent of superintendents indicated they are the primary providers of the orientation. Surprisingly, 62 percent of the large-district superintendents indicated they provide orientation. This might be because they perceive the problems of their districts to be much different than those in smaller districts. State school board associations probably base their orientation curriculum on the average district in their respective states (see **Table 5.2**).

Board member orientation is a very important activity, as often this is the point at which the working relationship between the superintendent and board begins. Since board members today are frequently elected on a special interest agenda, the board orientation is their first impression of the group consensus nature of district governance.

Community Participation

School district success depends significantly on community support. An indicator of community support is how actively large numbers of parents and citizens are involved in district activities, especially the decision-making processes. Most school boards and superintendents believe in community participation, but the level of involvement varies from district to district.

Each school community is different in terms of history and the traditional relationship between the schools, parents, non-parents, and private/public sector institutions. The type of participation engaged in by the community is typically based on history.

Heightened Need

In the 1992 AASA Study, the need for community involvement was perceived as more important than in 1982; 71.2 percent of superintendents indicated a very strong need, up from 59.8 percent in 1982. The 2000 Study specifically asked two questions about community involvement. The first was how actively superintendents sought community participation. Sixty-nine percent of the superintendents indicated they frequently or very often seek community involvement (see **Table 5.4**).

TABLE 5.6 IN LAST 10 YRS., HAVE COMMUNITY PRESSURE GROUPS EMERGED TO INFLUENCE THE BOARD?

	GROUP A: 25,000 OR MORE PUPILS		GROUP B: 3,000-24,999 PUPILS		GROUP C: 300-2,999 PUPILS		GROUP D: FEWER THAN 300 PUPILS		NATIONAL UNWEIGHTED PROFILE	
	No.	%	No.	%	No.	%	No.	%	No.	%
YES	86	90.5	378	69.6	712	53.3	104	41.8	1280	57.6
NO	9	9.5	165	30.4	625	46.7	145	58.2	944	42.4
TOTAL	95	100.0	543	100.0	1337	100.0	249	100.0	2224	100.0

TABLE 5.7 COMMUNITY PRESSURE GROUPS THAT INFLUENCE THE BOARD

PRESSURE GROUPS	CHECKED		NOT CHECKED.	
	No.	%	No.	%
COMMUNITY	703	31.1	1559	68.9
POLITICAL	361	16.0	1901	84.0
RELIGIOUS	346	15.3	1916	84.7
PRIVATE SECTOR	177	7.8	2085	92.2
GOVERNMENTAL	81	3.6	2181	96.4

TABLE 5.8 DOES YOUR DISTRICT CURRENTLY HAVE A SCHOOL-BUSINESS PARTNERSHIP?

	GROUP A: 25,000 OR MORE PUPILS		GROUP B: 3,000-24,999 PUPILS		GROUP C: 300-2,999 PUPILS		GROUP D: FEWER THAN 300 PUPILS		NATIONAL UNWEIGHTED PROFILE	
	No.	%	No.	%	No.	%	No.	%	No.	%
YES	89	94.7	421	77.7	544	40.8	43	17.3	1097	49.5
NO	5	5.3	121	22.3	789	59.2	206	82.7	1121	50.5
TOTAL	94	100.0	542	100.0	1333	100.0	249	100.0	2218	100.0

The second question asked their opinion as to how willing their communities were to participate in district decision making. Only 41.4 percent indicated their communities to be more willing to participate than in previous years. The larger the school district, the more likely superintendents are to indicate that community participation in decisions is needed to ensure continued community support. It is possible these data indicate that districts are feeling the effect of pressures to change and reform (see **Table 5.3**).

In very large districts, community support includes assistance from local property taxpayers, the private sector, and the media. Citizen advisory councils, parent/teacher organizations, and committees to help pass school finance measures were common vehicles of community support during the 1980s. In the 1990s, many of the larger school districts broadened the district governance by empowering local schools with site-based decision making.

Increased Willingness

The desire of superintendents to involve citizens in decision-making activities is apparent in the 2000 Study data. But how willing are citizens to participate in these activities? Superintendents say citizens are just as willing to participate in 2000 as they were in 1992 and 1982. This is true especially in the large districts. In fact, in many urban school districts, beginning in the 1960s and continuing to the present, parents have demanded they be allowed to participate in the decisions affecting the education of their children. Racial and ethnic conflict in many of these districts has been influential in heightening demands for involvement.

Over two-thirds (68.4 percent) of responding superintendents from very large districts (25,000 or more enrollment) think parents and citizens are willing to have a significant role in district decision making (see **Table 5.3**). Only 28.1 percent of superintendents in the very small districts think this is true for their districts. Overall, about one-third of superintendents think parents today are just as willing to participate in decision making as in 1982.

When is Participation Sought?

Superintendents can, to a limited extent, involve the community in district activities without permission of the board. However, when policy is discussed, the superintendent is likely to want board support before initiating projects involving the community. Superintendents indicated that their districts are involving citizens in a planning/advisory capacity, mostly in the strategic planning of district priorities and objectives.

The 1990s was a decade of increasing importance of high-stakes state assessment and testing programs. These programs have put substantial pressure on boards, superintendents, principals, and teachers to improve student achievement scores on both state and national instruments. Many more

TABLE 5.9 SUPERINTENDENTS' OPINIONS CONCERNING BOARD MEMBERS' GENERAL ABILITIES AND PREPARATION

PREPARATION	GROUP A: 25,000 OR MORE PUPILS		GROUP B: 3,000-24,999 PUPILS		GROUP C: 300-2,999 PUPILS		GROUP D: FEWER THAN 300 PUPILS		NATIONAL UNWEIGHTED PROFILE	
	No.	%	No.	%	No.	%	No.	%	No.	%
VERY WELL QUALIFIED	18	18.9	93	17.0	157	11.7	17	6.8	285	12.8
QUALIFIED	53	55.8	299	54.8	786	58.5	146	58.2	1284	57.4
NOT WELL QUALIFIED	19	20.0	141	25.8	373	27.8	78	31.1	611	27.3
INCOMPETENT	4	4.2	12	2.2	26	1.9	7	2.8	49	2.2
DON'T KNOW	1.1	.2	1	.2	1	.1	3	1.1	6	.3
TOTAL	95	100.0	546	100.0	1343	100.0	251	100.0	2235	100.0

superintendents indicated involving the community in program and curriculum matters in the 2000 Study than in 1992 and 1982. The same is true in the current study for school-based decision making, which was only in a developmental stage in many districts in 1992.

Also, the areas in which citizens participate appear to involve program/curriculum and efforts to mobilize community support for increased funding. Noticeably absent is the involvement of the community in the finance and budget activities of the district (see **Table 5.5**).

Community Pressure Groups

Most superintendents and school boards see community/school activities through a lens of involvement rather than as "pressure" politics. However, for various reasons, some community interest groups become pressure groups. A good example is found in communities where the school district relies heavily on local property taxes for funding. In many such communities, local residential taxpayer groups have pressured school boards over budget matters. In other districts, ad hoc pressure groups are formed to question an aspect of curriculum or to urge the board to fire or retain a staff member (often a coach).

The existence of such pressure groups in their school districts is confirmed by 57.6 percent of the superintendents. In the very large districts, where budget and political interests are strong, pressure groups are a reality for 90.5 percent of respondents (see **Table 5.6**).

Specific community groups were the largest numbers of special interest groups reported by the superintendents to have formed in their districts in the past 10 years. Seven hundred and seven superintendents (31.3 percent) reported that a religious or political pressure group had been active in their districts in the past decade. Issues such as school prayer and property taxes probably account for most of the 800 pressure groups mentioned by the superintendents.

The adept handling of pressure groups by the superintendent and the board is, to say the least, a serious task. Some studies of school boards have found that board members themselves often represent special interest or pressure groups. This tends to create board divisiveness and problems in district administration (Carter and Cunningham, 1997).

Board Abilities

School board members, according to superintendents in both the 2000 and 1992 studies, are generally "qualified" but not "well-qualified." Superintendents' complaints about uninformed board members and their inappropriate actions crop up frequently in "shop talk" at administrators' meetings (Carter and Cunningham, 1997). However, when asked on a more formal basis to rate board members' abilities, superintendents give generally positive appraisals.

TABLE 5.10 CHARACTERIZE YOUR SCHOOL BOARD	GROUP A: 25,000 OR MORE PUPILS		GROUP B: 3,000-24,999 PUPILS		GROUP C: 300-2,999 PUPILS		GROUP D: FEWER THAN 300 PUPILS		NATIONAL UNWEIGHTED PROFILE	
	No.	%	No.	%	No.	%	No.	%	No.	%
DOMINATED BY ELITE	1	1.1	17	3.1	36	2.7	5	2.0	59	2.6
REPRESENTS DISTINCT FACTION	30	32.3	107	19.6	251	18.7	35	13.9	423	19.0
ALLIGNED WITH COMMON INTERESTS	59	63.4	374	68.6	868	64.6	170	67.7	1471	65.9
NOT ACTIVE	3	3.2	47	8.7	188	14.0	41	16.4	279	12.5
TOTAL	93	100.0	545	100.0	1343	100.0	251	100.0	2232	100.0

Fewer superintendents in the very small districts indicated that their board members are "very well qualified" (6.8 percent) than did superintendents in very large districts (18.9 percent). However, for most other categories, responses were fairly even across the board (see **Table 5.9**).

Importantly, nearly 30 percent of the reporting superintendents indicated their boards to be underqualified for their jobs. The number of superintendents being evaluated as excellent or good by these same boards is 91.7 percent.

Seventy-four percent of superintendents in the largest districts felt their boards to be qualified despite the fact that board positions in these districts are very often subject to fierce political campaigning on the part of special interest groups.

In the 1990s, the increased complexity of board decisions, heavy responsibilities, public visibility, and substantial time commitment required have made school board membership less attractive in some communities. Business and professional persons sometimes lose business from school district conflicts that occur during their tenure on the board. Some board members find their employers unhappy with their frequent absences from work resulting from school district business. In general, the desirability of being a school board member has declined just at a point when high-quality lay leadership is most needed for school reform (IEL, 1992).

Superintendents Characterize Their School Boards

Only a small fraction of superintendents see their boards as being dominated by an elite group in the community. This means that the past literature on school boards, which indicates the presence in many communities of small elite groups controlling district policy is no longer relevant (Lutz and Mertz, 1992) in most school districts. Most superintendents indicated that their boards are generally aligned with a broad base of community interests. Only in the large districts do superinten-

TABLE 5.11 DO SUPERINTENDENTS HAVE A FORMAL JOB DESCRIPTION?

FORMAL JOB DESCRIPTION	GROUP A: 25,000 OR MORE PUPILS		GROUP B: 3,000-24,999 PUPILS		GROUP C: 300-2,999 PUPILS		GROUP D: FEWER THAN 300 PUPILS		NATIONAL UNWEIGHTED PROFILE	
	No.	%	No.	%	No.	%	No.	%	No.	%
YES	53	56.4	282	52.0	676	50.6	103	41.1	1114	50.2
NO	6	6.4	44	8.1	143	10.7	54	21.7	247	11.1

TABLE 5.12 IF YOU HAVE A FORMAL JOB DESCRIPTION, ARE YOU REALLY EVALUATED AGAINST ITS CRITERIA?

EVALUATED AGAINST CRITERIA	GROUP A: 25,000 OR MORE PUPILS		GROUP B: 3,000-24,999 PUPILS		GROUP C: 300-2,999 PUPILS		GROUP D: FEWER THAN 300 PUPILS		NATIONAL UNWEIGHTED PROFILE	
	No.	%	No.	%	No.	%	No.	%	No.	%
YES	53	60.2	282	56.6	676	56.7	103	52.8	1114	56.4
NO	35	39.8	216	43.4	517	43.3	92	47.2	860	43.6

TABLE 5.13 HOW OFTEN DOES THE BOARD EVALUATE YOUR JOB PERFORMANCE?

HOW OFTEN	GROUP A: 25,000 OR MORE PUPILS		GROUP B: 3,000-24,999 PUPILS		GROUP C: 300-2,999 PUPILS		GROUP D: FEWER THAN 300 PUPILS		NATIONAL UNWEIGHTED PROFILE	
	No.	%	No.	%	No.	%	No.	%	No.	%
ANNUALLY	70	74.5	423	77.6	1118	83.1	185	73.7	1796	80.3
SEMI-ANNUALLY	20	21.3	87	16.0	120	8.9	41	16.3	268	12.0
AT CONTRACT RENEWAL	1	1.1	13	2.4	42	3.1	13	5.2	69	3.1
NEVER	1	1.1	7	1.3	27	2.0	6	2.4	41	1.8
OTHER	2	2.0	15	2.7	39	2.9	6	2.4	62	2.8
TOTAL	94	100.0	545	100.0	1346	100.0	251	100.0	2236	100.0

dents see boards often representing distinct community factions. Nearly two-thirds of the superintendents indicated that their boards are aligned with community interests (see **Table 5.10**).

Elected or Appointed?

Almost all superintendents in the United States today are appointed to their positions by elected school boards. There are still a tiny handful of elected district superintendents. The same is true for appointed school boards. However, in some large districts, such as Chicago, Detroit, Cleveland, and Boston, board members are appointed by the mayor or other elected officials.

Evaluations and Job Descriptions

The superintendent/board relationship, regarding employment issues, is in most respects, similar to other executive leadership positions in the public or private sector. Slightly more than 90 percent of responding superintendents had written job descriptions in 1992. This was an increase over 1982, when 75.9 percent had written job descriptions. Due to the high percentage of superintendents having written job descriptions in the 1992 Study, the question was not asked in the 2000 questionnaire.

Only 50.2 percent of the superintendents overall said they are evaluated according to the criteria in the job description. In very small districts, 36.9 percent of superintendents think they are not evaluated against the job description. In 1982, 59 percent of responding superintendents thought they were being evaluated in accordance with their job descriptions.

The belief by a significant number of superintendents that they are not being evaluated against criteria in their job descriptions reinforces the notion that the quality of the interpersonal relationships between the superintendent and board members is really what counts. It also suggests the

TABLE 5.14 REASONS BOARD EVALUATES JOB PERFORMANCE

REASONS	GROUP A: 25,000 OR MORE PUPILS No.	%	GROUP B: 3,000-24,999 PUPILS No.	%	GROUP C: 300-2,999 PUPILS No.	%	GROUP D: FEWER THAN 300 PUPILS No.	%	NATIONAL UNWEIGHTED PROFILE No.	%
PERIODIC/SYSTEMATIC ACCOUNTABILITY	53	55.8	310	56.8	679	50.4	99	39.4	1141	51.0
IDENTIFY AREAS NEEDING IMPROVEMENT	16	16.8	99	18.1	304	22.6	67	26.7	486	21.7
POINT OUT STRENGTHS	4	4.2	29	5.3	118	8.8	23	9.2	174	7.8
DOCUMENT DISSATISFACTION	7	7.4	26	4.8	70	5.2	16	6.4	119	5.3
ESTABLISH PERFORMANCE GOALS	30	31.6	153	28.0	318	23.6	47	18.7	548	24.5
ASSESS PERFORMANCE WITH STANDARDS	35	36.8	195	35.7	396	29.4	62	24.7	688	30.7
COMPLY WITH BOARD POLICY	19	20.0	122	22.3	407	30.2	87	34.7	635	28.4
TO DETERMINE SALARY	7	7.4	49	9.0	103	7.7	19	7.6	178	8.0
OTHER	4	4.2	23	4.2	55	4.1	15	6.0	97	4.3

NOTE: Many respondents chose more than one response.

TABLE 5.15 WHAT KIND OF PROCEDURE DOES BOARD USE TO EVALUATE SUPERINTENDENTS JOB PERFORMANCE?

PROCEDURE	GROUP A: 25,000 OR MORE PUPILS No.	%	GROUP B: 3,000-24,999 PUPILS No.	%	GROUP C: 300-2,999 PUPILS No.	%	GROUP D: FEWER THAN 300 PUPILS No.	%	NATIONAL UNWEIGHTED PROFILE No.	%
FORMAL	64	68.1	294	53.9	726	54.0	113	45.6	1197	53.7
INFORMAL	4	4.3	51	9.4	160	11.9	44	17.7	259	11.6
BOTH	25	26.6	189	34.7	422	31.4	85	34.3	721	32.3
NOT EVALUATED	1	1.0	11	2.0	36	2.7	6	2.4	54	2.4
TOTAL	94	100.0	545	100.0	1344	100.0	248	100.0	2231	100.0

possibility that, in many districts, job descriptions are taken from books or manuals and used without much thought as to whether the criteria match what the board expects the superintendent to do.

Job descriptions can (or at least, should) be an important indicator as to what expectations boards hold for superintendent performance. The job description can be managerially focused but the actual board expectations can be more aligned with a chief executive model of leadership.

Several years ago, Illinois enacted legislation mandating that superintendent contracts be based upon student performance. This has also been the case in some of the larger districts, where student achievement gains are tied to superintendent evaluation. This may well be a trend for the 21st century. Whether or not superintendents can measurably affect student achievement has not been the subject of extensive research.

According to **Table 5.13**, almost all superintendents are evaluated annually: 80.3 percent have annual, and 12.0 percent have semi-annual evaluations.

The Why and How of Evaluation

Superintendents say the major reasons they are evaluated by boards is to ensure systematic accountability and to establish performance goals. Very few superintendents (5.3 percent) think the primary purpose of evaluation is for complaints prior to dismissal (see **Table 5.14**). The data from the 2000 Study are very similar to responses in 1992 and 1982.

The process of evaluation is usually is formal, using an evaluation instrument and often numerical point values. Only 502 superintendents indicated that their boards use a formal method of evaluation (see **Table 5.11**).

Specifically, board members sometimes use a numerical point system in conjunction with an appraisal by board members of communication and other skills that are not easily quantified. Superintendents agree that subjective opinions of board members often enter the informal process. Most board evaluation is done in executive sessions, and in most states is mandated by statute. Often the evaluation is given at the same meeting that the superintendent's contract is rolled forward or a new contract offered. Seldom are the results of the evaluation made public except in a general manner. Unfortunately, no known districts evaluate the board in conjunction with the superintendent. This would seem logical, since they constitute the district governance team. Logically, the performance of the entire governance team should be simultaneously evaluated.

What Counts with the Board?

The criteria used most often to evaluate superintendents according to the 2000 Study is that of periodic/systematic accountability, followed by assessing performance of district attempts to meet

TABLE 5.16 MOST RECENT EVALUATION RATING GIVEN TO YOU BY YOUR BOARD

	GROUP A: 25,000 OR MORE PUPILS		GROUP B: 3,000-24,999 PUPILS		GROUP C: 300-2,999 PUPILS		GROUP D: FEWER THAN 300 PUPILS		NATIONAL UNWEIGHTED PROFILE	
	No.	%	No.	%	No.	%	No.	%	No.	%
EXCELLENT	74	79.6	394	72.4	917	68.3	157	62.5	1542	69.1
GOOD	13	14.0	115	21.1	308	22.9	68	27.1	504	22.6
AVERAGE	4	4.3	11	2.0	38	2.8	6	2.4	59	2.6
BELOW AVERAGE	0	0.0	2	.5	7	.6	2	.8	11	.5
NOT EVALUATED	2	2.1	22	4.0	73	5.4	18	7.2	115	5.2
TOTAL	93	100.0	544	100.0	1343	100.0	251	100.0	2231	100.0

standards (state assessment) and compliance with board policy. Two related criteria are improving performance and needs assessment. The accountability theme is strong, and reflects a decade-long trend toward high-stakes testing across the nation.

The most-often-encountered criterion found on 1992 superintendent evaluations was that of "general effectiveness," which echoed the 1982 Study. Other top criteria included management functions, board/superintendent relationships, budget development, and educational leadership and knowledge. In the smaller districts, budget development ranked high. The criterion "board-superintendent relations" was ranked second in almost all categories of district size; in 1982, it ranked fourth.

According to conventional wisdom, as the district goes, so goes the superintendent's evaluation. Superintendents and professional associations in recent years have emphasized the necessity of developing appropriate evaluation forms for all employees, including superintendents (Robinson and Bickers, 1990). In some states, these efforts have resulted in statutes indicating criteria and modes of evaluation for various educators, which usually exclude superintendents. As mentioned earlier in this report, at least one state has legislated that superintendent and administrator performance be aligned to academic achievement.

Superintendent Evaluation Ratings

Of the 2,231 reporting superintendents on this item, fully 1,542, or 69.1 percent, indicated that their boards had given them a rating of excellent on their last formal evaluation. When considering the percentage that was never evaluated, this is a very impressive figure. Another 22.6 percent said their last rating was "good."

It is evident from the 2000 data that boards of education across the nation are satisfied with the performance of their superintendents. This is also true in the largest districts, where 79.6 percent of the superintendents reported an "excellent" rating.

Unfortunately, those districts that have serious conflicts with their superintendents, resulting in firing or a contract buyout, create a general impression counter to the data.

Board Expectations

Superintendents indicated that boards expect them to be both education leaders and general managers (see **Table 5.17**). This is not surprising, since the operation of a school district requires both educational and managerial skills. In the few large urban school districts that have hired non-educators as superintendents, there is usually a deputy superintendent assigned to be the educational leader, while the superintendent fills the role of chief executive officer.

TABLE 5.17 BOARD'S PRIMARY EXPECTATIONS OF SUPERINTENDENT

EXPECTATION	GROUP A: 25,000 OR MORE PUPILS RANK #1	%	GROUP B: 3,000-24,999 PUPILS RANK #1	%	GROUP C: 300-2,999 PUPILS RANK #1	%	GROUP D: FEWER THAN 300 PUPILS RANK #1	%	NATIONAL UNWEIGHTED PROFILE RANK #1	%
EDUCATIONAL LEADER	46	48.4	274	50.8	485	36.1	87	34.8	892	40.1
POLITICAL LEADER	15	15.8	97	18.0	150	11.2	21	8.4	283	12.7
MANAGERIAL LEADER	7	7.4	112	20.8	576	42.9	115	46.0	810	36.4
LEADER OF REFORM	8	8.4	23	4.3	27	2.1	4	1.6	62	2.8
OTHER	19	20.0	33	6.1	104	7.7	23	9.2	179	8.0
TOTAL	95	100.0	539	100.0	1342	100.0	250	100.0	2226	100.0

Interestingly, only 62 superintendents saw a board expectation that they be leaders of reform. Another 283 (12.7 percent) felt that their boards had high expectations for them to be political leaders in their communities.

Obviously, most superintendents are aware of the expectations of their boards and wish to meet those expectations. If the board has a high expectation for the superintendent to be a strong educational leader, activities associated with that role will become a daily routine. During the 1990s, boards not only began to ask superintendents, but also their principals, to become educational leaders. This trend toward "instructional leadership" did not lessen the importance or emphasis on managing the district (or school) in a competent manner. In many districts, the expectations for superintendents have increased, but neither support staff nor salary levels have been increased.

Do Boards Accept Policy Recommendations?

Most superintendents (88.6 percent) indicated in the 2000 Study that school boards accept their policy recommendations. Most of these recommendations were initiated by the superintendents. These data seem to be consistent with other study data portraying boards as being satisfied with superintendent performance.

The results in 2000 are very similar on these questions to the results in both the 1992 and 1982 studies.

Do Boards Favor Site-Based Management?

Generally, superintendents report their boards to be favorable to site-based decision making at the school level. This is very true at the large district level, where nearly 75 percent of superintendents indicated that their boards favored the concept. About a third of the districts (32.1 percent) were opposed or indifferent. This is understandable in districts with only a handful of schools (see **Table 5.20**).

TABLE 5.18 BOARD'S PRIMARY EXPECTATIONS OF SUPERINTENDENT ANALYZED BY AGE

EXPECTATION	AGE 30-35 %	AGE 36-40 %	AGE 41-45 %	AGE 46-50 %	AGE 51-55 %	AGE 56-60 %	AGE 61-65 %	AGE 66+ %	AGE TOTAL %
EDUCATIONAL LEADER	17.6	32.5	32.0	38.6	41.8	43.0	40.8	50.0	40.2
POLITICAL LEADER	5.9	10.0	12.0	13.8	12.6	11.7	14.0	13.6	12.7
MANAGERIAL LEADER	52.9	42.5	44.7	36.5	34.5	34.9	38.2	27.3	36.2
LEADER OF REFORM	0.0	2.5	3.3	3.0	3.4	1.5	1.9	0.0	2.7
OTHER	23.5	12.5	8.0	8.1	7.7	8.8	5.1	9.1	8.1

TABLE 5.19 HOW OFTEN BOARD OF EDUCATION ACCEPTS POLICY RECOMMENDATIONS

	GROUP A: 25,000 OR MORE PUPILS No.	%	GROUP B: 3,000-24,999 PUPILS No.	%	GROUP C: 300-2,999 PUPILS No.	%	GROUP D: FEWER THAN 300 PUPILS No.	%	NATIONAL UNWEIGHTED PROFILE No.	%
90-100%	78	83.0	483	89.1	1191	89.3	212	85.5	1964	88.6
80-89%	12	12.8	52	9.6	110	8.3	25	10.1	199	9.0
70-79%	1	1.1	7	1.3	23	1.7	8	3.2	39	1.8
60-69%	0	0.0	0	0.0	4	.3	2	.8	6	.3
50-59%	2	2.1	0	0.0	3	.2	0	0.0	5	.2
LESS THAN 50%	1	1.0	0	0.0	2	.2	1	.4	4	.1
TOTAL	94	100.0	542	100.0	1333	100.0	248	100.0	2217	100.0

Site-based management or decision making has been implemented in many forms in thousands of districts. Research has been generally unsupportive as to whether site-based management has positively affected student achievement scores. The system is one of many management reform initiatives adopted from the private sector.

In districts where site-based management has been implemented, the roles of superintendents and principals have been altered. Levels of responsibility have been changed, as have working relationships with boards.

Superintendents Working with Boards

Most superintendents indicated that their primary working relationship with their boards is that of professional advisor and initiator of policy initiatives. However, only about a third (36.2 percent) see themselves as managers. It appears that superintendents and boards view the superintendency as a position of political, reform, and educational advisor/leader (see **Tables 5.18 and 3.19**).

Hours Spent in Board Communication

Superintendents were asked to state the specific number of hours they spent per week in direct communication with board members. Most superintendents interpreted "direct communication" to mean verbal contact, while a few interpreted memoranda as direct communication.

Most research on effective superintendents (and leaders in other fields) stresses the importance of effective communication. The 2000 Study indicates that 62.1 percent of superintendents spend three or fewer hours per week communicating directly with board members. On a seven-member board this is about a half-hour per board member. Most superintendents likely spend more than a half-hour per week with the board chair, leaving very little time for other board members. A 1994 study showed that superintendents who were judged to be exemplary, spent more than double the amount of time reported in the 2000 Study (Carter, Glass and Hord, 1994).

The data from this item might identify an important source of problems between many superintendents and their boards. Many superintendents coming from the teaching ranks are suspicious of parents when they are teachers and board members when they become superintendents. This might be the reason why superintendents spend so few hours communicating with the board. Most superintendents would agree that board meetings are not ideal situations for communicating with board members.

Problems Board Members Face

In the 1982, 1992, and 2000 AASA studies, superintendents perceived similar problems facing board members in fulfilling board duties.

TABLE 5.20 IN YOUR OPINION, WHAT IS YOUR SCHOOL BOARD'S STANCE TOWARD SCHOOL-BASED DECISION MAKING?

	GROUP A: 25,000 OR MORE PUPILS		GROUP B: 3,000-24,999 PUPILS		GROUP C: 300-2,999 PUPILS		GROUP D: FEWER THAN 300 PUPILS		NATIONAL UNWEIGHTED PROFILE	
	No.	%	No.	%	No.	%	No.	%	No.	%
SUPPORTIVE	71	74.7	346	64.1	635	47.5	89	36.0	1141	51.4
INDIFFERENT	11	11.6	88	16.3	370	27.7	82	33.2	551	24.8
OPPOSED	7	7.4	49	9.1	93	7.0	14	5.7	163	7.3
NO OPINION	6	6.3	57	10.5	238	17.8	62	25.1	363	16.5

In the 1992 instrument, an additional response item asked whether "understanding appropriate role" is a serious problem for boards, and 21.9 percent of the superintendents said it was. By 2000, this figure had dropped to 16.5. In 1992, 39.3 percent of the respondents said finance issues were the most difficult for board members, up from 37.1 percent in 1982. In 2000, 35.2 percent of the superintendents see finance as a major problem for board members. Superintendents indicated that community pressure is about the same as in 1982, 1992, and 2000 as a problem for board members. The pattern of responses to these questions is similar across the districts (see **Tables 5.22** and **5.23**).

Citing finance as the biggest problem for superintendents and board members is in line with what was occurring in many states in the late 1980s and early 1990s. At those times, political support and community priorities for the welfare of children declined. The changing demographics of the 1990s have presented a severe challenge to many school boards. School enrollments in 2000 are the largest in the nation's history and are projected to increase at least for the next decade. Old buildings, teacher shortages, pressure for increased student achievement, and legal mandates all place financial pressure on local districts and their taxpayers.

Problems Superintendents Face

School finance is viewed by superintendents as the number one problem both they and their school boards face. Fully 96.7 percent (96.3 in 1992) of the total sample ranked finance as number one (see **Table 5.24**). Assessment and testing, as well as accountability and credibility, also are viewed as critical problems. Time management, according to superintendents, is a major problem inhibiting their job performance – and one that could be eradicated with additional funding for more central office staff.

TABLE 5.21 NUMBER OF HOURS PER WEEK SPENT IN DIRECT COMMUNICATION WITH BOARD MEMBERS

	GROUP A: 25,000 OR MORE PUPILS		GROUP B: 3,000-24,999 PUPILS		GROUP C: 300-2,999 PUPILS		GROUP D: FEWER THAN 300 PUPILS		NATIONAL UNWEIGHTED PROFILE	
	No.	%	No.	%	No.	%	No.	%	No.	%
0-1	5	5.3	43	7.9	268	20.0	79	31.6	395	17.7
2-3	16	16.8	230	42.4	624	46.5	119	47.6	989	44.4
4-5	30	31.6	139	25.6	256	19.1	33	13.2	458	20.5
6-7	16	16.8	65	12.0	99	7.4	13	5.2	193	8.7
8-9	11	11.6	21	3.9	34	2.5	2	.8	68	3.1
10+	17	17.9	45	8.2	60	4.5	4	1.6	126	5.6
TOTAL	95	100.0	543	100.0	1341	100.0	250	100.0	2229	100.0

TABLE 5.22 WHAT IS THE MOST DIFFICULT PROBLEM BOARD MEMBERS FACE?

PROBLEMS	GROUP A: 25,000 OR MORE PUPILS		GROUP B: 3,000-24,999 PUPILS		GROUP C: 300-2,999 PUPILS		GROUP D: FEWER THAN 300 PUPILS		NATIONAL UNWEIGHTED PROFILE	
	No.	%	No.	%	No.	%	No.	%	No.	%
FINANCIAL ISSUES	28	29.5	189	34.7	470	35.0	97	39.3	784	35.2
COMMUNITY PRESSURE	17	17.9	82	15.0	241	17.9	44	17.8	384	17.2
EMPLOYEE RELATIONS	3	3.2	16	2.9	65	4.8	15	6.1	99	4.4
CURRICULAR ISSUES	0	0.0	9	1.7	26	1.9	7	2.8	42	1.9
INTERNAL BOARD CONFLICT	11	11.6	37	6.8	63	4.7	3	1.2	114	5.2
UNDERSTANDING APPROPRIATE BOARD ROLE	19	20.0	97	17.8	223	16.6	30	12.1	369	16.5
AVOID MISMANAGEMENT	5	5.2	58	10.6	136	10.2	34	13.8	223	10.4
PRESSURE	10	10.5	47	8.6	88	6.6	10	4.1	155	7.0
OTHER	2	2.1	10	1.9	31	2.3	7	2.8	50	2.2
TOTAL	95	100.0	545	100.0	1343	100.0	247	100.0	2230	100.0

In the 1992 Study, large district superintendents expressed a greater concern with finances than those from smaller districts. Also, in the 1992 Study, small district superintendents indicated that they felt more pressure from too many demands on time. In the 2000 Study, however, all superintendents indicated a great deal of concern about the excessive demands on their time. The effect of state assessment programs and mandated reform legislation is reflected in superintendent responses on items concerning accountability/credibility, changing priorities in curriculum, and compliance. The number of items superintendents rank as major issues and challenges have significantly increased from the 1992 and 1982 studies. In these studies, finance, time demands, and board relations were focal points of issue and challenge.

It seems that superintendents in 2000 are saying that their jobs are more complex and more difficult due to the significant number of issues and problems. Data from **Table 5.24** might indicate that superintendents see their districts in continual crisis. This is probably not an accurate portrayal of the condition of the nation's school districts. However, at least 70 percent of responding superintendents do feel their districts are challenged on 15 of the 30 items listed. The knowledge and skills superintendents need to confront the issues require leadership and managerial attributes, as well as increased funding.

The superintendency is definitely a position that is more challenged than in past decades. The sum of these challenges has been an increase in superintendent stress levels, a pressure cooker job situation, and many vacancies in districts with long histories of problems (Carter and Cunningham, 1997).

Self-Perceptions

In terms of effectiveness, almost twice as many superintendents in the very large districts rated their performance as "very successful" as did superintendents in small districts (see **Table 5.25**). This was also true in 1992. The probable reasons for this might be that superintendents feel trapped in the small district, are expected to do everything, and know that many important tasks are not being completed due to lack of time. Another reason might be that some feel they are "less" superintendent-effective due to only being able to work in a small, less prestigious district.

Despite the problems with finance and time management, 97.1 percent of sampled superintendents think their overall effectiveness level is "very successful" or "successful." Only 0.5 percent indicated they were not successful or had no idea.

In the 1992 Study, 96.7 percent of superintendents felt themselves to be very successful or successful. This is roughly the same as in 1982.

TABLE 5.23 RANKING OF PROBLEMS BOARD MEMBERS FACE - 2000-1992 COMPARISONS

PROBLEMS	GROUP A: 25,000 OR MORE PUPILS		GROUP B: 3,000-24,999 PUPILS		GROUP C: 300-2,999 PUPILS		GROUP D: FEWER THAN 300 PUPILS		NATIONAL UNWEIGHTED PROFILE	
	2000 RANKING	1992 RANKING	2000 RANKING	1992 RANKING	2000 RANKING	1992 RANKING	2000 RANKING	1992 RANKING	2000 RANKING	1992 RANKING
FINANCIAL ISSUES	1	1	1	1	1	1	1	1	1	1
COMMUNITY PRESSURE	3	2	3	3	2	3	2	3	2	3
UNDERSTANDING AND FULFILLING APPROPRIATE BOARD ROLE	2	3	2	2	3	2	3	2	3	2
INTERNAL BOARD CONFLICT	4	4	6	4	7	5	6	4.5	6	4
EMPLOYEE RELATIONS	7	5	7	5	6	4	7	4.5	7	5
AVOID MISMANAGEMENT	6	-	4	-	4	-	4	-	4	-
PRESSURE	5	-	5	-	5	-	5	-	5	-

Self-perceptions, while not necessarily totally accurate, are important, since feelings of self-worth and competency play an important part in a superintendent's attitude toward job performance. In brief, superintendents in the study sample (1) receive high marks from their boards, (2) feel they are successful, and (3) are very satisfied with their jobs.

Factors that Inhibit Effectiveness

Even though superintendents, as a group, consider themselves to be quite effective, there are three definite areas of administration/management that they feel inhibit their performance. According to **Table 5.27**, the first and foremost of these areas is lack of finances. In 1982, 41.6 percent of superintendents indicated finance was the leading problem inhibiting their job effectiveness; in 1992, 59

TABLE 5.24 SUPERINTENDENT RANKING OF ISSUES AND CHALLENGES FACING THE SUPERINTENDENCY

ISSUE AND CHALLENGE	GROUP A: 25,000 OR MORE PUPILS		GROUP B: 3,000-24,999 PUPILS		GROUP C: 300-2,999 PUPILS		GROUP D: FEWER THAN 300 PUPILS		NATIONAL UNWEIGHTED PROFILE	
	RANKED	%	RANKED	%	RANKED	%	RANKED	%	RANKED	%
FINANCING SCHOOLS	4	93.6	1	97.4	1	96.9	1	95.2	1	96.7
ASSESSING & TESTING FOR LEARNER OUTCOMES	1	97.9	2	96.1	2	93.1	3	85.7	2	93.2
ACCOUNTABILITY/CREDIBILITY	2	95.7	3	92.2	3	86.7	6	78.7	3	87.5
DEMANDS NEW WAYS TEACHING OR OPERATING ED. PROGRAMS	6	89.4	4	89.5	5	85.7	7	78.4	4	85.9
CHANGING PRIORITIES IN CURRICULUM	13	80.4	5	89.0	4	85.8	8	78.3	5	85.5
ADMINISTRATOR/BOARD RELATIONS	7	87.9	6	85.7	7	82.1	4	80.7	6	83.1
COMPLIANCE W/ STATE AND FED. MANDATES	14	79.7	9	78.3	6	83.1	2	86.0	7	82.2
TEACHER RECRUITING	3	94.7	7	84.2	8	78.0	11	73.2	8	79.6
TIMELY/ACCURATE INFO. FOR DECISION MAKING	8	85.0	10	78.2	10	76.3	9	75.2	9	76.9
CHANGE SOCIETAL VALUES/ BEHAVIORAL NORMS	15	77.7	12	76.6	9	76.8	10	74.9	10	76.6
PARENT APATHY/CHILD ABUSE	19	73.9	19	67.9	11	75.2	5	79.9	11	73.9
LACK OF FUNDS FOR TECHNOLOGY	12	80.9	14	72.2	12	72.0	13	69.8	12	72.1
PERSONAL TIME MANAGEMENT	20	72.4	15	69.3	12	72.0	14	69.6	13	71.0
PROGRAMS CHILDREN AT RISK	10	81.9	8	78.6	13	69.6	17	57.1	14	70.9
PLANNING AND MISSION STATEMENTS	17	76.7	13	72.6	14	65.8	18	55.2	15	66.7
CALIBER OF PERSONS ASSIGNED OR REMOVED LOCAL BOARD	16	77.4	17	68.6	15	64.5	15	58.4	16	65.3
ADMINISTRATOR RECRUITING	9	83.9	11	76.7	16	62.8	25	43.2	17	64.9
AGING/INADEQUATE FACILITIES	18	76.3	20	65.5	17	62.3	16	58.0	18	63.2
COMMUNITY INVOLVEMENT IN DECISION MAKING	11	81.7	16	69.1	19	57.2	19	53.4	19	60.7
CALIBER OF RESPONSIBILITIES ASSIGNED OR REMOVED FROM LOCAL BOARD	21	67.8	21	61.6	20	56.7	22	49.6	20	57.6
RAPIDLY DECREASING/INCREASING ENROLLMENT	21	67.8	23	54.6	21	54.7	12	72.2	21	57.2
DRUGS AND ALCOHOL IN SCHOOLS	26	57.0	22	56.5	18	58.2	23	48.6	22	56.7
"CHOICE" PROGRAMS	24	63.0	25	52.7	22	531	21	50.8	23	53.2
CHANGING DEMOGRAPHICS	5	91.4	18	68.0	23	46.7	28	38.4	24	52.8
SCHOOL-BASED DECISION MAKING	23	64.9	24	54.4	24	46.0	24	45.2	25	48.8
STUDENT DISCIPLINE./GANGS	22	67.1	26	49.1	25	43.8	27	38.5	26	45.4
RESTRUCTURING OF DISTRICT	25	60.6	27	42.6	26	29.9	26	39.2	27	35.4
AFFIRMATIVE ACTION PROGRAMS	27	48.9	28	26.6	27	25.3	29	24.0	28	26.5
CONSOLIDATION OF DISTRICTS	28	22.6	29	17.1	28	25.2	20	51.6	29	26.1

percent identified it as the chief problem. In 2000, this number is down to 44.2 percent. Whether this indicates that additional funding has come to their districts, or they have made operational adjustments, is not clear.

The second area inhibiting effectiveness is having too many insignificant demands placed on them by the board, staff, and community. Of course, this problem might be eased with more support staff, again remembering that most districts are one- or two-person administrative offices.

The third, and more interesting area, is that of compliance with state-mandated reforms. It certainly is true in many states that reform mandates have not been completely state funded, thus causing already scarce district resources to be diverted to implementing mandates. The strain on the already thin ranks of administrators is likely to be felt by the superintendents.

Reasons to Leave a District

What reasons do superintendents give for leaving one district for another? The career patterns of superintendents suggest they often begin their superintendency careers in smaller districts, then move to larger and better financed ones. This fits with the concept of an upwardly mobile professional. Many times, superintendents of very large districts move from a central office position into a medium-sized district.

When asked why they left their last superintendency, 37.9 percent overall replied that they were "moving to a larger district." This was less than the 46.9 percent in 1992. A move to a larger district generally also means an increase in salary and benefits. Often, superintendents believe they have accomplished their goals in a district. They then seek the challenges of a new job situation in a larger district.

About 14.6 percent of superintendents indicated that a conflict with school boards precipitated their move. This was less than the 16.7 percent in 1992. Only 10.2 percent of the superintendents in the largest districts said this was the case. Surprisingly, 24.8 percent of superintendents in the smallest districts indicated they had left because of board conflict. In the category of districts with enrollments of 300 to 2,999, 15.1 percent of the superintendents said they left due to board conflict.

TABLE 5.25 IN GENERAL, RATE YOUR EFFECTIVENESS AS A SUPERINTENDENT

RATING	GROUP A: 25,000 OR MORE PUPILS		GROUP B: 3,000-24,999 PUPILS		GROUP C: 300-2,999 PUPILS		GROUP D: FEWER THAN 300 PUPILS		NATIONAL UNWEIGHTED PROFILE	
	No.	%	No.	%	No.	%	No.	%	No.	%.
VERY SUCCESSFUL	62	65.3	286	52.4	526	39.1	80	31.8	954	42.7
SUCCESSFUL	30	31.5	245	44.9	753	56.0	144	57.4	1172	52.4
SOMEWHAT SUCCESSFUL	3	3.2	14	2.6	58	4.3	25	10.0	100	4.4
NOT SUCCESSFUL	0	0.0	1	.1	2	.1	1	.4	4	.2
HAVE NO IDEA	0	0.0	0	0.0	5	.5	1	.4	6	.3
TOTAL	95	100.0	546	100.0	1344	100.0	251	100.0	2236	100.0

TABLE 5.26 IN GENERAL, RATE YOUR EFFECTIVENESS AS A SUPERINTENDENT COMPARISON 2000-1992

	GROUP A: 25,000 OR MORE PUPILS		GROUP B: 3,000-24,999 PUPILS		GROUP C: 300-2,999 PUPILS		GROUP D: FEWER THAN 300 PUPILS		NATIONAL UNWEIGHTED PROFILE	
	2000	1992	2000	1992	2000	1992	2000	1992	2000	1992
VERY SUCCESSFUL	65.3	60.4	52.4	58.5	39.1	48.5	31.9	36.1	42.7	51.2
SUCCESSFUL	31.6	36.8	44.9	40.8	56.0	47.2	57.4	58.2	52.4	45.7
SOMEWHAT SUCCESSFUL	3.2	2.8	2.6	0.7	4.3	4.1	10.0	5.6	4.5	3.0
NOT SUCCESSFUL	0.0	0.0	0.2	0.0	0.1	0.3	0.4	0.0	0.2	0.1
HAVE NO IDEA	0.0	0.0	0.0	0.0	0.4	0.0	0.4	0.0	0.3	0.0

Board elections also accounted for about 10 percent of superintendents moving on to a new district. This was a bit less than in 1992. This question was new in 1992, and no comparable data are available from the 1971 or 1982 studies (see **Table 5.28**). The data in this table do not suggest that superintendents are constantly being terminated or being asked to move on by their boards. In fact, the data align well with data on the items about board ratings and perceived effectiveness.

In the past decade, media stories indicate that superintendents have less than a 3-year tenure in their school districts. In particular, a story in the late 1980s used a 2.5-year figure (Rist, 1991). This statistic has gained a life of its own over the past 10 years, even though it is erroneous. True, many large urban superintendencies are often vacant, but others have superintendents who stay for a good number of years. It will be interesting to see the longevity of non-educator superintendents in these districts.

Reasons to Leave the Field

In the 2000 Study, no list of issues that might make superintendents leave the field was presented. However, data from other items make it clear that, in 2000, the issues superintendents find troubling are the very ones that might cause them to leave the field. Lack of adequate finances for school district operations is the leading reason that superintendents might leave the position. Second in importance is lack of community support, including the support of the board of education. In the 1971 and 1982 studies, the leading reasons for leaving the field were "attacks on the superintendent" and "negotiations and strikes." Financing of schools was ranked fourth in both of these two previous surveys. Relations with unions and negotiations ranked eleventh out of a possible twelve responses in 1992, indicating that superintendents are not as concerned with negotiations and strikes as they were a decade ago. However, they are very concerned about finance and public perception of schools. Perhaps the continual attacks on public school performance, which have gone on for the last 15 years in the media and political circles, is of sufficient concern to force some superintendents to leave the field or retire early.

TABLE 5.27 FACTORS THAT INHIBIT SUPERINTENDENTS' EFFECTIVENESS

RESPONSE CLASSIFICATIONS	GROUP A: 25,000 OR MORE PUPILS		GROUP B: 3,000-24,999 PUPILS		GROUP C: 300-2,999 PUPILS		GROUP D: FEWER THAN 300 PUPILS		NATIONAL UNWEIGHTED PROFILE	
	No.	%	No.	%	No.	%	No.	%	No.	%.
INADEQUATE FINANCING	40	42.1	244	44.7	594	44.1	111	44.2	989	44.2
TOO MANY INSIGNIFICANT DEMANDS	33	34.7	215	39.4	489	36.3	98	39.0	835	37.3
STATE REFORM MANDATES	15	15.8	131	24.0	362	26.9	71	28.3	579	25.9
COLLECTIVE BARGAINING AGREEMENTS	18	18.9	94	17.2	183	13.6	14	5.6	309	13.8
RACIAL/ETHNIC PROBLEMS	2	2.1	6	1.1	9	.7	1	.4	18	.8
TOO MUCH ADDED RESPONSIBILITY	2	2.1	66	12.1	191	14.2	55	21.9	314	14.0
INSUFFICIENT ADMINISTRATIVE SUPPORT	6	6.3	45	8.2	134	10.0	31	12.4	216	9.7
DIFFICULTY RELATIONS WITH BOARD MEMBERS	6	6.3	30	5.5	71	5.3	14	5.6	121	5.4
INEFFECTIVE STAFF MEMBERS	8	8.4	50	9.2	136	10.1	20	8.0	214	9.6
DISTRICT TOO SMALL	0	0.0	3	.5	51	3.8	33	13.1	87	3.9
LACK OF COMMUNITY SUPPORT	1	1.1	20	3.7	45	3.3	3	1.2	69	3.1
BOARD MICROMANAGEMENT	33	34.7	117	21.4	273	20.3	38	15.1	461	20.6
BOARD OF ELECTIONS-CHANGED EXPECTATIONS	15	15.8	76	13.9	126	9.4	10	4.0	227	10.1
OTHER	4	4.2	23	4.2	55	4.1	14	5.6	96	4.3

Fulfillment

Despite the problems caused by under-financing, community pressure groups, and demands for reform and higher test scores, superintendents from all district sizes indicate a good deal of satisfaction with their role as superintendent (see **Table 5.30**). Over half indicated considerable satisfaction in their jobs. However, superintendents in smaller districts generally are less satisfied than those in larger districts. One reason might be that superintendents in smaller districts perform many tasks they believe are inappropriate to their positions, and have little or no help in doing them. Small district superintendents also indicated more stress and tension with board members and the community than their counterparts in larger districts.

The media and academic press generally portray superintendents in large urban districts to be under fire at all times and periodically to burn out on the continual pressures of providing quality educational services to typically minority communities. If they are under fire and are subject to burnout, then the 2000 data strongly suggest they are receiving a great deal of job satisfaction doing their difficult jobs.

Prestige

Superintendents indicated that they think the prestige and status of the position has remained fairly constant in their communities. About 3 out of 10 (28.5 percent) indicated they think prestige is increasing, while only 19.4 percent think their position is diminishing in importance and influence (see **Table 5.31**).

TABLE 5.28 REASONS LEFT LAST SUPERINTENDENCY

REASONS	GROUP A: 25,000 OR MORE PUPILS		GROUP B: 3,000-24,999 PUPILS		GROUP C: 300-2,999 PUPILS		GROUP D: FEWER THAN 300 PUPILS		NATIONAL UNWEIGHTED PROFILE	
	No.	%	No.	%	No.	%	No.	%	No.	%.
LARGER DIST. SUPERINTENDENCY	32	65.3	130	52.0	214	34.9	10	9.5	386	37.9
CONFLICT WITH BOARD MEMBERS	5	10.2	25	10.0	93	15.1	26	24.8	149	14.6
RETIREMENT	1	2.0	13	5.2	35	5.7	11	10.5	60	5.9
LACK OF FUND	0	0.0	3	1.2	15	2.4	4	3.8	22	2.2
BOARD ELECTIONS	1	2.0	23	9.2	65	10.6	8	7.6	97	9.5
FAMILY CONSIDERATIONS	1	2.0	16	6.4	55	9.0	12	11.4	84	8.3
HIGHER EDUC. OPPORTUNITIES	1	2.0	0	0.0	2	.3	1	1.0	4	.4
JOB IN "BETTER" FINANCED DIST.	3	6.1	12	4.8	38	6.2	9	8.6	62	6.1
CONFLICT WITH COMMUNITY	0	0.0	1	.4	3	.5	0	0.0	4	.4
CONFLICT WITH EMPLOYEE	0	0.0	1	.4	9	1.5	0	0.0	10	1.0
LONG ENOUGH	2	4.1	15	6.0	36	5.9	12	11.4	65	6.4
OTHER	3	6.1	11	4.4	49	8.0	12	11.4	75	7.4
TOTAL	49	100.0	250	100.0	614	100.0	105	100.0	1018	100.0

TABLE 5.29 HOW MUCH SELF-FULFILLMENT DOES POSITION OF SUPERINTENDENT PROVIDE?

AMOUNT	GROUP A: 25,000 OR MORE PUPILS		GROUP B: 3,000-24,999 PUPILS		GROUP C: 300-2,999 PUPILS		GROUP D: FEWER THAN 300 PUPILS		NATIONAL UNWEIGHTED PROFILE	
	No.	%	No.	%	No.	%	No.	%	No.	%.
NONE	1	1.0	0	0.0	3	.2	2	.8	6	.3
LITTLE	4	4.3	21	3.9	78	5.8	25	10.0	128	5.7
MODERATE	19	20.2	172	31.6	531	39.5	114	45.6	836	37.4
CONSIDERABLE	70	74.5	351	64.5	734	54.5	109	43.6	1264	56.6
TOTAL	94	100.0	544	100.0	1346	100.0	250	100.0	2234	100.0

Stress

A certain amount of stress is present in any professional position. This is especially true in the superintendency, where management of fiscal and human resources within a lay governance structure creates unique organizational conditions. Pressures caused by lack of adequate funding, competing community and school groups, employee unions, state-legislated mandates, intrusive board members, and the public's perceived dissatisfaction with performance of schools can all cause stress for superintendents (see **Table 5.32**). Stress is not necessarily an unhealthy condition, but if frustrations become too extreme, and superintendents have no healthy ways to release them, stress can become disabling. Superintendents under high stress might make decisions without benefit of reflection and rational thought. Interpersonal relations typically suffer when leaders are under severe stress, and organizations such as school districts, in which leaders constantly are under substantial pressure, generally do not perform well when leaders are more preoccupied with handling stress than with developing the organization's potential.

Stress levels perceived by superintendents in the 2000 Study show a disturbing, but largely predictable trend. Fully 51.5 percent of all reporting superintendents indicated that they feel considerable or very great stress in the superintendency. Another 40.9 percent indicated a moderate level of stress.

TABLE 5.30 HOW MUCH SELF-FULFILLMENT DOES POSITION OF SUPERINTENDENT PROVIDE COMPARISON 2000-1992

AMOUNT	GROUP A: 25,000 OR MORE PUPILS		GROUP B: 3,000-24,999 PUPILS		GROUP C: 300-2,999 PUPILS		GROUP D: FEWER THAN 300 PUPILS		NATIONAL UNWEIGHTED PROFILE	
	2000	1992	2000	1992	2000	1992	2000	1992	2000	1992
NONE	1.1	0.0	0.0	0.3	2.8	0.4	.8	0.4	.3	0.3
LITTLE	4.3	2.1	3.9	2.0	5.8	2.8	10.0	5.5	5.7	2.9
MODERATE	20.2	20.7	31.6	28.6	39.5	38.4	45.6	44.3	37.4	34.3
CONSIDERABLE	74.5	77.2	64.5	69.1	54.5	58.3	43.6	49.8	56.6	62.5

TABLE 5.31 STATUS/PRESTIGE OF THE SUPERINTENDENCY

STATUS/PRESTIGE	GROUP A: 25,000 OR MORE PUPILS		GROUP B: 3,000-24,999 PUPILS		GROUP C: 300-2,999 PUPILS		GROUP D: FEWER THAN 300 PUPILS		NATIONAL UNWEIGHTED PROFILE	
	No.	%	No.	%	No.	%	No.	%	No.	%.
DECREASING IN IMPORTANCE AND INFLUENCE	10	10.5	86	15.8	278	20.7	58	23.1	432	19.4
REMAINING THE SAME	30	31.6	232	42.5	595	44.4	102	40.6	959	43.0
INCREASING IN IMPORTANCE/ INFLUENCE	52	54.7	189	34.7	335	25.0	60	23.9	636	28.5
DO NOT REALLY KNOW	3	3.2	38	7.0	133	9.9	31	12.4	205	9.1
TOTAL	95	100.0	545	100.0	1341	100.0	251	100.0	2232	100.0

TABLE 5.32 SUPERINTENDENTS' OPINIONS OF THE SUPERINTENDENCY AS A STRESSFUL OCCUPATION

DEGREE OF STRESS	GROUP A: 25,000 OR MORE PUPILS		GROUP B: 3,000-24,999 PUPILS		GROUP C: 300-2,999 PUPILS		GROUP D: FEWER THAN 300 PUPILS		NATIONAL UNWEIGHTED PROFILE	
	No.	%	No.	%	No.	%	No.	%	No.	%.
NO STRESS	0	0.0	2	.4	8	.6	1	.4	11	.5
LITTLE STRESS	7	7.4	41	7.5	97	7.2	14	5.6	159	7.1
MODERATE STRESS	45	47.4	203	37.3	559	41.6	105	42.0	912	40.9
CONSIDERABLE STRESS	30	31.6	237	43.6	540	40.2	100	40.0	907	40.6
VERY GREAT STRESS	13	13.6	61	11.2	139	10.4	30	12.0	243	10.9
TOTAL	95	100.0	544	100.0	1343	100.0	250	100.0	2232	100.0

In the 1982 AASA study, superintendents perceived the superintendency as a moderately stressful occupation. Some 84.6 percent of the sample said that "considerable" or "some" stress was present in the occupation. In 1992, 84 percent say they felt "considerable" or "moderate" stress, and only 7.8 percent indicated "very great stress." There are no significant differences among districts according to size with the exception again of the very large district superintendents who indicate less stress than colleagues in smaller districts. "Very great stress" is indicated a bit more frequently by superintendents of very small school districts (see **Table 5.33**).

Differences in stress perceived by superintendents of differing age groups are not significant. However, superintendents over 60 do indicate lower stress responses than younger superintendents. Most superintendents, however, retire by age 60. "Very great stress" is felt more often by superintendents in the 40- to 44-year-old category.

Some districts and boards encourage "wellness" programs for all employees, a strategy that can help offset the negative aspects of occupational stress. All prospective superintendents should be aware of occupational stress and its causes, as such stress can have a negative impact on marriage and family. Higher education preparation programs might consider incorporating stress management training within their educational administration coursework. Certainly, superintendents should have their health monitored on a regular basis by their physicians.

A relevant question is just how high stress levels will become in the 21st century superintendency. Are boards aware of the amount of stress placed on their superintendents?

TABLE 5.33 SUPERINTENDENTS' OPINIONS OF THE SUPERINTENDENCY AS A STRESSFUL OCCUPATION - 2000-1992 COMPARISONS

	GROUP A: 25,000 OR MORE PUPILS		GROUP B: 3,000-24,999 PUPILS		GROUP C: 300-2,999 PUPILS		GROUP D: FEWER THAN 300 PUPILS		NATIONAL UNWEIGHTED PROFILE	
	2000	1992	2000	1992	2000	1992	2000	1992	2000	1992
DEGREE OF STRESS	%	%	%	%	%	%	%	%	%	%
NO STRESS	0.0	0.0	.4	0.2	.6	0.6	.4	0.0	.5	0.3
LITTLE STRESS	7.4	13.8	7.5	6.8	7.2	7.5	5.6	7.9	7.1	7.8
SOME STRESS	47.4	40.0	37.3	43.8	41.6	40.8	42.0	40.1	40.9	41.7
CONSIDERABLE STRESS	31.6	37.2	43.6	42.3	40.2	43.9	40.0	40.9	40.6	42.3
VERY GREAT STRESS	13.7	9.0	11.2	6.9	10.3	7.2	12.0	11.1	10.9	7.8

TABLE 5.34 SUPERINTENDENTS' SOURCE OF INFORMATION RATED "VERY GREAT" AND "CONSIDERABLE"

	GROUP A: 25,000 OR MORE PUPILS		GROUP B: 3,000-24,999 PUPILS		GROUP C: 300-2,999 PUPILS		GROUP D: FEWER THAN 300 PUPILS		NATIONAL UNWEIGHTED PROFILE	
SOURCE	RANK	%	RANK	%	RANK	%	RANK	%	RANK	%
PRINCIPALS	3	90.4	2	96.5	1	92.5	3	81.4	1	92.3
SCHOOL BOARD MEMBERS	2	93.6	3	95.1	2	90.3	1	90.0	2	91.5
CENTRAL OFFICE STAFF	1	94.6	1	98.7	4	78.0	5	64.0	3	82.6
FELLOW SUPERINTENDENTS	6	57.2	5	72.6	3	82.8	2	86.8	4	79.6
TEACHERS	4	72.3	4	76.1	5	70.1	4	74.4	5	72.1
PARENTS	5	68.1	6	68.5	6	55.8	7	51.6	6	59.0
STUDENTS	9	34.4	9	40.1	8	38.1	8	39.7	7	38.6
OTHER	7	50.0	7	54.6	10	34.3	10	30.0	8	37.7
STATE OFFICE STAFF	11	27.5	13	25.7	7	39.7	6	51.7	9	37.1
COMMUNITY GROUPS	8	49.5	8	45.8	11	34.0	11	29.4	10	37.0
CONSULTANTS	10	29.4	11	31.6	9	37.0	9	35.3	11	35.2
PROFESSIONAL ORGANIZATION	12	27.2	12	30.7	12	29.2	12	28.9	12	29.5
POWER STRUCTURE	8	49.5	10	37.6	13	26.2	13	17.8	13	29.1

Communication Sources

It is vital that executives in organizations have reliable sources of information. Over 90 percent of superintendents surveyed listed board members as a powerful source of information. However, their chief source of information was the district's principals. Superintendents also say they place great importance on the information they receive from their central office staff. This is natural, since it is the role of these individuals to keep the superintendent directly informed. Superintendents also value the information they receive from fellow superintendents at informal gatherings and meetings of professional education organizations (see **Table 5.34**).

Just as superintendents say they place great importance on information from the school board, they think board members place an equal amount of importance on the information received from them

TABLE 5.35 BOARD MEMBERS' SOURCE OF INFORMATION RATED "VERY GREAT" AND "CONSIDERABLE"

SOURCE	GROUP A: 25,000 OR MORE PUPILS		GROUP B: 3,000-24,999 PUPILS		GROUP C: 300-2,999 PUPILS		GROUP D: FEWER THAN 300 PUPILS		NATIONAL UNWEIGHTED PROFILE	
	RANK	%	RANK	%	RANK	%	RANK	%	RANK	%
DISTRICT SUPERINTENDENT	1	93.6	1	95.8	1	95.6	1	93.3	1	95.3
PRINCIPALS	5	58.7	4	66.8	2	75.7	2	72.3	2	72.5
CENTRAL OFFICE STAFF	2	67.7	2	81.4	3	59.0	4	46.5	3	64.1
PARENTS	3	61.7	3	67.2	4	54.3	3	51.8	4	57.5
TEACHERS	6	50.0	5	50.9	5	42.5	5	45.4	5	45.2
COMMUNITY LOCAL POWER STRUCTURE	7	48.9	7	37.4	6	26.8	7	23.9	6	30.0
OTHER	4	60.0	6	43.3	7	24.5	6	24.0	7	29.0
STUDENTS	10	16.1	9	25.0	8	22.7	8	23.2	8	23.1
SPECIAL INTEREST GROUPS	8	30.9	8	27.0	9	21.8	9	17.7	9	22.9
CONSULTANTS	11	8.5	10	15.3	10	17.3	10	14.1	10	16.1
PRIVATE	9	26.6	11	13.3	12	6.6	12	6.7	11	9.1
BOARD MEMBERS OTHER DISTRICTS	12	5.4	13	5.9	11	8.0	11	8.9	12	7.5
RELIGIOUS GROUPS	11	8.5	12	7.2	13	4.6	13	4.1	13	5.4

TABLE 5.36 BOARD MEMBERS' SOURCES OF INFORMATION - 2000-1992 COMPARISON

	VERY GREAT WEIGHT		CONSIDERABLE WEIGHT		SOME WEIGHT		LITTLE WEIGHT		NO WEIGHT AT ALL.		DON'T KNOW	
	2000 %	1992 %	2000 %	1992 %	2000 %.	1992 %	2000 %.	1992 %	2000 %.	1992 %	2000 %	1992 %
DISTRICT SUPERINTENDENT	69.3	72.6	26.0	21.3	3.6	3.5	.6	08	.3	1.2	.2	0.6
PRINCIPALS	69.3	-	26.0	-	3.6	-	.6	-	.3	-	.2	-
CENTRAL OFFICE STAFF	16.8	22.2	47.3	48.0	23.0	20.9	5.5	3.5	2.4	3.2	5.0	2.2
PARENTS	13.4	13.9	44.1	50.1	39.1	31.4	3.1	3.6	.3	.6	.1	.4
TEACHERS	6.9	9.8	38.3	45.9	48.4	40.2	5.9	3.9	.3	.1	.2	.1
COMMUNITY LOCAL POWER STRUCTURE	7.6	12.3	22.4	30.1	39.0	36.5	24.0	15.4	4.1	3.9	2.9	1.8
OTHER	12.7	3.2	16.3	23.5	18.7	55.8	14.5	15.8	12.0	1.3	25.9	.3
STUDENTS	4.4	-	18.7	-	49.8	-	24.0	-	2.5	-	.7	-
SPECIAL INTEREST GROUPS	6.0	8.3	16.9	24.8	47.3	45.7	24.7	17.0	2.9	2.5	2.1	1.6
CONSULTANTS	1.5	-	14.6	-	33.9	-	28.2	-	17.0	-	4.7	-
PRIVATE	.8	-	8.3	-	38.2	-	34.6	-	13.3	-	4.8	-
BOARD MEMBERS OTHER DISTRICTS	.9	-	6.6	-	24.9	-	40.0	-	23.8	-	3.8	-
RELIGIOUS GROUPS	.9	-	4.5	-	25.5	-	41.9	-	22.4	-	4.8	-

and the principals. **Table 5.35** shows superintendents also think that central office staff, parents, and teachers are credible sources of information for school board members, as well as special interest groups and local power structures. Between 1982 and 2000, superintendents have lost some "weight" in terms of their degree of worth as a source of information to board members, though, for the most part, responses stayed the same. Interestingly, boards rely on community sources for information nearly to the same extent as the superintendent. But internal sources of information are of primary importance both for the board and superintendent (see **Table 5.36**).

If They Could Do It All Over Again

Two-thirds of superintendents responding to whether or not they would do it all over again indicated they would again seek the superintendency as a career choice (see **Table 5.37**). Only 14.9 percent indicated they would seek a career outside the field of education. The data clearly support data on other items concerning self-fulfillment in the superintendency, board ratings, and perceptions of effectiveness. Even superintendents who feel a good deal of stress in the superintendency feel that they are receiving sufficient intrinsic or extrinsic rewards to keep them in the profession.

Even though most superintendents are former principals, very few indicate they would seek a career in the principalship over the superintendency. A few would select a professorship over the superintendency.

Summary

In general, boards and superintendents get along quite well. Few superintendents are terminated, and few boards rate their superintendent less than good or excellent. Most superintendents feel they are doing an effective job in a very stressful position. Both boards and superintendents are concerned about district financial levels. Also, both groups are quite concerned about pressures from state assessment programs to constantly raise test scores. Both boards and superintendents acquire most of their information to do their jobs from inside the district. Superintendents are satisfied with the jobs and would select the superintendency again as a career choice.

TABLE 5.37 IF SUPERINTENDENTS HAD TO DO IT ALL OVER AGAIN, WOULD THEY CHOOSE CAREER AS:

CAREER CHOICE	GROUP A: 25,000 OR MORE PUPILS		GROUP B: 3,000-24,999 PUPILS		GROUP C: 300-2,999 PUPILS		GROUP D: FEWER THAN 300 PUPILS		NATIONAL UNWEIGHTED PROFILE	
	No.	%	No.	%	No.	%	No.	%	No.	%
SCHOOL SUPERINTENDENT	73	76.8	378	70.4	865	65.0	143	57.7	1459	66.0
OTHER CENTRAL OFFICE ADMINISTRATOR	5	5.3	27	5.0	49	3.7	3	1.2	84	3.8
CLASSROOM TEACHER	1	1.1	6	1.1	31	2.3	19	7.7	57	2.5
GUIDANCE COUNSELOR	0	0.0	1	.2	15	1.1	6	2.4	22	1.0
COLLEGE PROFESSOR	2	2.1	18	3.4	62	4.7	10	4.0	92	4.2
BUSINESS MANAGER	0	0.0	5	.8	12	.9	5	2.0	22	1.0
STATE AGENCY EMPLOYEE	0	0.0	2	.4	3	.2	1	.4	6	.3
INTERMEDIATE SCHOOL DISTRICT ADMINISTRATOR	0	0.0	2	.4	10	.8	1	.4	13	.6
PRINCIPAL	1	1.1	17	3.2	54	4.1	11	4.5	83	3.7
PRIVATE SCHOOL ADMINISTRATOR	1	1.1	3	.6	3	.2	3	1.2	10	.5
OUTSIDE OF EDUCATION	10	10.4	70	13.0	208	15.6	41	16.5	329	14.9
OTHER	2	2.1	8	1.5	19	1.4	5	2.0	34	1.5
TOTAL	95	100.0	537	100.0	1331	100.0	248	100.0	2211	100.0

Bibliography

Callahan, R.E. (1966). *The Superintendent of Schools: A Historical Analysis*. Eugene, OR: ERIC.

Carter, D., T. Glass and S. Hord. (1994). *Selecting, Preparing, Developing the School District Superintendent*. New York: Falmer Press.

Carter, G.R. and W.G. Cunningham. (1997). *The American School Superintendent: Leading in an Age of Pressure*. San Francisco: Jossey-Bass.

Goodman, R.H., L. Fullbright and W. Zimmerman. (1994). *Getting There from Here: School Board-Superintendent Collaboration: Creating a Governing Team*. Arlington, VA: Educational Research Service.

Griffiths, D.E. (1988). "Educational Administration: Reform Now or RIP." (UCEA Occasional Paper No. 8312). Tempe, AZ: University Council for Educational Administration.

Institute for Educational Leadership. (1992). *Governing Public Schools: New Times, New Requirements*. Washington. D.C.: IEL.

Institute for Educational Leadership. (1986). *Strengthening Grassroots Leadership*. Washington, D.C.: IEL.

Kowalski, T. (1995). *Keepers of the Flame: Contemporary Urban Superintendents*. Thousand Oaks, CA: Corwin Press.

Lutz, F. and C. Merz. (1992). *The Politics of School Community Relations*. New York: Teachers College Press.

McCurdy, D. (1992). *Superintendent and School Board Relations*. Arlington, VA: AASA.

Norton, J., D. Webb and W. Sybouts. (1996). *The School Superintendency: New Responsibilities, New Leadership*. Boston: Allyn and Bacon.

Pitner, N.J. and R. Ogawa. (Spring 1981). "Organizational Leadership: The Case of the Superintendent." *Educational Administration Quarterly* 17, 2.

Rist, M.C. (December 1991). "Race and Politics Rip Into the Urban Superintendent." *Executive Educator* 12, 13: 12-14.

Robinson, G. and P. Bickers. (1990). *Evaluation of Superintendents and School Boards*. Arlington, VA: Educational Research Service.

Tyack, D.B. and E.E. Hansot. (1982). *Managers of Virtue: Public School Leadership in America, 1820-1980*. New York: Basic Books.

CHAPTER **6**

Female Superintendents

C. Cryss Brunner

Overview

While the current number of women in the superintendency is larger than over the last 10 years, it is disturbing to see that a line graph of the percentages of women in the superintendency from each year over the last century is, essentially, flat (Blount, 1998). In no small measure, the superintendency has been a white, male-dominated position since it was first created by school boards in the late 19th century (Bell and Chase, 1995; Crowson, 1987; Tyack and Hansot, 1982.)

The fact that there are so few women in the superintendency means that the data gathered from a representative sample of female superintendents almost disappears when it is analyzed as a part of the full sample of superintendents. This fact makes it necessary to pull data on female superintendents out of the larger sample to describe the women accurately, which we have attempted to do here.

There are some who believe that having the data presented in one large category of "superintendent" is a gender-free method of reporting. In fact, there are those who suggest that articulating the differences between genders tends to reinforce gender bias. In addition, because men and women have been socialized differently in our culture, both men and women bring important and sometimes different attributes that enhance the role of superintendent of schools. But, there is an important reason for articulating the differences in the practice and demographics of female superintendents. Aspiring women facing inequities and inequalities need role models like themselves. Therefore, when women are handed information about other women in the role of superintendent of schools, there is an increased chance that they will pursue the role. In fact, "despite documented interest in the position, which is revealed [in] surveys and through an increase of women candidates for the superintendency in university training programs and internships throughout the country over the past two decades, the numbers of female superintendents remain consistently small (Grogan, 1996, p. 21). Thus, research and publications of this type are important for women who seek the position.

Personal Demographics

Gender and Race

Of the 2,262 superintendents responding to *The 2000 Study of the American School Superintendency*, only 297 are women (see Table 6.1). This number has more than doubled since the 1992 Study that reported only 115 or 6.6 percent of superintendents to be women. In the 1982 and 1971 studies, women represented only 1.2 and 1.3 percent of the total sample. Even though a few women and minorities hold the largest and highest salaried superintendencies in the nation, they are still underrepresented among the ranks of American public school superintendents. Certainly, male and female minority superintendents are sorely underrepresented.

As Banks (1995) notes: "Justification for increasing the number of women in educational administration is frequently based on the disproportionate number of women who hold administrative positions [whereas] increasing the number of minorities in educational administration is frequently justified on the basis of the growing number of students of color in the public schools (cited in Tallerico, 1999, p. 31).

As shown in Table 6.2, white men and women hold the majority of superintendencies in our nation. Minorities are dramatically underrepresented, with white men and women holding 95.3 percent and 91.6 percent of the superintendencies represented in this study. While 5.1 percent of female superintendents are minorities, only 2.0 percent of male superintendents are minorities.

TABLE 6.1 NUMBERS BY GENDER

GENDER	No.*
MALES	1953
FEMALES	297
TOTAL	2250

* Not all respondents indicated gender

TABLE 6.2 NUMBERS BY RACE

	MALE		FEMALE	
RACE	No.	%	No	%
BLACK	38	2.0	15	5.1
WHITE	1855	95.3	272	91.6
HISPANIC	27	1.4	4	1.3
NATIVE AMER.	15	0.8	2	0.7
ASIAN	3	0.2	2	0.7
OTHER	9	0.5	2	0.7
TOTAL	1947	100.0	297	100.0

TABLE 6.3 AGE BY GENDER

	MALE		FEMALE	
AGE GROUP	No.	%	No.	%
30-35	15	0.8	1	0.3
36-40	38	2.0	1	0.3
41-45	128	6.6	24	8.2
46-50	475	24.5	93	31.6
51-55	723	37.2	102	34.7
56-60	407	21.0	50	17.0
61-65	137	7.1	20	6.8
66+	18	0.9	3	1.0
TOTAL	1941	100.0	294	100.0

TABLE 6.4 MARITAL STATUS

	MALE		FEMALE	
STATUS	No.	%	No.	%
MARRIED	1834	94.7	226	76.9
SINGLE	102	5.3	68	23.1
TOTAL	1936	100.0	294	100.0

Age and Marital Status

Female superintendents, on the average, are older than the average male superintendent. While 39.8 percent of women are between the ages of 41 and 50, only 31.1 percent of the men are between those same ages (see **Table 6.3**). In interviews, many women report that they have waited for their children to get older before pursuing positions that make heavy demands on their time. As a result, these women generally enter their first administrative positions later than men and the superintendency even later.

Table 6.4 represents the marital status of the superintendents. More female superintendents than men reported being single. Twenty-three percent of the female superintendents are single, and 76.9 percent are married. In contrast, 94.7 percent of men reported being married and only 5.3 percent reported being single. Traditionally, many school boards silently prefer a "family" person to be superintendent (Tyack, D. and E. Hansot, 1982). This predilection could possibly select against a single person.

Years of Experience as Superintendent

The average number of years of total experience varies markedly between male and female superintendents participating in the 2000 Study. While 26.6 percent of men have 14 or more total years of experience, 74.9 percent of the female superintendents have 9 or fewer years of experience (see **Table 6.5**).

Type of Community Lived in Before College

As shown in **Table 6.6**, 70.3 percent of male and 62.2 percent of female superintendents lived in either a rural or small town before going to college. Only 16.1 percent of male superintendents lived in suburban areas, while 15.9 percent of females lived in large cities prior to attending college.

TABLE 6.5 YEARS OF EXPERIENCE

YEARS	MALE		FEMALE	
	No.	%	No.	%
1	115	5.9	38	12.9
2 – 3	234	12.0	69	23.5
4 – 5	224	11.5	64	21.8
6 – 7	251	12.9	49	16.7
8 – 9	239	12.3	27	9.2
10 – 11	237	12.2	19	6.5
12 – 13	130	6.7	11	3.7
14 – 15	472	24.2	12	4.1
16+	47	2.4	5	1.7
TOTAL	1949	100.0	294	100.0

TABLE 6.6 COMMUNITY BEFORE COLLEGE

STATUS	MALE		FEMALE	
	No.	%	No.	%
RURAL	710	36.5	82	27.7
SMALL TOWN	657	33.8	102	34.5
SUBURBAN	313	16.1	65	22.0
LARGE CITY	264	13.6	47	15.9
TOTAL	1944	100.0	296	100.0

Undergraduate major

Almost half of the female superintendents reported majoring in education as undergraduates, while roughly half of the male superintendents reported either majoring in education or social sciences. As seen in **Table 6.7**, only 23.7 percent of the males majored in education as undergraduates. This difference may indicate that more women intended to become teachers as they entered college, rather than choosing the career later because other plans did not work out. In fact, women fill the greater number of teaching positions. However, a majority of teacher preparation programs have elementary education majors while secondary teachers major in a subject area. A greater number of women teachers are in the elementary ranks.

Highest Degree Held

More female superintendents (56.8 percent) hold either Ed.D.s or Ph.D.s than do male superintendents (43.7 percent). Men hold more specialist degrees than women, and about 25 percent of both men and women have a master's degree plus graduate work (See **Table 6.8**). Less experienced superintendents, both men and women, hold doctoral degrees. In the last decade, many doctoral programs have become more accessible to part-time students. Also, many school boards favor hiring superintendents with doctoral degrees.

TABLE 6.7 UNDERGRADUATE MAJOR

MAJOR	MALE No.	MALE %	FEMALE No.	FEMALE %
AGRICULTURE	35	1.8	0	0
BUSINESS	104	5.4	9	3.1
EDUCATION (other than Phy. Ed.)	458	23.7	147	49.8
FINE ARTS	57	2.9	12	4.1
HUMANITIES	136	7.0	50	16.9
MATH	150	7.7	8	2.7
PHYSICAL ED.	233	12.0	9	3.1
PHYSICAL OR BIOLOGICAL SC.	202	10.4	9	3.1
SOCIAL SCIENCES	479	24.7	37	12.5
OTHER	82	4.2	14	4.7
TOTAL	1936	100.0	295	100.0

TABLE 6.8 HIGHEST DEGREE HELD

	MALE No.	MALE %	FEMALE No.	FEMALE %
BA OR BS	6	0.3	1	0.3
MASTER'S IN ED	155	8.0	18	6.1
MASTER'S NOT IN ED	9	0.5	1	0.3
MASTER'S + GRAD.	463	23.9	77	26.0
SPECIALIST DEGREE	460	23.7	31	10.5
ED. D or PH.D.	847	43.7	168	56.8
TOTAL	1,940	100.0	296	100.0

TABLE 6.9 POLITICAL PARTY AFFILIATION

	MALE No.	MALE %	FEMALE No.	FEMALE %
DEMOCRAT	658	34.4	116	39.6
INDEPENDENT	595	31.1	97	33.1
REPUBLICAN	659	34.5	80	27.3
TOTAL	1912	100.0	293	100.0

Political Affiliation and Posture

As shown in **Table 6.9,** female superintendents (39.6 percent) are more often Democrats than are their male colleagues. This is a decrease from the 1992 Study, in which 48.2 percent of women reported being Democrats. The number of male Democrats has also decreased from 33.6 percent in 1992 to 34.4 percent in 1999. The number of superintendents reporting themselves to be Independents has risen for both men and women since 1992. For both men and women combined, 53.1 percent reported themselves to be Independent in 1992, while now 62.2 percent report their political affiliation as Independent. Female superintendents are decidedly more liberal than their male counterparts. However, the majority of both groups indicated that they view themselves as political moderates (see **Table 6.10**).

Professional Organizations

About three-quarters of male and female superintendents belong to the American Association of Administrators at the national level, as well as their state organizations. In addition, more than half of the women sampled are members of the Association for the Supervision of Curriculum and Development (ASCD). Almost 20 percent more women than men belong to ASCD, an association focused on curriculum. In contrast, qualitative research focused on women indicates that they are more likely than their male counterparts to attend to curriculum and instruction (Brunner, 1998a, 1998b). The fact that 20 percent more women belong to ASCD seems to support this qualitative data. Overall, female superintendents belong to more professional organizations than do the male superintendents (see **Table 6.11**).

TABLE 6.10 POLITICAL POSTURE/VIEWS

	MALE		FEMALE	
	No.	%	No.	%
LIBERAL	179	9.3	65	22.0
MODERATE	1070	55.7	184	62.2
CONSERVATIVE	673	35.0	47	15.9
TOTAL	1922	100.0	296	100.0

TABLE 6.11 PROFESSIONAL ORGANIZATIONS

ORGANIZATION	MALE		FEMALE	
	No.	%	No.	%
AASA	1487	76.1	218	73.4
AASA (STATE)	1239	63.4	179	60.3
ASCD	758	38.8	170	57.2
NSBA	324	16.6	72	24.2
NASSP	186	9.5	32	10.8
ASBO	164	8.4	25	8.4
NAESP	56	2.9	20	6.7
NABSE	18	0.9	10	3.4
NEA	78	4.0	10	3.4
OTHER	334	17.1	57	19.2

District Demographics

Region and Type of Communities in Which Districts are Located

The percentage of women occupying superintendencies is highest in the Great Lakes and Mid-East Regions. These regions are followed closely by the Far West and Southwest regions (See **Table 6.12**). Almost half of the female superintendents work in rural areas, while a higher percentage of women than men are superintendents in suburban areas (see **Table 6.13**).

Enrollment and School-business Partnerships

From this sample, 201 women hold superintendencies in districts with enrollments of fewer than 3,000 students, while 1,390 men hold superintendencies in districts with enrollments of fewer than 3,000 students. Ninety-three women hold superintendencies in districts with enrollments higher than 3,000 students, while 508 men hold superintendencies in districts with enrollments higher than 3,000 students. However, from this sample, only one woman reported having a superintendency in a district of more than 100,000 students (see **Table 6.14**).

Just under half (48.5 percent) of male superintendents reported their districts as having a school-business partnership, while 54.8 percent of the women reported having school-business partnerships within their districts (see **Table 6.15**).

TABLE 6.12 REGION OF DISTRICT

REGION	MALE No.	%	FEMALE No.	%
NEW ENGLAND	86	4.4	27	9.1
ROCKY MOUNTAINS	80	4.1	16	5.4
SOUTHEAST	243	12.5	25	8.4
GREAT LAKES	458	23.5	56	18.9
MIDEAST	281	14.4	56	18.9
SOUTHWEST	226	11.6	38	12.8
PLAINS	416	21.3	34	11.5
FAR WEST	143	7.3	42	14.2
ALASKA	6	0.3	1	0.3
HAWAII	0	0	1	0.3
OTHER	11	0.6	0	0.0
TOTAL	1950	100.0	296	100.0

TABLE 6.13 COMMUNITY DESCRIPTION

COMMUNITY TYPE	MALE No.	%	FEMALE No.	%
URBAN	120	6.2	27	9.1
SUBURBAN	350	18.0	71	23.9
SUBURBAN/RURAL	329	16.9	53	17.8
RURAL	1135	58.2	144	48.5
OTHER	15	0.8	2	0.7
TOTAL	1949	100.0	297	100.0

Career Paths: The Road More Traveled

Length of Classroom Service, Subjects Taught, and Extracurricular Activities Before Entering Administration

Female superintendents, on the average, spend a longer time as classroom teachers than do men. Almost half of the men surveyed said they spent about five years as a teacher. About 60 percent of women have spent at least 10 years in the classroom (see **Table 6.16**).

As shown in **Tables 6.17** and **6.18**, 43.8 percent of the women surveyed taught in an elementary setting compared with only 17 percent of the men. Forty-three percent of the males began their educational careers teaching science, social studies, or physical education, usually at the high school level. Sixty-five percent of males coached athletics and 16.1 percent were club advisors, while 12.6 percent of female superintendents coached athletics and 33.6 percent were club advisors.

Elementary teachers have less access to activities leading to administrative positions than secondary teachers. There are usually no department chair positions and very few assistant principalships. Elementary teachers typically have to jump from teaching to a principalship or central office position. This generally takes more time than moving into a high school department chair position.

TABLE 6.14 ENROLLMENT: JAN. 1999

SIZE	MALE No.	%	FEMALE No.	%
FEWER THAN 300	199	10.3	52	17.7
300 - 999	536	27.7	56	19.0
1,000 – 2,999	655	33.8	93	31.6
3,000 – 4,999	234	12.1	37	12.6
5,000 – 9,999	152	7.8	25	8.5
10,000 – 24,999	83	4.3	15	5.1
25,000 – 49,999	55	2.8	11	3.7
50,000 – 99,999	16	0.8	4	1.4
100,000 OR MORE	8	0.4	1	0.3
TOTAL	1938	100.0	294	100.0

TABLE 6.15 SCHOOL-BUSINESS PARTNERSHIPS

	MALE No.	%	FEMALE No.	%
YES	934	48.5	159	54.8
NO	993	51.5	131	45.2
TOTAL	1927	100.0	290	100.0

TABLE 6.16 YEARS AS TEACHER BEFORE ENTERING ADMIN./SUPERVISION

YEARS AS TEACHERS	MALE No.	%	FEMALE No.	%
0-5	789	40.5	60	20.2
6-10	730	37.5	120	40.4
11-15	294	15.1	70	23.6
16-20	90	4.6	34	11.4
21-25	36	1.8	11	3.7
26+	8	0.4	2	0.7
TOTAL	1947	100.0	297	100.0

Age, Nature, and Level of First Administrative Position

Women are most often appointed to their first administrative position later than men are. Nearly 53 percent of men were appointed to their first administrative position before age 30. Only 21.1 percent of female superintendents had obtained their first administrative position before age 30 (See **Table 6.19**). The numbers of both men and women entering the superintendency before age 30 has decreased by 8 percent from the 1992 Study.

Most often, women have their first administrative experience in the position of coordinator. Second to coordinator, women's first administrative position is the principalship. Forty-two point two percent of male superintendents first served in a principalship, while only 30.3 percent of female superintendents gained a principalship as their first administrative position (See **Table 6.20**). This number, however, is up from 11.6 percent in the 1992 Study. None of the women sampled in this study began their administrative careers as business managers.

TABLE 6.17 SUBJECT TAUGHT FIRST FULL-TIME TEACHING POSITION

	MALE		FEMALE	
SUBJECT TAUGHT	No.	%	No.	%
ART	12	0.06	3	1.0
BUSINESS ED.	83	4.3	4	1.3
COMPUTER ED.	3	0.2	0	0.0
COUNSELING	9	0.5	2	0.7
DRIVERS ED	19	1.0	0	0.0
ELEMENTARY	332	17	130	43.8
ENGLISH	175	9.0	43	14.5
FOREIGN LANG.	22	1.1	12	4.0
HOME EC.	0	0.0	3	1.0
INDUST. ARTS	46	2.4	0	0.0
MATH	224	11.5	10	3.4
MUSIC	40	2.0	5	1.7
PE/HEALTH	137	7.0	11	3.7
SCIENCE	252	12.9	12	4.0
SOC. STUDIES	453	23.2	18	6.1
SP. ED.	59	3.0	33	11.1
VOC. AG.	27	1.4	0	0.0
VOC. ED.	15	0.8	3	1.0
OTHER	39	2.0	7	2.4
NO TEACH EX	5	0.3	1	0.3
TOTAL	1952	100.0	297	100.0

TABLE 6.18 EXTRACURRICULAR ACTIVITIES AS A TEACHER

	MALE		FEMALE	
ACTIVITY	No.	%	No.	%
COACHING ATHLETICS	1230	65.5	33	12.6
CLUB ADVISOR	303	16.1	88	33.6
CLASS ADVISOR	129	6.9	24	9.2
NEWSPAPER/ANNUAL	43	2.3	25	9.5
MUSIC GROUPS	56	3.0	22	8.
OTHER	118	6.3	70	26.7
TOTAL	1879	100.0	262	100.0

More women than men began their administrative careers at the elementary level. More than twice as many men as women began their administrative careers at the high school level, while more than twice the number of women as men began their administrative careers in a district office (see **Table 6.21**).

Career Pattern Prior to the Superintendency

Men and women differ in their educational career experience. Women report (in order of descending frequency) serving as elementary teachers, district coordinators, assistant superintendents, and high school teachers, while men report at least one year of experience serving as high school teachers, junior high/middle school teachers, assistant superintendents, and directors or coordinators.

A longitudinal study of 142 female aspirants to the principalship, conducted by Edson (1981, 1988, and 1995), found that women had greater success obtaining elementary rather than secondary principalships. Indeed, this study finds that three times more men than women have served as high

TABLE 6.19 AGE WHEN APPOINTED TO FIRST ADMINISTRATIVE POSITION

	MALE		FEMALE	
AGE	No.	%	No.	%
25-30	1025	52.8	62	21.0
31-35	540	27.8	77	26.2
35-40	237	12.2	81	27.6
41-50	105	5.4	48	16.3
51+	36	1.9	26	8.8
TOTAL	1943	100.0	294	100.0

TABLE 6.20 NATURE OF FIRST ADMINISTRATIVE POSITION

	MALE		FEMALE	
NATURE OF POSITION	No.	%	No.	%
ASSISTANT PRINCIPAL	695	35.8	79	26.9
DEAN OF STUDENTS	55	2.8	2	0.7
PRINCIPAL	819	42.2	89	30.3
DIR./COORDINATOR	217	11.2	90	30.6
ASSIST. SUP.	30	1.5	3	1.0
STATE AGENCY	13	0.7	4	1.4
BUSINESS OFF.	13	0.7	0	0.0
OTHER	98	5.1	27	9.2
TOTAL	1940	100.0	294	100.0

TABLE 6.21 TYPE OF SCHOOL OF FIRST ADMINISTRATIVE POSITION

	MALE		FEMALE	
SCHOOL TYPE	No.	%	No.	%
ELEM SCHOOL	459	23.5	113	38.0
JUNIOR HI	195	10.0	13	4.4
MID SCHOOL	135	6.9	17	5.7
HIGH SCHOOL	800	41.0	55	18.5
PAROCHIAL	14	0.7	2	0.7
COLLEGE	9	0.5	2	0.7
VOCATIONAL	25	1.3	3	1.0
DIST OFFICE	183	9.4	62	20.9
OTHER	132	6.8	30	10.1
TOTAL	1952	100.0	297	100.0

school principals for one full year or more. Further, almost twice as many female superintendents have served as district coordinators and assistant superintendents as their male counterparts (see **Table 6.22**).

The career patterns of female superintendents differ from men in that women more often jump from the classroom past the principalship directly into a central office position before becoming a superintendent. Women are less likely to follow the track of teacher and principal before becoming a superintendent. In addition, slightly fewer women than men follow the track of teacher, principal, and central office employee. However, since the 1992 Study, there has been an increase in the number of men and women who follow this career pattern (see **Table 6.23**).

The Search

Time it Took to Find First Superintendency

Men and women are finding superintendencies faster than reported in the 1992 Study. Over 70 percent of women and men find their first superintendency within one year, while in 1992 only 67.2 percent of males found a superintendency in one year or less (see **Table 6.24**).

TABLE 6.22 POSITIONS HELD FOR AT LEAST ONE FULL YEAR

POSITION	MALE		FEMALE	
	No.	%	No.	%
ELEM TEACHER	570	29.2	178	59.9
ELEMENTARY ASS'T. PRINCIPAL	124	6.3	37	12.5
ELEM PRINCIPAL	717	36.7	141	47.5
JR HI/MS TEAHCER, JUNIOR HIGH/MS	879	45.0	114	38.4
ASS'T PRINC, JUNIOR HIGH/MS	304	15.6	33	11.1
PRINCIPAL	593	30.4	42	14.1
HI SCH TEACHER	1216	62.3	119	40.1
HIGH SCH ASS'T PRINCIPAL	545	27.9	46	15.5
HI SCH PRINCIPAL	999	51.2	55	18.5
DIR/COORDINATOR	561	28.7	165	55.6
ASS'T SUPER	665	34.1	151	50.8
PROFESSOR1	78	9.1	50	16.8
COUNSELOR	171	8.8	29	9.8
SUPERVISIOR OR CONSULTANT	166	8.5	79	26.6
OTHER	125	6.4	39	13.1

TABLE 6.23 CAREER PATTERN PRIOR TO THE SUPERINTENDENCY

CAREER PATTERN	MALE		FEMALE	
	No.	%	No.	%
TEACHER, PRINCIPAL & CENTRAL OFFICE	956	49.0	136	45.9
PRINCIPAL & CENTRAL OFFICE	27	1.4	10	3.4
TEACHER & CENTRAL OFFICE	146	7.5	51	17.2
TEACHER & PRINCIPAL	641	32.8	61	20.6
CENTRAL OFFICE ONLY	22	1.1	5	1.7
PRINCIPAL ONLY	33	1.7	0	0.0
TEACHER ONLY	38	1.9	10	3.4
NOT SURE	90	4.6	23	7.8
TOTAL	1953	100.0	296	100.0

Agency that Managed the Search

For the most part, local school boards manage the search process for current superintendents; this has decreased, however, by roughly 6 percent since the 1992 Study. Professional search firms are also likely to have managed searches that result in the hiring of female superintendents. The use of professional search firms in the selection of superintendents has increased about 3 percent since the 1992 Study. In addition, state school board associations are being used more frequently to hire superintendents. The use of professional search firms results in the hiring of more women than men, while local school boards tend to hire more men than women (see **Table 6.25**).

Interestingly, a recent study conducted by Kamler and Shakeshaft (1999) had the expressed purpose of examining the role of the search consultant as the gatekeeper in promoting or preventing women from attaining a superintendency. In that study, the authors report they "found more advocacy and gender equity than they expected—and than had been evident in consultant's behavior, even a decade ago (Chase and Bell, 1994). Nevertheless, fewer than half (40 percent) of the consultants [in their study] spoke about their outreach to women and their involvement with women's organizations to encourage women to apply for the superintendency."

Influence of Old Boy/Old Girl Network and Other Factors that may Advance Women's Careers

In the 1992 Study, female superintendents indicated that the "old boy/old girl" network had significantly helped them. In short, someone made a concerted effort to help them get their positions. In the 1992 Study, 76.9 percent said they benefited from the influence of the these networks (see **Table 6.26**). Clearly, they are still important.

TABLE 6.24 LENGTH OF TIME SEEKING SUPERINTENDENCY AFTER CERTIFICATION

LENGTH OF TIME	MALE No.	%	FEMALE No.	%
LESS THAN ONE YR	1090	56.0	174	59.2
1 YEAR	301	15.5	46	15.6
2 YEARS	230	11.8	31	10.5
3 YEARS	101	5.2	18	6.1
4 YEARS	55	2.8	7	2.4
5+ YEARS	169	8.7	18	6.1
TOTAL	1946	100.0	294	100.0

TABLE 6.25 WHO MANAGED SEARCH PROCESS FOR PRESENT SUPERINTENDENCY

AGENCY	MALE No.	%	FEMALE No.	%
PROFESSIONAL SEARCH FIRM	333	17.1	62	21.2
STATE SCHOOL BOARD ASSOC.	373	19.2	56	19.1
LOCAL SCHOOL BOARD MEMBERS	1066	54.8	141	48.1
OTHER	173	8.9	34	11.6
TOTAL	1945	100.0	293	100.0

TABLE 6.26 GOOD-OLD BOY/GIRL NETWORK HELPS SUPERINTENDENTS GET POSITIONS

	MALE No.	%	FEMALE No.	%
YES	908	46.8	220	76.9
NO	677	36.3	28	9.8
DON'T KNOW	282	15.1	38	13.3
TOTAL	1867	100.0	286	100.0

Table 6.27 shows other factors that may advance career opportunities for women. Eighty-three point three percent of women and 61.7 percent of men agree that women's interpersonal skills are the most influential factor for advancing career opportunities for women. In addition, over 75 percent of the women believe that their ability to maintain organizational relationships and their responsiveness to the community are also important factors that may advance their careers. The literature on women in educational leadership supports the finding that women need to maintain organizational relationships. In fact, some literature on female superintendents refers to a leadership style of positive feminine qualities including nurturing, caring, cooperation, supportiveness, and attention to relationships (Brunner, 1998a, 1998b, in press; Helgesen, 1990; Rosener, 1990; Sherman and Repa, 1994). The same literature suggests that women are noted for the unusual priority that they give curriculum and instruction. In contrast, only 56 percent of the male superintendents believe that these are important factors for advancing women's careers.

TABLE 6.27 FACTORS THAT MAY ADVANCE CAREER OPPORTUNITIES FOR WOMEN

	IMPORTANT FACTOR		SOMEWHAT IMPORTANT FACTOR		NOT A FACTOR		DON'T KNOW	
	MALE	FEMALE	MALE	FEMALE	MALE	FEMALE	MALE	FEMALE
EMPHASIS PLACED ON IMPROVING INSTRUCTION	44.8	61.0	37.0	32.5	11.5	5.4	6.7	1.0
KNOWLEDGE OF INSTRUCTIONAL PROCESS	46.0	62.2	35.4	31.3	12.4	5.8	6.2	0.7
KNOWLEDGE OF CURRICULUM	44.4	60.2	37.9	36.0	12.1	3.5	5.6	0.3
ABILITY TO MAINTAIN ORGANIZATIONAL RELATIONSHIPS	50.6	76.1	33.6	21.2	9.6	1.7	6.2	1.0
INTERPERSONAL SKILLS	61.7	83.3	24.0	13.9	8.9	2.0	5.4	0.7
RESPONSIVENESS TO PARENTS AND COMMUNITY GROUPS	51.6	75.8	32.2	19.5	10.3	3.1	5.9	1.7

TABLE 6.28 BARRIERS LIMITING ADMINISTRATIVE OPPORTUNITIES FOR WOMEN

	IMPORTANT FACTOR		SOMEWHAT IMPORTANT FACTOR		NOT A FACTOR		DON'T KNOW	
	MALE	FEMALE	MALE	FEMALE	MALE	FEMALE	MALE	FEMALE
SCHOOL BOARDS DO NOT ACTIVELY RECRUIT WOMEN	7.9	22.9	29.3	48.5	51.8	23.9	10.9	4.8
LACK OF MOBILITY OF FAMILY MEMBERS	21.1	41.0	50.6	47.1	13.4	8.5	14.9	3.4
MID-MANAGEMENT CAREER "GLASS CEILING"	2.8	16.9	27.5	45.9	48.4	25.5	21.3	11.7
LACK OF OPPORTUNITIES TO GAIN KEY EXPERIENCES PRIOR TO SEEKING THE SUPERINTENDENCY	7.4	17.6	30.2	36.9	55.0	43.8	7.5	1.7
LACK OF PROFESSIONAL NETWORKS	3.9	22.6	31.8	43.5	52.5	30.1	11.8	3.8
PERCEPTION OF SCHOOL BOARD MEMBERS THAT WOMEN ARE NOT STRONG MANAGERS	6.7	38.1	35.9	43.5	43.3	15.3	14.1	3.1
PERCEPTION OF SCHOOL BOARD MEMBERS THAT WOMEN ARE UNQUALIFIED TO HANDLE BUDGETING AND FINANCES	3.6	33.7	22.5	43.2	60.5	19.4	13.3	3.7
PERCEPTION THAT WOMEN WILL ALLOW THEIR EMOTIONS TO INFLUENCE ADMINISTRATIVE DECISIONS	5.1	25.0	28.7	46.9	50.7	22.6	15.5	5.5
THE NATURE OF SUPERINTENDENTS WORK MAKES IT AN UNATTRACTIVE CAREER CHOICE	13.1	19.7	36.0	38.1	38.9	39.5	12.1	2.7
LACK OF MENTORS/MENTORING IN SCHOOL DISTRICTS	6.0	16.0	34.8	50.2	45.9	29.0	13.2	4.8

Discriminatory Practices and Barriers Limiting Opportunities for Women

According to the 1992 Study, female superintendents were much more likely than men were to think that discriminatory practices facing women were a problem. In fact, the 1992 Study found that female superintendents reported that discriminatory hiring practices were a problem four times more often than men did. Although this specific question was broken out into particular barriers to opportunities in the 2000 Study, the findings were similar. The majority of men in the 2000 sample believe that most of the barriers listed are not factors limiting administrative opportunities for women, while the women themselves reported all to be either important or somewhat important factors.

The significant difference between the female superintendents' views that discriminatory practices exist and the male superintendents' majority views that discriminatory practices and barriers are not a factor is troubling. Unless these practices and barriers are addressed, increasing the numbers of women in the position of superintendent of schools will be extremely difficult. It is, after all, most often the male superintendents who are mentors for others aspiring and entering the position. And, if male superintendents do not believe that women face discrimination and/or barriers that limit their administrative opportunities, they are less likely to understand the need for them to mentor and encourage women.

TABLE 6.29 SUCCESSOR TYPES: CAREER OR PLACEBOUND

SUCCESSOR TYPE	MALE		FEMALE	
	No.	%	No.	%
PLACE-BND (INSIDE)	606	31.2	107	36.3
CAREER-BND (OUTSIDE)	1337	68.8	188	63.7
TOTAL	1943	100.0	295	100.0

TABLE 6.30 HAVE YOU SPENT ENTIRE CAREER IN ONE DISTRICT?

	MALE		FEMALE	
	No.	%	No.	%
YES	171	8.8	30	10.1
NO	1782	91.2	267	89.9
TOTAL	1953	100.0	297	100.0

TABLE 6.31 REASON FOR LEAVING LAST SUPERINTENDENCY

REASON	MALE		FEMALE	
	No.	%	No.	%
LACK OF ADEQUATE FINANCING	20	2.1	3	3.4
MOVE TO LARGER DISTRICT	358	38.3	26	29.2
CONFLICT WITH BOARD MEMBERS	136	14.5	13	14.6
RETIREMENT	57	6.1	4	4.5
CHANGING BOARD/ELECTIONS	86	9.2	12	13.5
FAMILY CONCERNS	79	8.4	7	7.9
HI ED OPPORTUNITY.	3	0.3	1	1.1
POSITION IN "BETTER FINANCED" DISTRICT	53	5.7	10	11.2
CONFLICT WITH COMMUNITY GROUPS	3	0.3	1	1.1
CONFLICT WITH EMPLOYEE GROUPS	10	1.1	11.1	
BEEN IN DISTRICT LONG ENOUGH	62	6.6	4	4.5
OTHER	68	7.3	7	7.9
TOTAL	935	100.0	89	100.0

In an effort to identify the prevalence of particular discriminatory practices, the 2000 Study broke the question down into categories. In this study, both men (21.1 percent) and women (41.0 percent) thought that a woman's lack of mobility was the strongest barrier limiting career opportunities for women. The personal lives of women continue to weigh in as a perceived limitation for them. For men, often the assumption is that the family will move and benefit from the new career opportunity. In addition, 33.7 percent of women believe that boards of education discriminate against their perceived ability to act as strong managers (see **Table 6.28**).

It is important to note that qualitative open-ended questions asked of female superintendents about discriminatory practices and barriers that limit their opportunities often yield additional information.

Successor Types and Length of Time in One District

Female superintendents move into their positions from inside the district more often than male superintendents do. However, the placement of both men and women from within the district into superintendencies has slightly decreased since the 1992 Study. The majority of both genders came into the superintendency from another district (see **Table 6.29**). In fact, as shown in **Table 6.30**, very few women or men have spent their entire professional careers in the same district.

TABLE 6.32 IF YOU STARTED OVER, WOULD YOU CHOOSE A CAREER AS:

CAREER	MALE		FEMALE	
	No.	%	No.	%
SUPERINTENDENT	1289	66.9	176	59.7
OTHER CENTRAL OFFICE POSITION	61	3.2	23	7.8
CLASSRM TEACHER	45	2.3	10	3.4
GUIDANCE COUNSELOR	20	1.0	2	0.7
COLLEGE PROFESSOR	84	4.4	8	2.7
BUSINESS MANAGER	21	1.1	1	0.3
STATE AGENCY	6	0.3	0	0.0
INTERMEDIATE SCHOOL DISTRICT ADMIN.	12	0.6	1	0.3
PRINCIPAL	73	3.8	12	4.1
PRIVATE SCHOOL ADMINISTRATOR	7	0.4	3	1.0
OUTSIDE OF EDUCATION	278	14.4	55	18.6
OTHER	31	1.6	4	1.4
TOTAL	1927	100.0	295	100.0

TABLE 6.33 WHERE IN 5 YEARS?

IN FIVE YEARS	MALE		FEMALE	
	No.	%	No.	%
CONTINUE SUPERINTENDENT UNTIL RETIREMENT	1162	59.9	182	62.5
EARLY RETIREMENT	292	15.1	31	10.7
WORKING IN UNIVERSITY	62	3.2	16	5.5
WORKING OUTSIDE ED.	81	4.2	12	4.1
LEAVE SUPERINTENDENCY- NO LONGER DESIRABLE	17	0.9	1	0.3
OTHER	326	16.8	49	16.8
TOTAL	1940	100.0	291	100.0

Moving On

Reason for Leaving the Superintendency, Alternative Careers, and the Future

When superintendents were asked why they left their last superintendency, twice as many women reported moving to districts with better financial situations. Thirty-eight (38.3) percent of men and 29.2 percent of women report leaving their last superintendency to move to a larger district. As shown in **Table 6.31**, it appears as though women are more likely to leave a district due to board elections or changing boards than are male superintendents.

Numerous studies point out that female superintendents select a role as a change agent. Many times this is the most difficult (and contentious) role for a superintendent. More research needs to be done to assess what "superintendent" role women and men select and how that affects their tenure.

The majority of superintendents of both genders say they would become superintendents again if they could choose a career all over. As compared to the 1992 Study, slightly more men than women would repeat the path. Also compared to 1992, 2 percent fewer men and women would become superintendents again. Apparently, things have not changed all that much in terms of the percentage of those willing to do the job.

In terms of other career choices, the second most common response was a career outside of education (see **Table 6.32**). This may have something to do with the high stress level that superintendents report. When asked where they will be in five years, the vast majority of superintendents said they will still be in the role. However, more men than women would choose early retirement and are more dissatisfied with their positions (see **Table 6.33**).

Professional Development

Superintendents and Mentorship

Nearly all superintendents, men and women, consider themselves mentors, but more women than men report serving as mentors. Since the 1992 Study, overall, more superintendents are serving as mentors (see **Table 6.34**).

Female superintendents in the sample more often had mentors than did male superintendents. As shown in **Table 6.35**, women had mentors 71 percent of the time (in contrast to 59.1 in 1992), while

TABLE 6.34 DO YOU CONSIDER YOURSELF A MENTOR?

	MALE		FEMALE	
	No.	%	No.	%
YES	1503	77.0	247	83.2
NO	388	19.9	41	13.8
DON'T KNOW	60	3.1	9	3.0
TOTAL	1951	100.0	297	100.0

TABLE 6.35 DO YOU, OR DID YOU EVER, HAVE A MENTOR?

	MALE		FEMALE	
	No.	%	No.	%
YES	1099	56.3	211	71.0
NO	837	42.9	85	28.6
DON'T KNOW	15	0.8	1	0.3
TOTAL	1951	100.0	297	100.0

male superintendents had mentors 56.3 percent of the time. Since the 1992 Study, greater numbers of both men and women have mentors.

Evaluation of Preparation for Superintendency

Table 6.36 is evidence that the majority of both men and women rank graduate programs that train superintendents as either "excellent" or "good." In contrast to the 1992 Study, this study reports that more women ranked their programs as "good" rather than "excellent." Again, over half the men and women rank non-university professional development as either "very useful" or "useful." Women have a slightly higher opinion of non-university based professional development than do men (see **Table 6.37**).

Educational Research

When superintendents were asked their opinions of the usefulness of educational research, 10 percent more women than men found it highly useful. This number has decreased since the 1992 Study, however. Overall, well over half of both men and women find educational research useful or highly useful (see **Table 6.38**). Perhaps women find educational research more useful because they are still actively involved in academic higher education programs. **Table 6.39** indicates that the lengths of time since the women have earned their highest degrees are evenly distributed over the table's divisions of years. In fact, at least 21.9 percent of women are currently working on degrees or have just completed them in the last 5 years. On the other hand, 43.6 percent of male superintendents finished their highest degrees 11 or more years ago.

Contracts and Evaluation

Hiring and Expectations

Male superintendents reported the reasons they were hired in the following order: 1) their personal characteristics, such as honesty, tact, etc., 2) their potential to be change agents, and 3) their instructional leadership skills. In contrast and reverse order, women believe they were hired because of their: 1) instructional leadership skills, 2) potential to be change agents, and 3) personal characteristics (see **Table 6.40**).

TABLE 6.36 EVALUATION OF PROGRAM OF GRADUATE STUDIES AS PREPARATION FOR THE SUPERINTENDENCY

	MALE		FEMALE	
	No.	%	No.	%
EXCELLENT	509	26.2	76	25.9
GOOD	923	47.5	132	45.1
FAIR	424	21.8	66	22.5
POOR	86	4.4	19	6.5
TOTAL	1942	100.0	293	100.0

TABLE 6.37 EVALUATION OF NON-UNIVERSITY-BASED PROFESSIONAL DEVELOPMENT

YEARS	MALE		FEMALE	
	No.	%	No.	%
VERY USEFUL	530	27.4	115	39.4
USEFUL	494	25.5	55	18.8
SOMEWHAT USEFUL	812	42.0	111	38.0
NOT USEFUL	31	1.6	4	1.4
NO OPINION	68	3.5	7	2.4
TOTAL	1935	100.0	292	100.0

Table 6.41, which describes what the superintendents believe about their boards' primary expectations, falls in line with **Table 6.40**. Interestingly, superintendents report that boards of education expect women to be instructional leaders and strong change agents and, in contrast, expect men to be political leaders and managers.

Board Evaluations and Superintendent Effectiveness

Male and female superintendents alike rate themselves as either very successful or successful. Men give themselves a slightly higher success rating than do women (see **Table 6.42**). As shown in Table 6.43, women reported a slightly higher ranking on board evaluations than men reported.

When superintendents were asked to report two reasons they were evaluated by boards of education, the majority of men and women reported that their evaluations were primarily for the purpose of providing periodic and systematic accountability for the district. The second most often reported reason for evaluation, by both men and women, was for the purpose of assessing their performances in the role when compared to a set of established standards. Another finding from this survey question is that a slightly higher percent of women than men reported that their evaluations were closely linked to their salaries (see **Table 6.44**).

TABLE 6.38 OPINION OF USEFULNESS OF EDUCATIONAL RESEARCH

	MALE		FEMALE	
	No.	%	No.	%
HIGHLY USEFUL	565	29.0	117	39.8
USUALLY USEFUL	884	45.4	131	44.6
OCCASIONALLY USEFUL	470	24.2	45	15.3
IS NOT USEFUL	21	1.1	1	0.3
NO OPINION	5	0.3	0	0.0
TOTAL	1945	100.0	294	100.0

TABLE 6.39 HOW LONG SINCE YOU EARNED YOUR HIGHEST ACADEMIC DEGREE?

YEARS	MALE		FEMALE	
	No.	%	No.	%
0 – 5 YEARS AGO	266	13.6	65	21.9
6 – 10 YEARS AGO	445	22.8	86	29.0
11 – 15 YEARS AGO	408	20.9	74	24.9
15+ YEARS AGO	833	42.7	72	24.2
TOTAL	1952	100.0	297	100.0

TABLE 6.40 REASON YOU WERE HIRED

REASON	MALE		FEMALE	
	No.	%	No.	%
PERSONAL CHARACTERISTICS (HONESTY, ETC.)	816	42.0	79	26.7
POTENTIAL TO BE CHANGE AGENT	504	25.9	88	29.7
ABITLITY TO KEEP STATUS QUO	30	1.5	4	1.4
ABIILTIY TO BE INSTRUCTION LEADER	466	24.0	108	36.5
NO PARTICULAR IMPORTANT REASON	56	2.9	7	2.4
NOT SURE	72	3.7	10	3.4
TOTAL	1944	100.0	296	100.0

The study also asked about factors that inhibit superintendents' effectiveness. In their responses, the men and women in the sample agreed that the top three factors that inhibit their effectiveness are: 1) inadequate financing, 2) too many insignificant demands, and 3) board micro-management. However, as can been seen in **Table 6.45**, men and women disagree in some areas. Men felt that state mandates inhibited their effectiveness more often than women. Further, women were more concerned about insufficient administrative staff and the fact that expectations of members of their boards changed too frequently.

Board Demographics, Dynamics, and Decision Making

Board Demographics

When superintendents were asked to characterize their school boards, over half of both male and female respondents characterized their board as active and aligned with community interests, but not rigid. More men than women characterized their boards as status quo boards (see **Table 6.46**).

Most superintendents reported that they have four or fewer female school board members. Female superintendents reported a slightly higher percentage of female board members than did male superintendents (see **Table 6.47**).

TABLE 6.41 BOARD'S PRIMARY EXPECTATION OF SUPERINTENDENT

	MALE		FEMALE	
EXPECTATION	No.	%	No.	%
EDUCATION LEADER	742	38.2	152	51.4
POLITICAL LEADER	259	13.4	26	8.8
MANAGER LEADER	733	37.8	82	27.7
LEADER OF SCHOOL REFORM	52	2.7	10	3.4
OTHER	154	7.9	26	8.8
TOTAL	1940	100.0	296	100.0

TABLE 6.42 PERCEPTION OF EFFECTIVENESS

	MALE		FEMALE	
	No.	%	No.	%
VERY SUCCESSFUL	828	42.5	128	43.1
SUCCESSFUL	1038	53.2	141	47.5
SOMETIMES SUCCESSFUL	77	3.9	24	8.1
NOT SUCCESSFUL	3	0.2	1	0.3
HAVE NO IDEA	4	0.2	3	1.0
TOTAL	1950	100.0	297	100.0

TABLE 6.43 SUPERINTENDENT RATING ON LAST EVALUATION

	MALE		FEMALE	
	No.	%	No.	%
EXCELLENT	1341	68.8	207	70.2
GOOD	442	22.7	67	22.7
AVERAGE	55	2.8	4	1.4
BELOW AVERAGE	11	0.6	0	0.0
NOT EVALUATED	99	5.1	17	5.8
TOTAL	1948	100.0	295	100.0

Table 6.48 displays the average length of board membership with 36.3 percent of men reporting 7-8 years of membership, and 28.6 percent of women reporting 7-8 years of membership. The average length of membership for both men and women appears to be between 5 and 8 years.

School Board Decision Making and Board Dynamics

Superintendents were asked to articulate what their school boards think about school-based (site-based) decision making. Roughly half of both male and female superintendents reported that their boards are supportive of school-based decision making. However, more men than women believe that their school boards are indifferent to school-based decision making and around 5 percent more females than males indicated that their boards are supportive of school-based decision making (see **Table 6.49**).

TABLE 6.44 REASONS FOR BOARD EVALUATIONS (TOP TWO REASONS SELECTED)

REASON	MALE No.	%	FEMALE No.	%
TO PROVIDE PERIODIC AND SYSTEMATIC ACCOUNTABILITY	998	51.1	148	49.8
IDENTIFY AREAS IN NEED OF IMPROVEMENT	440	22.5	48	16.2
POINT OUT STRENGTHS	144	7.4	31	10.4
DOCUMENT GENERAL DISSATISFACTION WITH PERFORMANCE	99	5.1	19	6.4
HELP ESTABLISH RELEVANT PERFORMANCE GOALS	471	24.1	79	26.6
ASSESS PRESENT PERFORMANCE WITH PRESCRIBED STANDARDS	592	30.3	100	33.7
COMPLY WITH BOARD POLICY	562	28.8	76	25.6
DETERMINE SALARY FOR FOLLOWING YEAR	144	7.4	35	11.8
OTHER	85	4.4	14	4.7

TABLE 6.45 FACTORS THAT MAY INHIBIT EFFECTIVENESS

FACTORS	MALE No.	%	FEMALE No.	%
TOO MANY INSIGNIFICANT DEMANDS	743	38.0	96	32.3
TOO MUCH ADDED RESPONSIBILITY	273	14.0	42	14.1
INADEQUATE FINANCING OF SCHOOLS	876	44.9	118	39.7
STATE REFORM MANDATES	527	27.0	55	18.5
INEXPERIENCED, UNQUALIFIED, OR ILL-PREPARED STAFF	173	8.9	40	13.5
DIFFICULT RELATIONS WITH BOARD MEMBERS	111	5.7	11	3.7
DISTRICT TOO SMALL	71	3.6	16	5.4
COLLECTIVE BARGAINING AGREEMENTS	270	13.8	41	13.8
RACIAL/ETHNIC PROBLEMS	16	0.8	2	0.7
LACK COMMUNITY SUPPORT	61	3.1	9	3.0
INSUFFICIENT ADMIN. STAFF	168	8.6	49	16.5
BOARD MICROMANAGEMENT	398	20.4	63	21.2
BOARD ELECTIONS; CHANGED EXPECTATIONS	180	9.2	48	16.2
OTHER	84	4.3	13	4.4

In addition, Table 6.50 suggests that women seek community participation slightly more often than men do. As can be seen, none of the female superintendents marked "never" and only 2.4 percent marked "seldom," while 4.7 percent of the males marked "never" or "seldom."

The sampled superintendents were asked who takes the lead in developing policy. When this question was asked in the 1992 survey, both male and female superintendents reported that, about two-thirds of the time, they took the lead in developing district policy. In the 2000 Study, the percentages are more evenly distributed among different stakeholders. Evidently, policy development has become an activity that is shared with more people. Certainly this is a goal of many reforms (Hallinger, 1992; Mohrman, 1993; Wohlseterr, Smyer, and Mohrman, 1994; Crowson, 1992)

In this study, 43.5 percent of the male and 35.4 percent of the female superintendents lead in policy development. Both men and women reported that they share policy development a little over one-third of the time. Slight differences occur in terms of with whom the two groups share the responsibility. Women tend to share the responsibility of policy development slightly more with central office and board members; while men tend to share the responsibility slightly more with principals

TABLE 6.46 HOW YOU CHARACTERIZE YOUR SCHOOL BOARD

CHARACTERISTIC	MALE		FEMALE	
	No.	%	No.	%
DOMINATED BY ELITE IN COMMUNITY	50	2.6	10	3.4
REPRESENTS DISTINCT FACTIONS IN THE COMMUNITY	356	18.3	70	23.6
ACTIVE, ALIGNED WITH COMMUNITY INTEREST, NOT RIGID	1285	66.0	192	64.6
NOT ACTIVE, ACCEPTING OF RECCOMENDATIONS MADE BY PROF. STAFF	256	13.1	25	8.4
TOTAL	1947	100.0	297	100.0

TABLE 6.47 WOMEN ON BOARDS

NUMBER	MALE SUPT		FEMALE SUPT	
	No.	%	No.	%
0	173	8.9	16	5.4
1	464	23.8	47	15.8
2	574	29.4	90	30.3
3	397	20.3	73	24.6
4	185	9.5	41	13.8
5	85	4.4	18	6.1
6	28	1.4	7	2.4
7	14	0.7	3	1.0
BLANK	33	1.7	2	0.7

TABLE 6.48 LENGTH OF BOARD MEMBERSHIP

YEARS	MALE		FEMALE	
	No.	%	No.	%
1 - 4	172	8.9	32	10.9
4 - 5	193	10.0	42	14.3
5 - 6	440	22.9	66	22.4
7 - 8	698	36.3	84	28.6
9+	419	21.8	70	23.8
TOTAL	1922	100.0	294	100.0

(see **Table 6.51**). It is important to note that all the data in the survey are self-reports. This fact is especially important when the information gathered is related to a superintendent's interaction with others. Consider, for example, the case of policy development. In the survey, both men and women report that they share in policy development about one-third of the time. It is difficult to know with any great certainty that this is what happens without visiting the district. What we can say is that this is what individual superintendents perceive. Interestingly, the numbers are fairly consistent across gender in the case of who takes the lead in policy development.

Table 6.52 contains the percentage of times that boards of education accept recommendations from their superintendents. Almost all of the superintendents had an acceptance rate of 70 percent or greater. While some literature on female superintendents suggests that it is more difficult for women to gain acceptance of their recommendations, in this study's sample, no gender difference appears.

When superintendents were asked what they believed to be the most difficult job facing school boards, 35.7 percent of the men and 31.2 percent of the women answered "financial issues." However, when totaling some of the other difficulties facing boards (inter-board conflict, understanding board roles, and avoiding micro-management), it becomes clear that superintendents believe that board members create some of their greatest difficulties (totals of the three areas show 31 percent of

TABLE 6.49 SCHOOL BOARD'S OPINION OF SCHOOL-BASED DECISION MAKING

	MALE		FEMALE	
OPINION	No.	%	No.	%
SUPPORTIVE	983	50.9	164	55.6
INDIFFERENT	492	25.5	58	19.7
OPPOSE	142	7.3	22	7.5
NO OPINION	315	16.3	51	17.3
TOTAL	1932	100.0	295	100.0

TABLE 6.50 SEEKING CITIZEN PARTICIPATION IN DECISION MAKING

	MALE		FEMALE	
FREQUENCY	No.	%	No.	%
ALL THE TIME	260	13.4	40	13.5
FREQUENTLY	1061	54.7	186	62.8
WHEN REQUIRED	528	27.2	63	21.3
NEVER	3	0.2	0	0.0
SELDOM	87	4.5	7	2.4
TOTAL	1939	100.0	296	100.0

TABLE 6.51 WHO DEVELOPS POLICY?

	MALE		FEMALE	
	No.	%	No.	%
PRINCIPALS	31	1.6	2	0.7
CENTRAL OFF. STAFF	186	9.6	37	12.6
SUPERINTENDENT	850	43.8	104	35.4
SCHOOL BOARD	143	7.4	34	11.6
SCHOOL BOARD CHAIR	4	0.2	2	0.7
SHARED RESPONSIBILITY	710	36.6	112	38.1
OTHER	16	0.8	3	1.0
TOTAL	1940	100.0	294	100.0

men and 38 percent of women rated them the most difficult). Slightly more female superintendents acknowledged internal board conflict and reported feeling micro-managed than male superintendents (see **Table 6.53**).

Finally, superintendents were asked for a general opinion of how well their board members were prepared to serve on the board. In the same vein, superintendents were asked if their board members had the ability to handle their duties. On one hand, as shown in **Table 6.54**, over half of the superintendents—both male and female—believe that their school boards are qualified concerning their general abilities and preparation. On the other hand, only 12.5 percent of men and 14.5 percent of the women ranked them as "very well" qualified. In addition, 26.6 percent of men and 31.6 percent of women ranked school boards as "not well" qualified.

Stress, Self-Fulfillment, and Prestige

In the 1992 Study, 11.6 percent of women and 7.5 percent of men noted that they were under "very great stress." In the same year, 42 percent of men and women said they experienced "considerable"

TABLE 6.52 PERCENT OF RECOMMENDATIONS FROM SUPERINTENDENT ACCEPTED BY BOARD

	MALE		FEMALE	
PERCENT	No.	%	No.	%
90 –100%	1709	88.4	264	89.8
80 – 89%	178	9.2	22	7.5
70 – 79%	35	1.8	4	1.4
60 – 69%	5	0.3	1	0.3
50 – 59%	5	0.3	1	0.3
LESS THAN 50%	2	0.1	2	0.7
TOTAL	1934	100.0	294	100.0

TABLE 6.53 SUPERINTENDENT PERCEPTION OF THE MOST DIFFICULT JOB FACING SCHOOL BOARDS

	MALE		FEMALE	
JOB	No.	%	No.	%
FINANCIAL ISSUES	695	35.7	92	31.2
COMMUNITY PRESSUE	332	17.1	52	17.6
EMPLOYEE RELATIONS	89	4.6	11	3.7
CURRICULUM	41	2.1	1	0.3
INTER BOARD CONFLICT	96	4.9	18	6.1
UNDERSTANDING BOARD ROLES	321	16.5	53	18.0
AVOIDING MICROMANAGEMENT	191	9.8	42	14.2
PRESSURE FROM SPECIAL INTEREST GROUPS	134	6.9	21	7.1
OTHER	46	2.4	5	1.7
TOTAL	1945	100.0	295	100.0

TABLE 6.54 GENERAL OPINION OF BOARD PREPARATION AND ABILITY TO HANDLE DUTIES

	MALE		FEMALE	
OPINION	No.	%	No.	%
VERY WELL QUALIFIED	243	12.5	44	14.8
QUALIFIED	1140	58.5	150	50.5
NOT WELL QUALIFIED	519	26.6	94	31.6
INCOMPETENT	41	2.1	8	2.7
DO NOT KNOW	5	0.3	1	0.3
TOTAL	1948	100.0	297	100.0

stress. Similarly, in this study, slightly more women identified themselves as under "considerable" or "very great stress"—56.7 women and 50.8 men marked these categories (see **Table 6.55**) Even though both men and women find the superintendency a stressful position, over half of them derive considerable satisfaction from the job (see **Table 6.56**).

Table 6.57 identifies the degree of status or prestige that the men and women in the study believe the position of superintendent of schools holds. As in 1992, the majority of men and women believe that the position has as much status or prestige as in the past. More women believe the position is gaining in status. It is difficult to know whether this is a reflection of personal experience or a belief that there is a difference in the perception of others toward the role.

TABLE 6.55 AMOUNT OF STRESS IN THE SUPERINTENDENCY

	MALE		FEMALE	
AMOUNT OF STRESS	No.	%	No	%
NO STRESS	13	0.7	0	0.0
LITTLE STRESS	147	7.9	13	4.4
MODERATE STRESS	795	40.9	114	38.9
CONSIDERABLE STRESS	789	40.6	121	41.3
VERY GREAT STRESS	198	10.2	45	15.4
TOTAL	1942	100.0	293	100.0

TABLE 6.56 SELF-FULFILLMENT OF THE SUPERINTENDENCY

	MALE		FEMALE	
FULFILLMENT	No.	%	No	%
NONE	6	0.3	0	0.0
LITTLE	114	5.9	14	4.8
MODERATE	735	37.8	101	34.5
CONSIDERABLE	1089	56.0	178	60.8
TOTAL	1944	100.0	293	100.0

TABLE 6.57 STATUS/PRESTIGE OF THE SUPERINTENDENCY

	MALE		FEMALE	
STATUS/PRESTIGE LEVEL	No.	%	No	%
DECREASING	379	19.4	54	18.4
ABOUT THE SAME	858	44.0	109	37.1
INCREASING	535	27.4	103	35.0
DO NOT KNOW	178	9.1	28	9.5
TOTAL	1950	100.0	294	100.0

Bibliography

Banks, C. M. (1995). "Gender and race as factors in educational leadership and administration." In J. A. Banks and C. A. McGee Banks (Eds.). *Handbook of Research on Multicultural Education*. New York: Macmillan.

Bell, C., and S. Chase. (1995). "The underrepresentation of women in school leadership." In C. Marshall (Ed.), *The New Politics of Race and Gender: Yearbook of the Politics of Education Association*. Washington, DC: Falmer.

Blount, J. M. (1998). *Destined to Rule the Schools: Women and the Superintendency*. Albany, NY: State University of New York Press.

Bredeson, P., and R. Faber. (1994). "What do superintendents mean when they say they are involved in curriculum and instruction?" Paper presented at the annual meeting of the American Educational Research Association. New Orleans, LA.

Brunner, C. C. (in press). *Principles of Power: Women Superintendents and the Riddle of the Heart*. Albany, NY: State University of New York Press.

Brunner, C. C. (1998a). "Can power support and "ethic of care?" An examination of the professional practices of female superintendents." *Journal for a Just and Caring Education* 4,2: 142-75.

Brunner, C. C. (1998b). "Female superintendents: Strategies for success." *The Journal of Educational Administration* 36, 2: 160-182.

Chase, S., and C. Bell. (1994). "How search consultants talk about female superintendents." *The School Administrator* 51, 92: 36-42.

Crowson, R. (1987). "The local school district superintendency: A puzzling administrative role." *Educational Administration Quarterly* 23, 3: 49-69.

Crowson, R. (1992). *School-community Relations, Under Reform*. Berkeley, CA: McCutchan Publishing Corporation.

Edson, S. (1981). "'If they can, I can: Women aspirants to administrative positions in public schools." In P. Schmuck, W. Charters, and R. Carlson (Eds.), *Educational Policy and Management: Sex Differentials*. New York: Academic Press.

Edson, S. (1988). *Pushing the Limits: The Female Administrative Aspirant*. Albany, NY: State University of New York Press.

Edson, S. (1995). "Ten years later: Too little, too later?" In D. Dunlap and P. Schumuck (Eds.), *Women Leading in Education*. Albany, NY: State University of New York Press.

Grogan, M. (1996). *The Voices of Women Aspiring to the Superintendency*. Albany, NY: State University of New York Press.

Hallinger, P. (1992). "The evolving role of American principals: From managerial to instructional to transformational leaders." *Journal of Educational Administration* 30, 3: 35-48.

Helgesen, S. (1990). *The Female Advantage: Women's Ways of Leadership*. Garden City, NY: Doubleday.

Kamler, E., and C. Shakeshaft. (1999). "The role of search consultants." In C. C. Brunner (Ed.), *Sacred Dreams: Women and the Superintendency*. Albany, NY: State University of New York Press.

Mohrman, S. A. (1993). "School based management and school reform: Comparisons to private sector organizational renewal." Paper presented at the annual meeting of the Association of Public Policy Analysis and Management. Washington, DC.

Rosener, J. (1990). "Ways women lead." *Harvard Business Review* 68, 6: 119-25.

Sherman, D., and T. Repa. (1994). "Women at the top: The experiences of two superintendents." *Equity and Choice* 10, 2: 59-64.

Tallerico, M. (1999). "Women and the superintendency: What do we really know?" In C. C. Brunner (Ed.), *Sacred Dreams: Women and the Superintendency*. Albany, NY: State University of New York Press.

Tyack, D., and E. Hansot. (1982). *Managers of Virtue: Public School Leadership in America: 1820-1980*. New York: Basic Books

Wohlseterr, P., R. Smyer, and S. A. Mohrman. (1994). "New boundaries for school-based management: The high involvement model." *Education Evaluation and Policy Analysis* 16, 3: 268-86.

CHAPTER **7**

Ethnic Minority Superintendents

C. Cryss Brunner

Overview

In no small measure, minorities in the superintendency are severely underrepresented. And as with the underrepresentation of women, the small numbers of minorities get lost within the larger sample, making it impossible to tell if their responses differ in any significant way from the responses of the non-minorities. Thus, for the first time in the history of the AASA Ten-Year Studies, a chapter has been designated to describe the responses of minority superintendents.

As with the chapter on female superintendents, this chapter on minority superintendents has limited space in which to report the responses to all of the questions. As a result, a subset of questions has been pulled out as representative of the responses submitted by minority superintendents.

This chapter is somewhat limited in scope, because all races and ethnicities categorized as minority are grouped together in the study, reducing individual and particular racial group identity. This grouping of minority and non-minority also reifies a "we/they" mentality, rather than reflecting the fuller diversity across both categories. There is also danger of reifying racial bias when people are cast into categories based on race. This is true for the male/female grouping in Chapter 6. However, there is value in articulating—to make public—the uniqueness along race and ethnic lines.

To be sure, whatever its limitations, this information is potentially important to minorities who aspire to or currently practice in the position of superintendent of schools. Role models from all ethnic groups are few and far between. Indeed, research with a focus on minorities in the superintendency is comparatively rare.

Personal Demographics

Race and Gender

Of the 2,262 superintendents responding to the 2000 Study, only 117 are minorities. African Americans account for 5.3 percent of the sample (2.0 percent male, 5.1 percent female) followed by 2.7 percent Hispanic superintendents (1.4 percent male, 1.3 percent female). These numbers have increased by roughly 2 percent since the 1992 Study (see **Table 7.1**). Still, the percentage of minority superintendents probably has not risen at the same rate as increased percentages of minority students.

Age

Most of the minority superintendents (87.2 percent) are between the ages of 46 and 60. Almost 83 percent of non-minorities fall between these same ages. Most of the superintendents who are younger than 46 are white males (see **Tables 7.2** and **6.3**).

Minority superintendents appear from these data to have about the same professional age track as non-minority superintendents.

Marital Status

Almost 88 percent of minority superintendents are married compared with 92.6 percent of non-minority superintendents. In addition, 12.1 percent of minority superintendents are single, 23.1 of female superintendents are single, and 7.4 percent of non-minority superintendents (men and women calculated together) are single (see **Table 7.3**). Again, minority superintendents do not differ in marital status from non-minority superintendents.

Years of Experience as Superintendent

About 75 percent of minorities have been in the superintendency for 9 or fewer years, which compares closely with the 84.1 percent of women who have been in the position for 9 or fewer years (see **Table 6.5**). In contrast, 57.5 percent of non-minorities have been in the position nine or fewer years and the remaining 42.5 percent have been in the position for more than 9 years (see **Table 7.4**).

Type of Community Lived in Prior to College

Table 7.5 demonstrates that the percentage (29.3 percent) of minorities who have lived in large cities prior to college is twice the percentage (13.1) of non-minorities who have lived in large cities prior to college. This is probably attributable to greater access to higher education in large urban areas for both minority and majority educators.

Highest Degree Held

Minorities have fewer specialist degrees than non-minorities, but a greater number of Ed.D.s and Ph.D.s than non-minorities (see **Table 7.6**).

TABLE 7.1 ETHNICITY BY GENDER

RACE	MALE		FEMALE	
	No.	%	No	%
BLACK	38	2.0	15	5.1
WHITE	1855	95.3	272	91.6
HISPANIC	27	1.4	4	1.3
NATIVE AMER.	15	0.8	2	0.7
ASIAN	3	0.2	2	0.7
OTHER	9	0.5	2	0.7
TOTAL	1947	100.0	297	100.0

TABLE 7.2 AGE BY ETHNICITY

AGE GROUP	NON-MINORITY		MINORITY	
	No.	%	No.	%
30-35	15	0.7	1	0.9
36-40	38	1.8	0	0.0
41-45	147	7.0	3	2.6
46-50	531	25.1	36	30.8
51-55	786	37.2	38	32.5
56-60	429	20.3	28	23.9
61-65	148	7.0	9	7.7
66+	19	0.9	2	1.7
TOTAL	2113	100.0	117	100.0

This may reflect the fact that larger urban districts hire many minority superintendents and many universities offer minority fellowships .

Political Party Affiliation and Political Postures

While non-minority male and female superintendents are fairly evenly distributed across political party affiliation categories, over half of the minority superintendents are Democrats, 24.3 percent are independents, and only 16.5 percent are Republicans (see **Table 7.7**). This percentage reflects the political affiliation of the communities in which they work.

Table 7.8 shows that almost twice as many non-minority superintendents, 33.2 percent, compared to 17.5 percent of minority superintendents are conservatives. In addition, 5 percent more minorities than non-minorities report their political posture as liberal. However, over half of all superintendents sampled for this survey report their political posture as moderate.

Professional Organizations and Professional Journals Read

Minorities report belonging to more professional organizations than do non-minorities. In addition, a larger percentage of minorities are members of the National School Board Association (see **Table 7.9**).

Table 7.10 reflects that the percentages of minorities and non-minorities reading specific professional journals are comparable.

District Demographics

Region Where School District is Located

Table 7.11 identifies the regions in which the school districts sampled are located. The greatest numbers of districts with minorities serving as superintendents are in the Southwest (24.8 percent). The Far West and the Southeast follow the Southwest. Most non-minority superintendents are serving in districts in the Great Lakes region (23.3 percent) followed by the Plains states and the

TABLE 7.3 MARITAL STATUS

STATUS	NON-MINORITY		MINORITY	
	No.	%	No.	%
MARRIED	1956	92.6	102	87.9
SINGLE	156	7.4	14	12.1
TOTAL	2112	100.0	116	100.0

TABLE 7.4 YEARS OF EXPERIENCE

YEARS	NON-MINORITY		MINORITY	
	No.	%	No.	%
1	141	6.6	12	10.4
2 – 3	288	13.6	13	11.3
4 – 5	267	12.6	21	18.3
6 – 7	269	12.7	29	25.2
8 – 9	255	12.0	11	9.6
10 – 11	246	11.6	10	8.7
12 – 13	135	6.4	5	4.3
14 – 15	471	22.2	13	11.3
16+	51	2.4	1	0.9
TOTAL	2123	100.0	115	100.0

Midwest. Minority superintendents are found in areas that have large minority enrollments. There are relatively few minority superintendents serving majority districts.

Type of Community Lived in Prior to College/ Type of Community in Which School District Is Located

The content of **Table 7.12** is a repeat of **Table 7.5**. It is repeated purposely here to show the possible connection between the type of community superintendents live in prior to college and the type of community in which a superintendent eventually serves (see **Table 7.13**). About 30 percent of minority superintendents, in contrast to 13.1 percent non-minorities, lived in large cities prior to college, and 23.7 percent of minority superintendents, in contrast to 5.6 percent of non-minorities, are currently working in urban areas.

TABLE 7.5 COMMUNITY BEFORE COLLEGE

COMMUNITY TYPE	NON-MINORITY		MINORITY	
	No.	%	No.	%
RURAL	758	35.8	34	29.3
SMALL TOWN	718	33.9	37	31.9
SUBURBAN	366	17.3	11	9.5
LARGE CITY	277	13.1	34	29.3
TOTAL	2119	100.0	116	100.0

TABLE 7.6 HIGHEST DEGREE HELD

DEGREE	NON-MINORITY		MINORITY	
	No.	%	No.	%
BA OR BS	7	0.3	0	0.0
MASTER'S IN ED	161	7.6	11	9.4
MASTER'S NOT IN ED	9	0.4	1	0.9
MASTER'S + GRAD.	508	24.0	31	26.5
SPECIALIST DEGREE	476	22.5	14	12.0
ED. D or Ph.D.	953	45.1	60	51.3
TOTAL	2114	100.0	117	100.0

TABLE 7.7 POLITICAL PARTY AFFILIATION

AFFILIATION	NON-MINORITY		MINORITY	
	No.	%	No.	%
DEMOCRAT	706	33.8	68	59.1
INDEPENDENT	720	34.5	19	16.5
REPUBLICAN	662	31.7	28	24.3
TOTAL	2088	100.0	115	100.0

TABLE 7.8 POLITICAL POSTURE/VIEWS

POSTURE	NON-MINORITY		MINORITY	
	No.	%	No.	%
LIBERAL	226	10.8	18	15.8
CONSERVATIVE	698	33.2	20	17.5
MODERATE	1178	56.0	76	66.7
TOTAL	2102	100.0	114	100.0

District Enrollment and School-Business Partnerships

Enrollment data as of January 1999 (see **Table 7.14**), show that white male and female superintendents are serving in districts that have smaller enrollments than districts where minorities are serving as superintendents. Fully 72.5 percent of non-minorities are serving in districts with fewer than 3,000 students, while 51.4 percent of minorities are serving in districts with enrollments greater than 3,000. However, a majority of the largest districts in the nation have minority superintendents.

Table 7.15 gives the percentage of districts that participate in school-business partnerships. A higher percentage of women (54.8 percent) and minorities (61.4 percent) report participating in school-business partnerships, while 48.5 percent of non-minority superintendents (men and women) report participating in school-business partnerships. Minority superintendents often serve economically depressed communities where business partners provide needed resources and role models for economically disadvantaged students.

Career Paths—The Road More Traveled

Nature and Type of School of First Administrative Position

Approximately 65 percent of minority superintendents began their administrative careers as either an assistant principal or principal, while almost 80 percent of non-minorities began their careers as an assistant principal or principal. This difference is accounted for by considering that 22.2 percent of minorities began their administrative careers as some type of coordinator, while only 13.3 percent of non-minorities began their careers as coordinators (see **Table 7.16**). Many of these coordinator positions were for programs with categorical funding and minority participation.

TABLE 7.9 PROFESSIONAL ORGANIZATIONS

ORGANIZATION	NON-MINORITY		MINORITY	
	No.	%	No.	%
AASA	1613	75.8	87	73.7
AASA (STATE)	1350	63.5	64	54.2
ASCD	872	41.0	54	45.8
NSBA	365	17.2	29	24.6
NASSP	198	9.3	20	16.9
NABSE	10	0.5	18	15.3
ASBO	178	8.4	11	9.3
NAESP	68	3.2	8	6.8
NEA	80	3.8	8	6.8
OTHER	366	17.2	24	20.3

TABLE 7.10 PROFESSIONAL JOURNALS READ FREQUENTLY

JOURNAL	NON-MINORITY		MINORITY	
	No.	%	No.	%
AMERICAN SCHOOL BOARD JOURNAL	917	46.1	55	47.8
EDUCATION WEEK	866	45.7	66	62.3
EDUCATIONAL LEADERSHIP	949	48.9	62	56.9
KAPPAN	635	36.0	37	37.8
NASSP BULLETIN	225	14.3	19	21.6
PRINICIPAL	54	3.8	11	13.8
THE SCHOOL ADMINISTRATOR	1066	53.9	56	50.9
OTHER	107	68.2	7	63.6

Table 7.17 illustrates that about the same percentage of minorities (28 percent) and non-minorities (25.3 percent) gain their first administrative positions at the elementary level. When considering gender, however, it can be seen that more women (38 percent) (see **Table 6.21**) than minorities and non-minority men gained their first administrative position at the elementary level. Higher percentages of women and minorities than non-minorities also began their administrative careers at the district office level.

Type of Position with at Least One Full Year of Experience

A slightly higher percentage of minorities than non-minorities have had one full year or more of experience as a teacher or principal at the elementary level. Minorities have served as assistant superintendents or consultants for a year or longer more often than non-minorities. In addition, almost 5 percent more minorities than non-minorities have been college professors (see **Table 7.18**).

TABLE 7.11 REGION OF DISTRICT

REGION	NON-MINORITY No.	%	MINORITY No.	%
NEW ENGLAND	110	5.2	3	2.6
ROCKY MOUNTAINS	91	4.3	5	4.3
SOUTHEAST	250	11.8	18	15.4
GREAT LAKES	495	23.3	17	14.5
MIDEAST	319	15.0	16	13.7
SOUTHWEST	235	11.1	29	24.8
PLAINS	442	20.8	7	6.0
FAR WEST	164	7.7	21	17.9
ALASKA	7	0.3	0	0.0
HAWAII	0	0.0	1	0.9
OTHER	11	0.5	0	0.0
TOTAL	2124	100.0	117	100.0

TABLE 7.12 DESCRIPTION OF COMMUNITY LIVED IN PRIOR TO COLLEGE

COMMUNITY TYPE	NON-MINORITY No.	%	MINORITY No.	%
RURAL	758	35.8	34	29.3
SMALL TOWN	718	33.9	37	31.9
SUBURBAN	366	17.3	11	9.5
LARGE CITY	277	13.1	34	29.3
TOTAL	2119	100.0	116	100.0

TABLE 7.13 COMMUNITY DESCRIPTION SCHOOL DISTRICT IS LOCATED

COMMUNITY TYPE	NON-MINORITY No.	%	MINORITY No.	%
URBAN	119	5.6	28	23.7
SUBURBAN	403	19.0	16	13.6
SUBURBAN/RURAL	362	17.1	19	16.1
RURAL	1223	57.6	54	45.8
OTHER	16	0.8	1	0.8
TOTAL	2123	100.0	118	100.0

Career Pattern Prior to the Superintendency

Table 7.19 shows that minorities' and non-minorities' career paths are similar. The largest difference occurs in the path that moves from teacher to principal to superintendent. About 10 percent more non-minorities follow this path than do minorities — who more often follow the path of teacher, principal, central office, and then superintendent.

Length of Time to Secure First Superintendency After Certification, and Agency that Managed Search

While 57.4 percent of non-minorities secure a superintendency position within 1 year after certification, only 38.1 percent of minorities secure a position in the same amount of time. In fact, 12.7 percent of minorities report that it took them 5 or more years to secure a superintendency, while 8.1 percent of non-minorities report it taking 5 or more years after certification (see Table 7.20).

Table 7.21 identifies who managed the search for the superintendents in the sample. As with female superintendents, professional search firms hired slightly more of the sampled minorities than the sampled non-minorities.

The data in Table 7.22 reveal what superintendents think about the "good-old boy/girl" networks in relation to their ability to help superintendents secure positions. Although over half of all superintendents believe the "good-old boy/girl" networks help them secure positions, a higher percentage of minorities (65.2 percent) than non-minorities (51.6 percent) report that the networks helped them to secure a position as a superintendent. The percentage of minority and non-minority superintendents who report receiving help from the networks has decreased slightly since the 1992 Study.

Discrimination in Hiring

Minority superintendents think discriminatory hiring practices are a major problem, while their non-minority colleagues perceive this quite differently. In fact, 46.9 percent of minority superintendents report that discriminatory hiring practices are a major problem, compared to only 10.1 percent of non-minorities. In the 1992 Study, 59.7 percent of minorities and 16.6 percent of non-minorities saw this as a major problem (see Table 7.23).

TABLE 7.14 ENROLLMENT: JAN. 1999

SIZE	NON-MINORITY		MINORITY	
	No.	%	No.	%
FEWER THAN 300	242	11.5	7	6.1
300 - 999	569	26.9	23	20.0
1,000 – 2,999	720	34.1	27	23.5
3,000 – 4,999	251	11.9	18	15.7
5,000 – 9,999	168	8.0	9	7.8
10,000 – 24,999	89	4.2	9	7.8
25,000 – 49,999	51	2.4	15	13.0
50,000 – 99,999	15	0.7	5	4.3
100,000 OR MORE	7	0.3	2	1.7
TOTAL	2112	100.0	115	100.0

TABLE 7.15 SCHOOL-BUSINESS PARTNERSHIPS

	NON-MINORITY		MINORITY	
	No.	%	No.	%
YES	1021	48.7	70	61.4
NO	1077	51.3	44	38.6
TOTAL	2098	100.0	114	100.0

No literature or research could be found revealing whether minority superintendents frequently apply often in districts with a non-minority population.

Moving On?

When superintendents in this sample were asked if they were willing to do it all over again, the vast majority reported that they would choose the superintendency again if they had the opportunity. Minority superintendents responded at about the same percentage rate as women and non-minorities. They would make the same choice again, even though they report enduring many problems and challenges and a great deal of stress. The stress they report may account for their second most often chosen response, that is, if they had it to do all over again, they would choose a career "outside of education" (see **Table 7.24**). The numbers of superintendents selecting this response has increased by about three percent since the 1992 Study.

Table 7.25 shows the responses given by superintendents when they were asked where they thought they would be in five years. Fully 65.8 percent of minority superintendents and 60 percent of non-minority superintendents sampled said they will continue in the superintendency until they retire. Minorities (8.8 percent) are twice as likely as non-minorities (3.2 percent) to say they will leave the superintendency for a desirable position at a university. A few more minorities than non-minorities expressed an interest in leaving the superintendency to pursue a career outside of education.

Table 7.26 indicates that a greater percentage of minorities than non-minorities stated that they left the last superintendency because they either moved to a larger district or had a conflict with board members.

TABLE 7.16 NATURE OF FIRST ADMINISTRATIVE POSITION

NATURE OF POSITION	NON-MINORITY		MINORITY	
	No.	%	No.	%
ASSISTANT PRINCIPAL	734	34.8	40	34.2
DEAN OF STUDENTS	48	2.3	9	7.7
PRINCIPAL	867	41.1	36	30.8
DIR./COORDINATOR	281	13.3	26	22.2
ASSIST. SUP.	32	1.5	1	0.9
STATE AGENCY	17	0.8	0	0.0
BUSINESS OFF.	12	0.6	1	0.9
OTHER	121	5.7	4	3.4
TOTAL	2112	100.0	117	100.0

TABLE 7.17 TYPE OF SCHOOL OF FIRST ADMINISTRATIVE POSITION

SCHOOL TYPE	NON-MINORITY		MINORITY	
	No.	%	No.	%
ELEM SCHOOL	538	25.3	33	28.0
JUNIOR HI	199	9.4	9	7.6
MID SCHOOL	141	6.6	11	9.3
HIGH SCHOOL	815	38.3	36	30.5
PAROCHIAL	14	0.7	1	0.8
COLLEGE	11	0.5	0	0.0
VOCATIONAL	27	1.3	1	0.8
DIST OFFICE	224	10.5	21	17.8
OTHER	157	7.4	6	5.1
TOTAL	2126	100.0	118	100.0

Again, many minority superintendents do not have the opportunity to work in districts that have affluent and cohesive communities. Communities in crisis are more prone to conflict as are such school districts. Superintendency tenure is often linked to the frequency of conflicts arising in the school district and/or the community.

TABLE 7.18 TYPE OF POSITION WITH AT LEAST ONE FULL YEAR EXPERIENCE

POSITION	No.	%	NON-MINORITY No.	%	MINORITY	
ELEM. TEACHER		701	33.0		46	39.0
ELEMENTARY ASS'T. PRINC		146	6.9		15	12.7
ELEM PRINC		802	37.7		53	44.9
JR HI/MS TEAHCER		942	44.3		47	39.8
JUNIOR HIGH/MS ASS'T PRINC		316	14.9		21	17.8
JUNIOR HIGH/MS PRINCIPAL		597	28.1		35	29.7
HI SCH TEACHER		1271	59.8		60	50.8
HIGH SCH ASS'T PRINC		562	26.4		29	24.6
HI SCH PRINC		1003	47.2		47	39.8
DIR/COORDINATOR		679	31.9		46	39.0
ASS'T SUPER		761	35.8		54	45.8
PROFESSOR		211	9.9		17	14.4
COUNSELOR		181	8.5		19	16.1
SUPERVISIOR OR CONSULTANT		222	10.4		23	19.5
OTHER		155	7.3		9	7.6

TABLE 7.19 CAREER PATTERN PRIOR TO THE SUPERINTENDENCY

CAREER PATTERN	NON-MINORITY No.	%	MINORITY No.	%
TEACHER, PRINCIPAL & CENTRAL OFFICE	1027	48.3	62	52.5
PRINCIPAL & CENTRAL OFFICE	33	1.6	4	3.4
TEACHER & CENTRAL OFFICE	182	8.6	15	12.7
TEACHER & PRINCIPAL	674	31.7	26	22.0
CENTRAL OFFICE ONLY	27	1.3	0	0.0
PRINCIPAL ONLY	31	1.5	2	1.7
TEACHER ONLY	46	2.2	1	0.8
NOT SURE	106	5.0	8	6.8
TOTAL	2126	100.0	118	100.0

TABLE 7.20 LENGTH OF TIME SEEKING SUPERINTENDENCY AFTER CERTIFICATION

LENGTH OF TIME	NON-MINORITY No.	%	MINORITY No.	%
LESS THAN ONE YEAR	1216	57.4	45	38.1
1 YEAR	323	15.3	23	19.5
2 YEARS	240	11.3	21	17.8
3 YEARS	114	5.4	5	4.2
4 YEARS	53	2.5	9	7.6
5+ YEARS	171	8.1	15	12.7
TOTAL	2117	100.0	118	100.0

Professional Development

Are Superintendents Mentors? Did They Have Mentors?

Table 7.27 demonstrates that 89.9 percent of minorities have served as, or considered themselves, mentors. This percentage is over 10 percent greater than that reported by non-minorities (77.1 percent), and over 5 percent greater than that reported by minority and non-minority women (83.2 percent) in the sample. Some minorities report in conversations that since there are so few of them, they need and want to serve more frequently as mentors.

Approximately the same percentage of minorities (59.3 percent) and non-minorities (58.2 percent) had mentors (see **Table 7.28**). However, more women (minority and non-minority) (71 percent) than minorities or non-minority men had mentors.

Opinion of Usefulness of Educational Research

Minority superintendents in this sample find educational research significantly more useful than non-minorities. Fully 53.9 percent of minorities indicated that educational research is highly useful, while only 29.3 percent of non-minorities indicated that educational research is highly useful (see **Table 7.29**). These findings are consistent with the 1992 Study.

Table 7.30 shows the answers to a question that asked the superintendents to indicate the types of preservice and/or inservice training that are important and whether they should be included in the training of superintendents during preservice, inservice, both, or neither. Out of the 27 types of training listed, 4 were of particular interest to minorities. In other words, around 50 percent or higher of minorities marked that 4 of the types of training listed were important enough to be offered in both preservice and inservice professional development.

TABLE 7.21 WHO MANAGED SEARCH PROCESS FOR PRESENT SUPERINTENDENCY

	NON-MINORITY		MINORITY	
AGENCY	No.	%	No.	%
PROFESSIONAL SEARCH FIRM	369	17.4	24	20.9
STATE SCHOOL BOARD ASSOC.	408	19.3	21	18.3
LOCAL SCHOOL BOARD MEMBERS	1150	54.3	55	47.8
OTHER	191	9.0	15	13.0
TOTAL	2118	100.0	115	100.0

TABLE 7.22 GOOD-OLD BOY/GIRL NETWORK HELPS SUPERINTENDENTS GET POSITIONS

	NON-MINORITY		MINORITY	
	No.	%	No.	%
YES	1051	51.6	73	65.2
NO	681	33.4	23	20.5
DON'T KNOW	304	14.9	16	14.3
TOTAL	2036	100.0	112	100.0

TABLE 7.23 EXTENT THAT DISCRIMINATORY HIRING & PROMOTIONAL PRACTICES LIMIT CAREER OPPORTUNITIES

	NON-MINORITY		MINORITY	
	No.	%	No.	%
MAJOR PROBLEM	209	10.1	53	46.9
MINOR PROBLEM	745	35.9	33	29.2
LITTLE PROBLEM	725	34.9	16	14.2
NO PROBLEM	397	19.1	11	9.7
TOTAL	2076	100.0	113	100.0

First, 50.5 percent of minorities believe that both preservice and inservice training should be given to superintendents on the topic of "changing demographics: social and cultural issues such as race relations, and integration/segregation." Approximately the same percentage of non-minorities agreed with this assertion.

Second, 48.6 percent of minorities believe that both preservice and inservice training should be given to superintendents on the topic of "restructuring of districts." Close to 40 percent of non-minorities — around 10 percent fewer than minorities — agreed with this choice.

Third, 57.8 percent of minorities suggested that both preservice and inservice training should be given to superintendents on the topic of "developing and funding institutional programs for children at risk." About the same percentage of non-minorities made this choice.

And finally, 66.1 percent of minorities responded that both preservice and inservice training should be given to superintendents on the topic of "aging and inadequate facilities." Around 60 percent of non-minorities responded in the same way.

Length of Time Since Earning Highest Academic Degree

Close to 44 percent of minorities earned their highest academic degrees within the last 10 years. Fewer (37.9 percent) non-minorities and more (50.9 percent) women earned their highest academic degrees within the last 10 years. About 41 percent of non-minorities earned their highest academic degrees over 15 years ago (see **Table 7.31**).

TABLE 7.24 IF YOU STARTED OVER, WOULD YOU CHOOSE A CAREER AS:

CAREER	NON-MINORITY		MINORITY	
	No.	%	No.	%
SUPERINTENDENT	1385	65.9	77	67.0
OTHER CENTRAL OFFICE POSITION	77	3.7	7	6.1
CLASSRM TEACHER	52	2.5	3	2.6
GUIDANCE COUNSELOR	20	1.0	2	1.7
COLLEGE PROFESSOR	87	4.1	4	3.5
BUSINESS MANAGER	22	1.0	0	0.0
STATE AGENCY	6	0.3	0	0.0
INTER SCH DIST ADM.	13	0.6	1	0.0
PRINCIPAL	84	4.0	1	0.9
PRIVATE SCH ADM	8	0.4	2	1.7
OUTSIDE ED.	315	15	17	14.8
OTHER	33	1.6	2	1.7
TOTAL	2102	100.0	115	100.0

TABLE 7.25 WHERE WILL YOU BE IN 5 YEARS?

IN FIVE YEARS	NON-MINORITY		MINORITY	
	No.	%	No.	%
CONT. SUPER TILL RETIRE	1267	60.0	75	65.8
EARLY RETIREMENT	317	15.0	7	6.1
IN UNIVERSITY WORK	68	3.2	10	8.8
WORK OUTSIDE OF ED	85	4.0	7	6.1
LEAVE SUPERINTENDENCY- NO LONGER DESIRABLE	17	0.8	1	0.9
OTHER	359	17.0	14	12.3
TOTAL	2113	100.0	114	100.0

Contracts and Evaluation

Hiring and Board Expectations

As reported in **Table 7.32**, almost half of the minority superintendents believe they were hired primarily for their potential to be change agents; much more than non-minorities (25.5 percent) or women (29.7 percent). The second reason minorities believe they were hired was their ability to be educational leaders. Again, minority superintendents are first hired in districts having large numbers of minority members, a lack of fiscal resources, and seemingly perpetual conflict. It is not surprising that boards would be looking for change agents to resolve conflict and move the district toward reaching national means in achievement and graduation rates.

While 39.4 percent of non-minorities consider the board's primary expectation of them to be educational leaders, 49.1 percent of minorities see this as the primary expectation of their boards. In addition, 37.2 percent of non-minorities consider managerial leadership a primary expectation, while only 24.1 percent of minorities see this as a primary expectation of their boards (see **Table 7.33**).

TABLE 7.26 REASON FOR LEAVING LAST SUPERINTENDENCY

REASON	NON-MINORITY No.	%	MINORITY No.	%
LACK OF ADEQUATE FINANCING	22	2.3	1	2.1
MOVE TO LARGER DISTRICT	362	37.2	20	42.6
CONFLICT WITH BOARD MEMBERS	140	14.4	9	19.1
RETIREMENT	59	6.1	2	4.3
CHANGING BOARD/ELECTIONS	90	9.2	7	14.9
FAMILY CONCERNS	84	8.6	2	4.3
HI ED OPPORTUNITY.	4	0.4	0	0.0
POSITION IN "BETTER FINANCED" DISTRICT	61	6.3	2	4.3
CONFLICT WITH COMMUNITY GROUPS	4	0.4	0	0.0
CONFLICT WITH EMPLOYEE GROUPS	11	1.1	0	0.0
BEEN IN DISTRICT LONG ENOUGH	63	6.5	3	6.4
OTHER	74	7.6	1	2.1
TOTAL	974	100.0	47	100.0

TABLE 7.27 DO YOU CONSIDER YOURSELF A MENTOR?

	NON-MINORITY No.	%	MINORITY No.	%
YES	1639	77.1	106	89.8
NO	419	19.7	10	8.5
DON'T KNOW	67	3.2	2	1.7
TOTAL	2125	100.0	118	100.0

TABLE 7.28 DO YOU, OR DID YOU EVER, HAVE A MENTOR?

	NON-MINORITY No.	%	MINORITY No.	%
YES	1236	58.2	70	59.3
NO	874	41.1	47	39.8
DON'T KNOW	15	0.7	1	0.8
TOTAL	2125	100.0	118	100.0

Superintendent Effectiveness and Board Evaluations

Table 7.34 shows that 95 percent of non-minorities sampled perceive themselves to be very successful or successful, while 94.1 percent of minorities sampled perceive themselves to be very successful or successful. However, on their last board evaluation, only 69.9 percent of non-minorities and 58.5 percent of minorities were given an "excellent" rating. Further, 22.4 percent of non-minorities and 28.8 percent of minorities were rated as "good" by their boards (see **Table 7.35**).

When the sampled superintendents were asked to indicate why their boards evaluated them, minorities and non-minorities were in agreement. They indicated that the most important reason for a superintendent's evaluation was to establish periodic and systematic accountability to the

TABLE 7.29 OPINION OF USEFULNESS OF EDUCATIONAL RESEARCH

	NON-MINORITY		MINORITY	
	No.	%	No.	%
HIGHLY USEFUL	620	29.3	62	53.9
USUALLY USEFUL	976	46.1	35	30.4
OCCASIONALLY USEFUL	496	23.4	18	15.7
IS NOT USEFUL	22	1.0	0	0.0
NO OPINION	5	0.2	0	0.0
TOTAL	2119	100.0	115	100.0

TABLE 7.31 HOW LONG SINCE YOU EARNED YOUR HIGHEST ACADMIC DEGREE?

YEARS	NON-MINORITY		MINORITY	
	No.	%	No.	%
0 – 5 YEARS AGO	307	14.4	24	20.5
6 – 10 YEARS AGO	500	23.5	27	23.1
11 – 15 YEARS AGO	458	21.5	24	20.5
15+ YEARS AGO	862	40.5	42	35.9
TOTAL	2127	100.0	117	100.0

TABLE 7.32 REASON YOU WERE HIRED

REASON	NON-MINORITY		MINORITY	
	No.	%	No.	%
PERSONAL CHARACTERISTICS (HONESTY, ETC.)	865	40.8	28	23.9
POTENTIAL TO BE CHANGE AGENT	541	25.5	49	41.9
ABITLITY TO KEEP STATUS QUO	33	1.6	1	0.9
ABIILTIY TO BE INSTRUCTION LEADER	544	25.7	29	24.8
NO PARTICULAR IMPORTANT REASON	59	2.8	4	3.4
NOT SURE	76	3.6	6	5.1
TOTAL	2118	100.0	117	100.0

TABLE 7.33 BOARD'S PRIMARY EXPECTATION OF SUPERINTENDENT

EXPECTATION	NON-MINORITY		MINORITY	
	No.	%	No.	%
EDUCATION LEADER	834	39.4	57	49.1
POLITICAL LEADER	274	13.0	11	9.5
MANAGER LEADER	786	37.2	28	24.1
LEADER OF SCHOOL REFORM	57	2.7	5	4.3
OTHER	164	7.8	15	12.9
TOTAL	2115	100.0	116	100.0

board for job performance. Other reasons they listed included (in order of significance): to assess present performance in accordance with prescribed standards, to comply with board policy, and to help establish relevant performance goals (see **Table 7.36**).

Table 7.37 displays the top two reasons that the sample of superintendents chose when asked what factors inhibit their effectiveness. Inadequate financing of districts and too many insignificant demands were the two factors most often selected by both minority and non-minority superintendents. In addition, both groups indicated that board issues — such as board relationship, changing boards, and board micro-management — are also significant factors that may inhibit their effectiveness.

Board Demographics, Dynamics, and Decision Making

Board Demographics

Superintendents in the sample were asked to characterize their school boards. As with most of the non-minority men and women, 59 percent of minority superintendents characterized their boards as being aligned with community interests. However, a higher percentage of minorities (26.5 percent) as compared to 18.6 percent of non-minorities characterized their boards as representing distinct factions (see **Table 7.38**)

Minority superintendents have a higher percentage of women on their school boards than do non-minorities, but a slightly lower percentage of women on their school boards than do female superintendents (see **Table 7.39**).

According to **Table 7.40**, 30.5 percent of minorities report having no minorities serving on their school boards; in contrast, 75.7 percent of non-minorities have no minorities serving on their school boards. Further, almost half of the minorities reported that they have one to four minorities on their school boards, while only 21.8 percent of non-minorities reported having one to four minorities serving on their school boards.

TABLE 7.34 PERCEPTION OF OVERALL EFFECTIVENESS

	NON-MINORITY		MINORITY	
	No.	%	No.	%
VERY SUCCESSFUL	897	42.2	58	49.2
SUCCESSFUL	1122	52.8	53	44.9
SOMETIMES SUCCESSFUL	94	4.4	7	5.9
NOT SUCCESSFUL	4	0.2	0	0.0
HAVE NO IDEA	7	0.3	0	0.0
TOTAL	2124	100.0	118	100.0

TABLE 7.35 SUPERINTENDENT RATING ON LAST EVALUATION

	NON-MINORITY		MINORITY	
	No.	%	No.	%
EXCELLENT	1475	69.6	69	58.5
GOOD	474	22.4	34	28.8
AVERAGE	55	2.6	4	3.4
BELOW AVERAGE	11	0.5	0	0.0
NOT EVALUATED	105	5.0	11	9.3
TOTAL	2120	100.0	118	100.0

Decision Making

Superintendents were asked what they thought their school boards' opinion was of school-based decision making. **Table 7.41** shows that 59.1 percent of minority superintendents reported that their boards are supportive of school-based decision making. This percentage is slightly higher than the level of support reported by non-minorities. On the other side of the issue, 3.5 percent of minorities reported that their school boards are opposed to school-based decision making.

When superintendents were asked how often their boards seek citizen participation in decision making, slightly more minorities and women than non-minority men reported that their boards seek citizen participation "all the time" (see **Table 7.42**).

Superintendents in the study were also asked who takes the lead in policy development (see **Table 7.43**). In response, 42.4 percent of minority superintendents indicated that this is a shared responsibility. This large percentage could be because minority superintendents often have larger districts with larger boards. In slight contrast, 38.1 percent of the female superintendents sampled reported that they share the lead in policy development and 36.4 percent of non-minority men reported sharing this responsibility. In fact, it appears that minority superintendents (28.8 percent) are around half as likely to develop policy alone as non-minorities (43.4 percent). When contrasted with 1992, it is seen that, in 2000, more superintendents report sharing the responsibility for policy development.

Table 7.44 shows the percentage of the time that the superintendents' boards accept their recommendations. The minorities sampled in this study reflect a somewhat lower percentage of board accepted recommendations than non-minorities reported.

When the superintendents were asked to identify the most difficult job facing their boards, 25.2 percent of minorities and 35.7 of non-minorities identified "financial issues" (see **Table 7.45**). The percentage for non-minorities is consistent with the 1992 Study, while the percentage for the minorities has dropped around 14 percent.

TABLE 7.36 BOARD EVALUATION REASONS (TOP TWO REASONS SELECTED)

REASON	NON-MINORITY		MINORITY	
	No.	%	No.	%
TO PROVIDE PERIODIC AND SYSTEMATIC ACCOUNTABILITY	1072	50.4	72	61.0
IDENTIFY AREAS IN NEED OF IMPROVEMENT	463	21.8	24	20.3
POINT OUT STRENGTHS	168	7.9	7	5.9
DOCUMENT GENERAL DISSATISFACTION WITH PERFORMANCE	109	5.1	8	6.8
HELP ESTABLISH RELEVANT PERFORMANCE GOALS	525	24.7	24	20.3
ASSESS PRESENT PERFORMANCE WITH PRESCRIBED STANDARDS	654	30.7	38	32.2
COMPLY WITH BOARD POLICY	607	28.5	31	26.3
DETERMINE SALARY FOR FOLLOWING YEAR	173	8.1	6	5.1
OTHER	92	4.3	6	5.1

A greater percentage of minorities (22.6 percent) contrasted with of non-minorities (16.8 percent) reported that dealing with "community pressures" is the most difficult job facing their school boards. Interestingly, over one-third of both minorities (40.1 percent) and non-minorities (37.1 percent) indicated that the most difficult jobs facing school boards come from within the board itself — internal conflict, understanding board roles, and board micro-management.

Table 7.46 displays the general opinion held by superintendents regarding their boards' preparation and ability to handle board duties. When viewing all the data, it can be seen that minorities report their boards to be somewhat less qualified than non-minorities. While 70.7 percent of non-minorities believe that their boards are either very well qualified or qualified, only 62.1 percent of minorities feel the same way. In fact, 33.6 percent of minorities reported that their boards are not well qualified contrasted with 26.9 percent of non-minorities reporting the same thing.

TABLE 7.37 FACTORS THAT MAY INHIBIT EFFECTIVENESS (TWO MOST IMPORTANT FACTORS)

FACTORS	NON-MINORITY		MINORITY	
	No.	%	No.	%
TOO MANY INSIGNIFICANT DEMANDS	801	37.7	36	30.5
TOO MUCH ADDED RESPONSIBILITY	307	14.4	7	5.9
INADEQUATE FINANCING OF SCHOOLS	945	44.4	48	40.7
STATE REFORM MANDATES	561	26.4	20	16.9
INEXPERIENCED, UNQUALIFIED, OR ILL-PREPARED STAFF	194	9.1	19	16.1
DIFFICULT RELATIONS WITH BOARD MEMBERS	115	5.4	5	4.2
DISTRICT TOO SMALL	83	3.9	4	3.4
COLLECTIVE BARGAINING AGREEMENTS	287	13.5	22	18.6
RACIAL/ETHNIC PROBLEMS	14	0.7	4	3.4
LACK COMMUNITY SUPPORT	65	3.1	6	5.1
INSUFFICIENT ADMIN.STAFF	211	9.9	6	5.1
BOARD MICROMANAGEMENT	425	20.0	33	28.0
BOARD ELECTIONS; CHANGED EXPECTATIONS	209	9.8	18	15.3
OTHER	89	4.2	7	5.9

TABLE 7.38 HOW YOU CHARACTERIZE YOUR SCHOOL BOARD

CHARACTERISTIC	NON-MINORITY		MINORITY	
	No.	%	No.	%
DOMINATED BY ELITE IN COMMUNITY	53	2.5	7	6.0
REPRESENTS DISTINCT FACTIONS IN THE COMMUNITY	394	18.6	31	26.5
ACTIVE, ALIGNED WITH COMMUNITY INTEREST, NOT RIGID	1404	66.2	69	59.0
NOT ACTIVE, ACCEPTING OF RECCOMENDATIONS MADE BY PROF. STAFF	271	12.8	10	8.5
TOTAL	2122	100.0	117	100.0

Stress, Fulfillment, Prestige, and Challenges of the Superintendency

Stress

As reported in **Table 7.47**, the amount of stress that superintendents feel seems to have increased by roughly 10 percent since the 1992 Study. The 1992 Study indicated that less than half of the superintendents surveyed felt that they suffered "considerable" to "very great stress." The 2000 Study shows that over half of the minority and non-minority superintendents alike suffer "considerable" to "very great stress" in their positions.

Self-Fulfillment

The amount of self-fulfillment that superintendents gain from their work has decreased since the 1992 Study. In 1992, 62.1 percent of non-minorities and 74.6 of minorities said they gained considerable self-fulfillment serving as superintendents. This year's study shows that only 56.4 percent of

TABLE 7.39 WOMEN ON BOARDS

	NON-MINORITY		MINORITY	
	No.	%	No.	%
0	181	8.5	8	6.8
1	485	22.8	24	20.3
2	634	29.8	26	22.0
3	442	20.8	29	24.6
4	211	9.9	15	12.7
5	96	4.5	7	5.9
6	32	1.5	3	2.5
7	16	0.8	1	0.8
BLANK	30	1.4	5	4.2

TABLE 7.40 MINORITIES ON BOARDS

	NON-MINORITY		MINORITY	
	No.	%	No.	%
0	1610	75.7	36	30.5
1	288	13.5	16	13.6
2	109	5.1	14	11.9
3	51	2.4	13	11.0
4	18	0.8	15	12.7
5	13	0.6	9	7.6
6	3	0.1	4	3.4
7	4	0.2	5	4.2
BLANK	31	1.5	6	5.1
TOTAL	2127	100.0	118	100.0

TABLE 7.41 SCHOOL BOARD'S OPINION OF SCHOOL-BASED DECISION MAKING

	NON-MINORITY		MINORITY	
OPINION	No.	%	No.	%
SUPPORTIVE	1079	51.2	68	59.1
INDIFFERENT	524	24.9	23	20.0
OPPOSE	159	7.5	4	3.5
NO OPINION	345	16.4	20	17.4
TOTAL	2107	100.0	115	100.0

non-minorities and 63.2 percent of minorities derive a considerable amount of self-fulfillment from the superintendency. Overall, minorities enjoy slightly more self-fulfillment from their positions than do their non-minority colleagues (see **Table 7.48**).

Prestige

Table 7.49 shows that a much higher percentage of minority superintendents (44.1 percent) than non-minority superintendents (27.6 percent) believe that the status or prestige of the superintendency is increasing. These percentages are significantly down since the 1992 Study, however, when 65.7 percent of minorities and 34.7 percent of non-minorities believed that the prestige of the superintendency was increasing.

Challenges Facing the Superintendency

One question in the 2000 survey asked superintendents to rate the level of significance (great, significant, limited, little or none, don't know) of a list of challenges to the superintendency today. An examination of the results reveals that there are differences (from slight to large) between minority and non-minority responses to 19 of the 29 listed issues and challenges. **Table 7.50** illustrates these data.

TABLE 7.42 SEEKING CITIZEN PARTICIPATION IN DECISION MAKING

FREQUENCY	NON-MINORITY		MINORITY	
	No.	%	No.	%
ALL THE TIME	243	13.4	18	15.7
FREQUENTLY	1177	55.7	65	56.5
WHEN REQUIRED	562	26.6	28	24.3
NEVER	3	0.1	0	0.0
SELDOM	90	4.3	4	3.5
TOTAL	2115	100.0	115	100.0

TABLE 7.43 WHO DEVELOPS POLICY?

	NON-MINORITY		MINORITY	
	No.	%	No.	%
PRINCIPALS	31	1.5	2	1.7
CENTRAL OFF. STAFF	210	9.9	13	11.0
SUPERINTENDENT	917	43.4	34	28.8
SCHOOL BOARD	160	7.6	18	15.3
SCHOOL BOARD CHAIR	6	0.3	0	0.0
SHARED RESPONSIBILITY	769	36.4	50	42.4
OTHER	18	0.9	1	0.8
TOTAL	2111	100.0	118	100.0

TABLE 7.44 PERCENT OF RECOMMENDATIONS FROM SUPERINTENDENT ACCEPTED BY BOARD

PERCENT	NON-MINORITY		MINORITY	
	No.	%	No.	%
90–100%	1877	89.1	94	81.0
80–89%	184	8.7	13	11.2
70–79%	35	1.7	4	3.4
60–69%	6	0.3	0	0.0
50–59%	3	0.1	3	2.6
LESS THAN 50%	2	0.1	2	1.7
TOTAL	2107	100.0	116	100.0

To begin, in response to the challenge of "changes in societal values and behavioral norms," most of the minorities and non-minorities chose "significant." However, fewer minorities (45.1 percent) than non-minorities (50.7 percent) responded this way. The reverse is true under the response labeled "limited." More minorities (26.5 percent) than non-minorities (19.9 percent) chose the response "limited."

The challenge identified as "accountability credibility" had the largest percentage of minorities (48.7 percent) for selecting the response "great." The largest percentage of non-minorities (52.3 percent) chose the response "significant."

When ranking the challenge of "community involvement in school-district decision making" both minorities (53.2 percent) and non-minorities (48.6 percent) most often ranked it as "significant," with about 5 percent more minorities ranking it "significant." Just the reverse is true for those who ranked it as "limited." More non-minorities (36.5 percent) and fewer minorities (27 percent) selected the response "limited."

Interestingly, while minorities (47.3 percent) and non-minorities (49 percent) most often selected "limited" for the response to "affirmative action programs and Title IX," a critically larger percentage of minorities (35.7 percent) than non-minorities (22.2 percent) ranked this challenge as "significant." Further, a much smaller percentage of minorities (9.8 percent) as contrasted to non-minorities (24.8 percent) indicated that this challenge had little or no significance.

The challenge of "student discipline/gangs" evoked the following percentages of responses in the "significant" category: minorities (48.2 percent) and non-minorities (34.9 percent). The difference between these percentages is noteworthy.

TABLE 7.45 SUPERINTENDENT PERCEPTION OF THE MOST DIFFICULT JOB FACING SCHOOL BOARDS

JOB	NON-MINORITY		MINORITY	
	No.	%	No.	%
FINANCIAL ISSUES	758	35.7	29	25.2
COMMUNITY PRESSUE	357	16.8	26	22.6
EMPLOYEE RELATIONS	94	4.4	6	5.2
CURRICULUM	40	1.9	2	1.7
INTER BOARD CONFLICT	103	4.9	10	8.7
UNDERSTANDING BOARD ROLES	355	16.7	18	15.7
AVOIDING MICROMANAGEMENT	214	10.1	18	15.7
PRESSURE FROM SPECIAL INTEREST GROUPS	151	7.1	4	3.5
OTHER	49	2.3	2	1.7
TOTAL	2121	100.0	115	100.0

TABLE 7.46 GENERAL OPINION OF BOARD PREPARATION AND ABILITY TO HANDLE DUTIES

OPINION	NON-MINORITY		MINORITY	
	No.	%	No.	%
VERY WELL QUALIFIED	268	12.6	17	14.7
QUALIFIED	1235	58.1	55	47.4
NOT WELL QUALIFIED	572	26.9	39	33.6
INCOMPETENT	43	2.0	5	4.3
DO NOT KNOW	6	0.3	0	0.0
TOTAL	2124	100.0	116	100.0

Both minorities (38.1 percent) and non-minorities (47.1 percent) ranked the challenge of "strategic planning and mission statements" as "significant."

The challenge of "administrator-board relations" is more important to the largest percentage of minorities (45.4 percent), who ranked it as "great," than to the largest percentage of non-minorities (44.5 percent), who ranked it as "significant."

The differences between the rankings of minorities and non-minorities in response to the challenge of "developing and funding institutional programs for children at risk" show up in two categories. First, about 16 percent more minorities (38.4 percent) than non-minorities (22.6 percent) ranked this challenge as "great." Second, about 9 percent more non-minorities (25.1 percent) than minorities (16.1) ranked it as "limited."

The largest percentage of minorities (49.5 percent) ranked the issue of "teacher recruiting and selection" as "great" and the largest percentage of non-minorities (46.2 percent) ranked it as "significant." The fact that minorities more often work in urban areas than do non-minorities may account, in part, for this difference.

Eleven percent more minority superintendents (33.9 percent) than non-minorities (23 percent) believe that "obtaining timely and accurate information for decision making" is a "great" challenge facing superintendents.

TABLE 7.47 AMOUNT OF STRESS IN THE SUPERINTENDENCY

DEGREE OF STRESS	NON-MINORITY		MINORITY	
	No.	%	No.	%
NO STRESS	12	0.6	1	0.9
LITTLE STRESS	152	7.2	9	7.8
MODERATE STRESS	865	40.9	43	37.4
CONSIDERABLE STRESS	856	40.5	50	43.5
VERY GREAT STRESS	230	10.9	12	10.4
TOTAL	2115	100.0	115	100.0

TABLE 7.48 SELF-FULFILLMENT OF THE SUPERINTENDENCY

SELF-FULLFILLMENT	NON-MINORITY		MINORITY	
	No.	%	No.	%
NONE	5	0.2	1	0.9
LITTLE	120	5.7	8	7.0
MODERATE	799	37.7	33	28.9
CONSIDERABLE	1194	56.4	72	63.2
TOTAL	2118	100.0	114	100.0

TABLE 7.49 STATUS/PRESTIGE OF THE SUPERINTENDENCY

AMOUNT	NON-MINORITY		MINORITY	
	No.	%	No.	%
DECREASING	415	19.6	16	13.6
ABOUT THE SAME	923	43.5	42	35.6
INCREASING	586	27.6	52	44.1
DO NOT KNOW	197	9.3	8	6.8
TOTAL	2121	100.0	118	100.0
STRESS	230	10.9	12	10.4
TOTAL	2115	100.0	115	100.0

Twelve percentage points separate minorities and non-minorities in their response to the issue of "aging and inadequate facilities." Fully 40.2 percent of minorities reported this as a "great" challenge, while 28.2 percent of non-minorities reported it as "great." Again, the greater percentage of minority superintendents in urban areas may account for some of this discrepancy. Only 12.5 percent of minorities ranked this issue as of "limited" significance, while 25.7 percent of non-minorities ranked it as "limited."

About 12 percent more minorities (29.2 percent) than non-minorities (17.6 percent) ranked the issues of "legislative and local efforts to implement choice programs" as of "great significance."

Almost 45 percent of minorities ranked "insufficient funds to purchase and use technology" as a "significant" challenge, while 39 percent of non-minorities ranked it "significant."

TABLE 7.50 ISSUES AND CHALLENGES FACING THE SUPERINTENDENCY TODAY

LEVEL OF SIGNIFICANCE	GREAT		SIGNIFICANT		LIMITED		LITTLE OR NONE		DON'T KNOW	
	NON-MIN.	MIN.	NON-MIN.	MIN.	NON-MIN.	MIN.	NON-MIN.	MIN.	NON-MIN.	MIN.
CHANGES IN SOCIETAL VALUES AND BEHAVIORAL NORMS	26.2	25.7	50.7	45.1	19.9	26.5	3.1	2.7	0.1	0.0
ACCOUNTABILITY/CREDIBILITY	35.3	48.7	52.3	40.7	11.7	10.6	0.7	0.0	0.0	0.0
COMMUNITY INVOLVEMENT IN SCHOOL-DISTRICT DECISION MAKING	11.5	18.9	48.6	53.2	36.5	27.0	3.3	0.9	0.0	0.0
AFFIRMATIVE ACTION PROGRAMS AND TITLE IX	3.5	7.1	22.2	35.7	49.0	47.3	24.8	9.8	0.4	0.0
STUDENT DISCIPLINE/GANGS	9.8	12.5	34.9	48.2	39.6	30.4	15.3	8.9	0.4	0.0
STRATEGIC PLANNING AND MISSION STATEMENTS	19.4	33.6	47.1	38.1	28.1	22.1	5.2	6.2	0.2	0.0
ADMINISTRATOR-BOARD RELATIONS	38.6	45.4	44.5	38.9	14.2	12.0	2.5	3.7	0.1	0.0
DEVELOPING AND FUNDING INSTITUTIONAL PROGRAMS FOR CHILDREN AT RISK	22.6	38.4	47.7	42.9	25.1	16.1	4.4	2.7	0.1	0.0
TEACHER RECRUITING AND SELECTION	33.4	49.5	46.2	34.2	17.5	13.5	2.8	6.3	0.1	0.0
OBTAINING TIMELY AND ACCURATE INFORMATION FOR DECISION-MAKING	23.0	33.9	53.7	50.0	20.5	15.2	2.7	0.9	0.2	0.0
AGING AND INADEQUATE FACILITIES	28.2	40.2	34.1	38.4	25.7	12.5	11.8	8.0	0.2	0.9
LEGISLATIVE AND LOCAL EFFORTS TO IMPLEMENT CHOICE PROGRAMS	17.6	29.2	35.0	38.1	35.1	26.5	11.6	6.2	0.8	0.0
INSUFFICIENT FUNDS TO PURCHASE AND USE TECHNOLOGY	32.5	37.5	39.2	44.6	22.3	14.3	5.9	3.6	0.1	0.0
SCHOOL-BASED DECISION MAKING	9.8	23.0	38.6	34.5	40.8	33.6	10.6	8.0	0.3	0.9
CHANGING DEMOGRAPHICS: SOCIAL-CULTURAL ISSUES SUCH AS RACE RELATIONS, INTEGRATION, SEGREGATION	22.2	42.5	29.9	20.0	25.5	23.0	22.1	13.3	0.4	0.9
RESTRUCTURING OF DISTRICTS	11.4	22.6	23.0	28.7	31.4	21.7	33.4	26.1	0.9	0.9
CHANGING PRIORITIES IN CURRICULUM	30.6	44.7	54.9	39.5	12.3	14.0	2.2	0.9	0.0	0.9
DEMANDS FOR NEW WAYS OF TEACHING OR OPERATING THE EDUCATIONAL PROGRAM	34.9	46.9	50.9	41.6	12.9	8.8	1.2	1.8	0.0	0.9
ASSESSING AND TESTING FOR LEARNER OUTCOMES	46.5	60.4	46.6	34.2	6.3	5.4	0.5	0.0	0.1	0.0

A surprising 13 percentage points mark the difference between minorities and non-minorities in their ranking of "school-based decision making." Twenty-three percent of minorities and about 10 percent of non-minorities believe the issue to be of "great" significance.

The greatest percentage difference — under a single rank — between minority and non-minority superintendents' responses can be seen under the issue of "changing demographics: social-cultural issues such as race relations, integration or segregation." A full 20 percentage point spread exists between minorities (42.5 percent) and non-minorities (22.2 percent) who ranked the issue to be of "great" significance.

When ranking the challenge "restructuring of districts," 11 percent more minorities (22.6 percent) than non-minorities (11.4 percent) ranked it as of "great significance."

Two issues had the second greatest percentage difference between minority and non-minority superintendents' responses under a single rank. One is the issue of "changing priorities in curriculum." Fourteen percentage points separate the minorities (44.7 percent) and non-minorities (30.6 percent) who ranked this challenge as of "great" significance.

The second issue with a 14 percentage point spread — under the ranking of "great" significance — between minority (60.4 percent) and non-minority superintendents (46.5 percent) is the challenge of "assessing and testing for learner outcomes."

Finally, 46.9 percent of minorities and 34.9 percent of non-minorities ranked the challenge of "demands for new ways of teaching or operating the educational program" as of "great" significance.

Bibliography

Alston, J. (in press). "Missing from action. Where are the black female school superintendents?" Special Issue: Women of Color and the Superintendency. *Urban Education.*

Alston, J. (1999). "Climbing hills and mountains: Black females making it to the superintendency." In C. Cryss Brunner (Ed.), *Sacred Dreams: Women and the Superintendency.* Albany, NY: State University of New York Press.

Brunner, C. C. and L. M. Caire. (in press). "The importance of representation for aspiration." Special Issue: Women of Color and the Superintendency. *Urban Education.*

Chase, S. (1995). *Ambiguous Empowerment: The Work Narratives of Women School Superintendents.* Amherst: University of Massachusetts Press.

Grogan, M. (in press). "A black woman tells." Special Issue: Women of Color and the Superintendency. *Urban Education.*

Grogan, M. (1999). "A feminist posttructuralist account of collaboration: A model for the superintendency." In C. Cryss Brunner (Ed.), *Sacred Dreams: Women and the Superintendency.* Albany, NY: State University of New York Press.

Jackson, B. (1999). "Getting inside history—against all odds: African-American women school superintendents." In C. Cryss Brunner (Ed.), *Sacred Dreams: Women and the Superintendency.* Albany, NY: State University of New York Press.

Kalbus, J. (in press). "Path to the superintendency." Special Issue: Women of Color and the Superintendency. *Urban Education.*

Mendez-Morse, S. E. (in press). "Claiming forgotten leadership." Special Issue: Women of Color and the Superintendency. *Urban Education.*

Mendez-Morse, S. E. (1999). "Redefinition of self: Mexican-American women becoming superintendents." In C. Cryss Brunner (Ed.), *Sacred Dreams: Women and the Superintendency.* Albany, NY: State University of New York Press.

Murtada, K. (in press). "Cleaning up and maintenance: In the wake of an urban school administration tempest." Special Issue: Women of Color and the Superintendency. *Urban Education.*

Ortiz, F. I. (in press *a*). "Who controls succession in the superintendency? A minority perspective." Special Issue: Women of Color and the Superintendency. *Urban Education.*

Ortiz, F. I. (in press *b*). "Hispanic females' school leadership: Cases of super-intending." *The New Superintendency: Advances in Research and Theories of School Management and Educational Policy.* Salt Lake, UT: JAI Press.

Ortiz, F. I. (1999). "Seeking and selecting Hispanic female superintendents." In C. Cryss Brunner (Ed.), *Sacred Dreams: Women and the Superintendency.* Albany, NY: State University of New York Press.

Simms, M. (in press). "Impressions of leadership: Through a Native woman's eyes." Special Issue: Women of Color and the Superintendency. *Urban Education.*

Chapter 8

Professional Preparation and Training

Lars Björk

Overview

The importance of the preparation arm of a profession cannot be discounted. The socialization of initiates influences the way the work of the profession is carried out. It is true that professional administrators acquire significant skills and experiences during their tenure as teachers and principals. However, many of their attitudes, beliefs, and skills are molded in university classrooms in preparation for programs leading to licensing and certification.

In this last chapter of the 2000 Study, the current debates concerning quality and relevance are discussed before data collected from the sample group is presented. There is an interesting paradox created by the data concerning the perceived relevance and worth of superintendent preparation programs. Surveyed superintendents generally believe their preparation programs were "good." Only about a third thought them to be "fair or poor." However, the current literature on superintendent and administrator preparation quality is almost universally negative. The same is true of positions and policy positions taken by professional associations serving administrators. Most likely the programs are not as bad as their critics claim, but are genuinely in need of substantial restructuring. The restructuring or rebirth of superintendent preparation and inservice training is certainly one of the two or three most serious challenges facing the profession in the 21st century, and well warrants the extensive discussion and analysis that follow.

Superintendents are confronted by simultaneous and often contradictory demands for continuity and change. Society has always looked to those in the superintendency as conservators of community values and educational change agents when the magnitude of problems threatens community well-being. In an age characterized by rapid and continuous change, it is important that superintendents, as well as those who prepare them, continue to evolve, addressing the new realities of schooling and governance. The closely entwined themes of school reform and reforming administrator preparation programs affirm the notion that when one element of a system changes, other parts must readjust to conform to new circumstances. When this dynamic interrelationship is ignored, the well-being of these organizations may be threatened.

The social, economic, political, and technological changes that have unfolded in the United States over the past several decades continue to have a tremendous impact on the nature and conduct of schooling, and raise serious questions about how the next generation of school leaders should be prepared. It is clear that societal changes are increasing the complexity of schooling and are correspondingly calling for changes in the way superintendents lead schools. It is, however, equally clear that these changes may be viewed as either a crisis, or an opportunity for reconceptualizing the superintendency and restructuring how the next generation of superintendents are identified, prepared, and selected.

Accomplishing these tasks will be neither simple nor easy. The ability of university-based professional preparation programs to adjust rapidly is constrained by state statutes, state department of education regulations, accreditation association requirements, institutional procedures, and norms of the professorate. In addition, these programs are influenced by federal and state program initiatives, state legislation, changing mandates, and activities of professional associations related to training and licensure standards. Also, pressures to move toward free market systems contribute to the uncommon complexity of the task. Although collaborative efforts of different stakeholders have forged a new direction for professional preparation and licensure in the United States over the past decade, work directed toward reconceptualizing the superintendency and reconfiguring professional preparation is still underway.

Formal Academic Training and Degrees

Professional preparation in the field of educational administration has a rather brief history (McCarthy, 1999) in comparison with other professions such as law, medicine, and dentistry. It is neither as orderly nor as well-defined a process as is customary in these established professions that have national and state boards that heavily influence program standards, content, instructional processes, and licensing. Preparation in these fields tends to rely on graduate education programs, which provide a foundation for practice. They are characterized by the acquisition of professional and technical knowledge, extended internships, comprehensive practice-oriented initial licensure examinations, and continuing staff development delivered by professional associations that focus on maintaining technical competency and re-licensure requirements.

Historically, superintendent preparation programs have been university-based. Administrators enter the superintendency through academic degrees and state certification. State certification requires at least one academic degree, since entry into teaching in all states requires at least a bachelor's degree. A master's degree is required for administrative certification in nearly all states, except those that do not have administrative certificate programs.

Content, quality, and relevance of professional preparation, as well as national standards, are important aspects of any profession. The Interstate School Leadership Licensure Consortium (ISLLC) standards for the superintendency, which were released in 1999, hold promise for guiding future preparation and licensure. The ISLLC standards integrate AASA's performance standards and NCATE's standards for school administrators forged by the National Policy Board for Educational Administration (NPBEA), a consortium of education associations. Although over 30 states are using ISLLC standards in some fashion, many states continue to dictate the structure and content of educational administration programs through state teacher/administrator certification codes.

In addition, most superintendents are recommended for certification by universities in which they are enrolled in graduate level/certification courses after completing a state defined and approved program of study. These higher education courses and programs of study vary greatly in subject

TABLE 8.1 HIGHEST DEGREE ATTAINED BY SUPERINTENDENTS: 1971, 1982, 1992, AND 2000

	1971	1982	1992	2000
B.A. or B.S.	2.1	0.9	0.5	0.3
MASTER'S	55.1	44.3	4.5	8.1
MASTER'S + ADDITIONAL GRADUATE WORK	NA	NA	24.0	24.1
SPECIALIST DEGREE	13.4	14.9	15.8	22.0
Ed.D or Ph.D.	29.2	39.5	36.0	45.3
OTHER	0.2	0.4	19.2	0.2

content, degree of difficulty, and required field/clinical experiences. The practicum/internship, if required at all, tends to be neither comprehensive nor extensive and usually provides a brief, one semester snapshot of superintendents' work. Although intensive, yearlong internships in the superintendency are highly desirable, they are currently a rare exception.

The preparation of American school superintendents is dissimilar to other professions like medicine, law, and dentistry that typically require full-time study before being licensed to practice. Superintendents' professional career patterns often limit the range of training options. A superintendent's career generally begins as a classroom teacher, later moving up through building-level administration, and then often into a central office position or directly into the superintendency. Preparation and licensure is usually protracted over several years and is characterized as serving individuals who are mid-career, in their mid-thirties to mid-forties, and who are married and have commitments to provide for their families. These conditions typically produce part-time, commuter students who pursue graduate degrees or administrator certification during evenings and in summer school.

Once superintendents complete their graduate degree or administrator certification program, most participate in professional development programs periodically over their careers to maintain technical currency in the field. Many of these programs are delivered by professional associations, universities, state departments of education, state "leadership academies," internship programs mandated by state school-reform legislation (as is the case in Kentucky), and private sector organizations.

Although the successive steps on the professional career ladder help individuals acquire many of the skills and competencies required in the superintendency, they are incomplete and tend to prepare individuals to reproduce current practices. In addition, inservice programs, while skill focused and touted as being more relevant than university-based models, are classroom oriented and in a like manner are separated from district contexts. Opportunities for aspiring superintendents to gain new perspectives and fill gaps in their knowledge and skills may require dramatically different approaches than are currently in place in universities, professional associations, and state departments of education. New practices will most surely require greater relevancy, attention to adult learning theory, and more extensive field experience than is currently the case.

The Educational Reform Reports

During the past several decades, widespread concern for the quality of public education launched what is arguably the most intense, comprehensive, and sustained effort to improve education in American history. Compelling arguments for improving classroom instruction and fundamentally altering the manner in which schools are structured, managed, and governed not only challenged conventional assumptions about the nature of schooling, but also increased awareness of the impor-

TABLE 8.2. HIGHEST DEGREE ATTAINED, ANALYZED BY NUMBER OF YEARS SINCE ATTAINING HIGHEST DEGREE

DEGREE	0-5 YEARS AGO		6-10 YEARS AGO		11-15 YEARS AGO		15+ YEARS AGO		NATIONAL SAMPLE	
	No.	%	No.	%	No.	%	No.	%	No.	%
BA OR BS	0	0.0	1	14.3	0	0.0	6	85.7	7	0.3
MASTER'S IN EDUCATION	11	6.3	44	25.3	31	17.8	88	50.6	174	7.8
MASTER'S NOT IN EDUCATION	0	0.0	0	0.0	2	20.0	8	80.0	10	0.5
MASTER'S + GRADUATE WORK	59	10.9	105	19.4	114	21.4	263	48.6	541	24.1
SPECIALIST DEGREE	92	18.6	139	28.1	110	22.3	153	31.0	494	22.0
DOCTORATE	171	16.8	240	23.6	225	22.1	380	37.4	1016	45.3
TOTAL	333	100.0	529	100.0	482	100.0	898	100.0	2242	100.0

tance of school and district leadership. Peterson and Finn (1985) observed that, "at a time when the nation is deeply concerned about the performance of its schools, and near-to-obsessed with the credentials and careers of those who teach in them, scant attention has been paid to the preparation and qualifications of those who lead them" (p.42).

While most educational reform reports focus on improving classroom instruction and programs, several underscore the importance of principals in facilitating the change process. Several key reports, including the Carnegie Task Force Report (1986) and the report of the Holmes Group (1986), brought attention to this issue by emphasizing the need for reforming education at the local and building level, identifying the principal as the key to success, and discussing how the preparation of school administrators may be improved. Reform reports released by the American Association of Colleges of Teacher Education (1988) and the National Governor's Association (1986), acknowledged that school principals were key to creating a supportive reform environment. The notion that the principal is a pivotal actor in facilitating school change was echoed in research findings indicating that, without their assistance, significant and lasting reform would be unlikely (Björk, 1993).

The Educational Administration Reports

As the nature of educational reform shifted toward more complex issues associated with restructuring American education, conventional ways of doing administration were called into question. These concerns launched a national debate among scholars, policymakers, and reformers on how the superintendency is changing or may change (Crowson, 1988) and how the next generation of initiates should be prepared.

Pressure for reforming university-based educational administration programs during the 1980s-1990s came from a number of sources: the school reform movement; the recognition that school principals were key to change; the realization that many administrators did not have adequate knowledge of instructional practices and change methods; the disillusionment with the theory movement and social science frameworks; the criticism that university-based preparation programs are disconnected from the reality of schools; and the lack of improvement of administrative practice (Murphy, 1987).

During the 1980s and early 1990s, educational administration programs were scrutinized in reports released by associations, national commissions and task forces, including the National Association of Elementary School Principals (NAESP), 1990; National Policy Board for Educational Administration (NPBEA), 1989; the Commission on Excellence in Educational Administration (NCEEA), 1987; the Carnegie Forum on Educational and the Economy, 1986; and the University Council of Education Administration (UCEA), 1989. Reports released by these and other groups examined the nature and content of educational administration programs, clarified the relationship between the school reform movement and the preparation of educational leaders, and identified key areas for improving the preparation of competent educational leaders. Common recommendations emerging from these reports have significant implications for restructuring educational administration programs.

An evaluation of the Danforth Foundation initiative to improve the preparation of school leaders during the 1980s and 1990s found that most educational administration programs are not programs per se, but are sequences of separate and unconnected courses that give little thought "to effective teaching, adult learning theory, linkages with school districts, field experiences that help bridge the theory-practice gap, content closely aligned with desired outcomes, or rigorous evaluation" (Milstein, 1993, p. 18). These findings provide a framework for both criticism of prevailing practice and a template for restructuring professional preparation in the field.

Strengthening Field Connections

The history of professional preparation in the field points to changes in the professorate and subsequent shifts in the intensity of linkages with the field. Before the 1960s, the majority of faculty in educational administration programs served as school administrators and joined university faculties toward the end of their careers. In the 1950s, these programs drew substantial criticism from colleagues in the arts and sciences for recruiting practitioners who taught using personal experiences and anecdotes (Marland, 1960) and who had little interest in research and theory (McCarthy, 1999). The quest for a science of administration, the theory movement, contributed to preparation programs placing greater emphasis on building a professional knowledge base, recruiting faculty discipline-based scholars from the social sciences (Griffiths, 1964), and changing course content and curriculum away from a focus on the execution of technical tasks.

Several national reports released in the 1980s concur that the weakest threads in the fabric of professional preparation programs are found in university/school linkages as well as connections to other education stakeholders (Carver, 1988; NCEEA, 1987; NPBEA, 1989). A marked decline in faculty support for the value of theory, and widespread criticism that programs fail to attend to problems of practice, changed departmental hiring practices (Miklos, 1983; McCarthy, 1999; McCarthy and Kuh, 1997). In the 1980s, hiring faculty with social science backgrounds, rather than practitioner experience, peaked and by 1994, 33 percent of faculty had school administrator experience. More than half of those faculty hired by educational administration departments between 1989 - 1994 had been school administrators (McCarthy, 1999). These new faculty were committed to strengthening linkages with schools and facing problems of practice (McCarthy, 1999), and 80 percent of faculty surveyed in 1994 reported that service to schools should be more highly regarded by universities (McCarthy and Kuh, 1997).

NCEEA (1987) recognized the importance of reconnecting with the field, arguing that schools should share the responsibility for preparing the next generation of school leaders. In addition, NPBEA (1989) suggested that long-term, formal relationships be established between universities and school districts to create partnership sites for clinical experiences, field residencies, principal apprenticeship programs, and action research. Although efforts to reconnect with the field to enhance program relevance is of critical importance, the nature of how that is being accomplished is significantly different from approaches used before the 1950s. Many program reforms and initiatives are moving toward fundamentally restructuring school-state agency-university relationships.

Revising Course Content

Although an increasing number of school administrators are becoming educational administration faculty and are helping to reconnect preparation to the field, the fundamental structure of educa-

TABLE 8.3. HIGHEST DEGREE HELD BY SUPERINTENDENT

DEGREE	GROUP A: 25,000 OR MORE PUPILS No.	%	GROUP B: 3,000-24,999 PUPILS No.	%	GROUP C: 300-2,999 PUPILS No.	%	GROUP D: FEWER THAN 300 PUPILS No.	%	NATIONAL UNWEIGHTED PROFILE No.	%
BA OR BS	0	0.0	1	0.2	2	0.1	4	1.6	7	0.3
MASTER'S IN EDUCATION	2	2.1	17	3.1	116	8.7	37	14.7	172	7.7
MASTER'S NOT IN EDUCATION	1	1.1	4	0.7	3	0.2	2	0.8	10	0.4
MASTER'S + GRADUATE WORK	11	11.6	75	13.8	367	27.4	85	33.9	538	24.1
SPECIALIST DEGREE	2	2.1	54	9.9	354	26.5	81	32.3	491	22.0
DOCTORATE	79	83.2	393	72.2	496	37.1	42	16.7	1010	45.3
TOTAL	95	100.0	544	100.0	1338	100.0	251	100.0	2228	100.0

tional administration programs is more difficult to change. Pohland and Carlson (1993) found that titles of required courses in 1993 were consistent with titles of courses used in 1976. These courses include school business finance/budgeting, educational law, school community relations, district administration, leadership, administrative behavior (theory), and organizational development. Thus, a number of observers suggest that programs have not appreciably changed since the 1960s (McCarthy, 1999). The content and course emphasis, however, are frequently updated as individual faculty members strive to reflect changes in the field. In this regard, continuity in program structures and course titles may mask changes in course content.

A number of factors hinder change in institutions of higher education. Change is inhibited by drawn out institutional review processes; powerful influences of state administrator licensure requirements that lock programs into specific courses; faculty hiring linked to content specialization; faculty resistance to radical changes that may jeopardize employment, and educational administration program emphasis on basic managerial aspects of the job (Cooper and Boyd, 1988; McCarthy, 1999).

Analyses of the national commission reports on the preparation of educational administrators identified several recommendations for change. A major emphasis is placed on examining course sequences and course content to reflect a coherent and integrated curriculum that is contextually linked to the field of practice. McCarthy et. al (1988) observed that reorganizing educational administration curricula and revising course content were the field's most crucial needs and were important backdrops for changes in other areas. The Danforth foundation initiatives helped to influence professional preparation programs' shift away from an emphasis on management to a focus on leadership. This shift was consistent with emerging responsibilities of school leaders to act as facilitators and mentors and to work in decentralized systems characterized by shared governance, participatory decision making, school-based councils (Danforth Foundation, 1987). The work of school and district leaders also shifted towards the centrality of student learning (Cambron-McCabe, 1993) requiring them to develop expert knowledge in instruction, curriculum, teaching and learning, and the social context of schooling (Murphy, 1993).

Revising Instructional Strategies

Analyses of instructional strategies used in educational administration programs suggest there is considerable room for improvement. Studies show that before the 1960s, instruction tended to rely on anecdotes, personal experiences, and was highly prescriptive. Although the shift toward the

TABLE 8.4 UNDERGRADUATE MAJOR OF SUPERINTENDENTS

MAJOR	GROUP A: 25,000 OR MORE PUPILS		GROUP B: 3,000-24,999 PUPILS		GROUP C: 300-2,999 PUPILS		GROUP D: FEWER THAN 300 PUPILS		NATIONAL UNWEIGHTED PROFILE	
	No.	%	No.	%	No.	%	No.	%	No.	%
AGRICULTURE	1	1.1	3	0.6	26	1.9	6	2.4	36	1.6
BUSINESS	5	5.3	20	3.7	69	5.2	18	7.2	112	5.0
EDUCATION (NOT PHYS ED.)	25	26.6	159	29.2	347	26.0	74	29.6	605	27.2
FINE ARTS	3	3.2	17	3.1	40	3.0	9	3.6	69	3.1
HUMANITIES	12	12.8	59	10.8	101	7.6	13	5.2	185	8.3
MATHEMATICS	6	6.4	35	6.4	95	9.1	23	9.2	159	7.2
PHYSICAL EDUCATION	5	5.3	47	8.6	160	12.0	28	11.4	240	10.8
PHYSICAL OR BIOLOGICAL SCIENCES	12	12.8	54	9.9	127	9.5	18	7.2	211	9.5
SOCIAL SCIENCE	22	23.4	126	23.2	315	23.6	48	19.2	511	23.0
OTHER	3	3.2	24	4.4	55	4.1	13	5.2	95	4.3
TOTAL	94	100.0	544	100.0	1335	100.0	250	100.0	2223	100.0

social sciences during the 1970s - 1980s altered course content, few instructional innovations accompanied these changes. The lecture method is dominant (McCarthy, 1999; Murphy, 1992), a format and approach least conducive to adult learning (AACTE, 1988; Murphy, 1990; Erlandson and Witters-Churchill, 1988). Strong theoretical and empirical evidence support the use of instructional strategies substantively grounded in the reality of schools and appropriate to adults preparing to become school administrators. These strategies include: simulations, case studies, practice-based and problem-based strategies, collaborative action research (Milstein et al, 1993), integration of formal knowledge, and field-based activities throughout program coursework (Björk, 1999). The strategies also include using more student-centered rather than professor-centered instructional approaches.

Bridges and Hallinger (1991) and Murphy (1990a) echo several key national commission reports in calling for increasing the relevance of administrator preparation programs by orienting the curriculum and instruction more explicitly toward problems of practice. This approach emphasizes organizing knowledge of research and best practice around problems, rather than presenting information in unconnected course segments. Problem-based instruction relies on students to assume responsibility for their own learning, and emphasizes small groups and collaborative problem solving rather than lectures and competition for grades. This approach is directed towards decreasing "isolated, passive, and sterile knowledge acquisition as the primary activity of preparation programs, and increase the knowledge that can be adopted to the wide variety of situations that will confront the practitioner" (Prestine, 1992, p.23).

Redesigning program content, changing instructional strategies, and integrating clinical components through cooperative school/university linkages are consistent with education reform reports released during the 1980s (AACTE, 1988; NASSP, 1985; NCEEA, 1987) that called for greater emphasis on reality-oriented instructional formats.

Integrating instruction and clinical experiences

Although refocusing program curricula, revising course content, and changing instructional strategies are fundamental to reconstructing leadership preparation programs, effectively integrating formal knowledge and experiential knowledge gained in clinical settings is equally crucial (Griffiths, 1988). In consideration of the characteristics of aspiring administrators, finding a way to provide substantive field-based experiences remains a difficult problem facing those responsible for preparing school leaders. Most educational administration programs include a field-based preservice practicum, typically following the completion of licensure program coursework. In some instances, educational administration programs are being directed toward integrating formal

TABLE 8.5 MAJOR OF SUPERINTENDENT'S HIGHEST DEGREE

MAJOR	GROUP A: 25,000 OR MORE PUPILS		GROUP B: 3,000-24,999 PUPILS		GROUP C: 300-2,999 PUPILS		GROUP D: FEWER THAN 300 PUPILS		NATIONAL UNWEIGHTED PROFILE	
	No.	%	No.	%	No.	%	No.	%	No.	%
EDUCATIONAL ADMIN./SUPERVISION	84	89.4	484	89.3	1200	89.6	216	87.1	1984	89.2
SECONDARY EDUCATION	0	0.0	8	1.5	36	2.7	6	2.4	50	2.2
PHYSICAL EDUCATION	0	0.0	1	0.2	6	0.4	1	0.4	8	0.4
HUMANITIES/FINE ARTS	1	1.1	2	0.4	6	0.4	3	1.2	12	0.5
SCIENCE OR ENGINEERING	0	0.0	3	0.5	9	0.7	0	0.0	12	0.5
BUSINESS	0	0.0	0	0.0	4	0.3	0	0.0	4	0.2
MATHEMATICS	0	0.0	3	0.6	7	0.5	0	0.0	10	0.4
ELEMENTARY EDUCATION	0	0.0	7	1.3	13	1.0	6	2.4	26	1.2
OTHER	9	9.6	34	6.3	58	4.3	16	6.5	117	5.3
TOTAL	94	100.0	542	100.0	1339	100.0	248	100.0	2223	100.0

knowledge and field-based experiences throughout leadership preparation, rather than using the practicum as a capstone experience.

The University of Kentucky redesigned its principal and superintendent practicum to follow the annual work cycle of these administrators. The cycle of principals' and superintendents' work is used as a template to define instructional content, instructional sequencing, field experiences, and integration of state-mandated training modules delivered by the state department of education and professional associations. This strategy allows for the integration of formal and experiential knowledge in a manner that coincides with events in the administrator work cycle. Eleven school districts comprising the Central Kentucky Educational Cooperative provide time for aspiring administrators to participate in field-based and training activities. This "backward mapping" (Odden, 1992) approach reorients prevailing instructional practices to fit the reality of administrators' work. Björk (1996, 1999) and Ashe, Haubner, and Troisi (1991) contend that field-based activities may serve as a vehicle for including other stakeholders in the preparation enterprise, integrating formal and experiential knowledge, enhancing adult learning, and contributing higher levels of knowledge transference to school settings.

In most states, licensure requirements are limited to completion of a state-approved planned program of study that includes minimal school-based work. Although some states have implemented internship programs that provide yearlong, substantive involvement in school-based administrative settings, they vary greatly in form. For example, North Carolina provides internships while students are completing licensure programs, while Kentucky requires initial licensure before being hired as a principal. Principals are required to participate in a supervised intern program during the first year of employment. If they successfully complete their internship, they are required to complete the second administrative licensure stage within a five-year period. Both the North Carolina and Kentucky models address a significant limitation faced by educational administration programs since their inception: placing aspiring administrators in supervised administrative settings on a full-time basis.

TABLE 8.6 LENGTH OF SERVICE AS A CLASSROOM TEACHER PRIOR TO BECOMING AN ADMINISTRATOR: 1971, 1982, 1992, AND 2000

	1971	1982	1992	2000
0-5	47.7	NA	47.9	37.7
6-10	33.3	NA	36.1	37.9
11-15	13.8	NA	12.1	16.2
16+	5.8	NA	3.8	8.2

TABLE 8.7 LENGTH OF SERVICE AS CLASSROOM TEACHER PRIOR TO ENTERING ADMINISTRATION OR SUPERVISION

YEARS AS TEACHER	GROUP A: 25,000 OR MORE PUPILS		GROUP B: 3,000-24,999 PUPILS		GROUP C: 300-2,999 PUPILS		GROUP D: FEWER THAN 300 PUPILS		NATIONAL UNWEIGHTED PROFILE	
	No.	%	No.	%	No.	%	No.	%	No.	%
0-5	57	60.0	242	44.6	487	36.2	55	22.2	841	37.7
6-10	32	33.7	212	39.0	523	38.9	80	32.3	847	37.9
11-15	4	4.2	71	31.1	226	16.8	61	24.6	362	16.2
16-20	2	2.1	15	2.8	73	5.4	34	13.7	124	5.6
21-25	0	0.0	2	0.4	30	2.2	15	6.0	47	2.1
26+	0	0.0	1	0.2	7	0.5	3	1.2	11	0.5
TOTAL	95	100.0	543	100.0	1346	100.0	248	100.0	2232	100.0

Recruiting Student Cohorts

NPBEA, in its report *Improving the preparation of school administrators* (1989), recommended that vigorous recruiting efforts be put in place to attract the "best and brightest" candidates who reflect the diverse ethnic, racial, and gender differences in our society. In addition, they argue for an increase in entrance standards to ensure that students possess strong analytical abilities, high administrative potential, and demonstrated success in teaching. This position was echoed by AACTE (1988) and Carver (1988) who recognized the need for strengthening the linkages between schools and universities to recruit highly qualified candidates. Commission reports and studies emphasize the importance of using a variety of means of identifying and recruiting potential school leaders to participate in innovative preparation programs. Joint action in identifying the "best and brightest" candidates is essential to establishing highly motivated cohorts, increase the commitment of the partners, and establishing a sense of shared responsibility.

An important structural change in educational leadership programs over the past decade is the move toward admitting students to graduate degree and licensure programs in cohort groups. Although the cohort model is not considered an innovation in the field, McCarthy (1999) notes that when it is used as a means of understanding the nature and dynamics of communities of learners, and examining and refining the use of collaborative leadership techniques, it can be transformed into a powerful instructional strategy. In addition, cohorts provide support systems that cultivate a sense of community among students and faculty that positively influence academic performance, commitment, persistence, reflection, and may directly affect their leadership practices as school administrators (Barnett, Basom, Yerkes, and Norris, 2000; Norton, 1995; Hill, 1995).

Cohort groups also tend to demand more from faculty, tend to challenge conventional instructional approaches, and question the relevance of course content, creating tension between faculty and students (Barnett and Muse, 1993). In addition, non-cohort students enrolled in more conventional instructional groupings are resentful when they perceive others receiving learning experiences and resources not available to them (Barnett and Muse, 1993). Norton (1995) also notes that cohort models tend to increase faculty workloads and create tension among department faculty. Not withstanding the disadvantages, Norton (1995) found that 50 percent of the institutions in the UCEA use cohorts at the master's degree level and 80 percent used them at the doctoral degree level. In a study that sampled a broader range of institutions, McCarthy and Kuh (1995) found that 50 percent of the students in Ed. D. programs, and 25 percent of students in Ph.D. and masters degree programs, were enrolled in cohorts.

Evaluation of University-Based Programs

There does not appear to be a shortage of critics of professional preparation in the field. Although there are few empirical studies on how practitioners view the effectiveness of their preparation

TABLE 8.8 LENGTH OF SERVICE AS CLASSROOM TEACHER PRIOR TO ENTERING ADMINISTRATION OR SUPERVISION, ANALYZED BY GENDER

YEARS AS TEACHER	MALE		FEMALE		NATIONAL SAMPLE	
	No.	%	No.	%	No.	%
0-5	789	40.5	60	20.2	849	37.8
6-10	730	37.5	120	40.4	850	37.9
11-15	294	15.1	70	23.6	364	16.2
16-20	90	4.6	34	11.4	124	5.5
21-25	36	1.8	11	3.7	47	2.1
26+	8	0.4	2	0.7	10	0.4
TOTAL	1947	100.0	297	100.0	2244	100.0

(how it contributes to perceptions of school or district effectiveness, or its relationship to student learning outcomes), sweeping statements that preparation is "seriously deficient" (Thompson, 1989, p.372) appear frequently in the press and public policy forums. Sweeping statements such as this often go beyond reasonable interpretations of data and are infrequently balanced by positive evaluations of innovative programs launched over the past decade. The notion that excellent leaders are needed for excellent schools has captured the imagination of the American public. It has consequently increased interest, scrutiny, and competition from a range of agencies, associations, and public sector organizations. The range of concerns, and increasing strength of vested interest groups (states, professional associations, and private business), has fueled the debate on the value, direction, and options for delivering professional preparation programs. Unfortunately, the combination of uninformed critique and vested interests provide powerful ingredients for bad policy.

Critiques of university-based professional preparation programs are often strident and assert that they have failed to produce leaders in sufficient number and quality to meet the changing needs of schools. A more reasoned approach may call for examining the indictments leveled at principal and superintendent programs and the data that support or refute claims.

On a cautionary note, evaluation data on professional preparation programs tend to survey principals and superintendents who completed graduate degree and licensure programs much earlier. For example, 40.2 percent of superintendents in this study had completed their highest degree more than 15 years earlier, with an additional 21.5 percent completing their degrees between 11 and 15 years prior to the survey. Thus 61.5 percent of individuals surveyed completed degree and licensure programs prior to educational reform initiatives taking place in the field. Although these studies are historically appropriate for understanding the evolution of professional preparation programs, indictments based on out-of-date findings are less than suitable for framing cogent public policy.

A survey of educational administration graduate students from 62 university-based programs conducted by McCarthy, Kuh and Beckman (1979) found that half regarded their preparation as being irrelevant to school practice. In addition, Hoyle (1985) found that veteran administrators saw significant differences between what they learned and what they do, and concurred with Pitner (1982) that educational administration programs needed to be improved. These findings, in combination with education commission reports and those specifically focused on educational administration during the mid- to late-1980s, raised serious questions about conventional assumptions and practices and concurred that professional preparation programs must address the issues that confront school administrators.

National commission and task force reports on administrator preparation programs have played a significant role in heightening concern and raising questions about conventional assumptions and practices. Many critics added their voices to assertions made by the National Commission for the Principalship (1990) convened by the National Association of Secondary School Principals (NASSP), that university-based preparation programs were outmoded, that licensing requirements did not reflect current work, and that programs should face the issues that confront school administrators. In view of the fact that superintendent preparation programs are embedded in the same departmental structures as principal preparation, many of these criticisms are likely to be pertinent.

The debate on administrator preparation is being fueled by wide indictments, including questions raised by cost-benefit analysis studies as to whether programs should be discontinued altogether (Brent and Haller, 1998); the lack of field-relevant preparation (Achilles, 1998); opportunities for more field-relevant licensure created by ISLLC standards (Van Meter and Murphy, 1997); charges that graduate-level education has minimal impact on teacher perceptions of administrator effectiveness (Haller, Brent, and McNamara, 1997); claims of an absence of a relationship between graduate education and instructional leadership (Zheng, 1996); calls for department-level self-analysis and improvement (Downey, 1998); recognition of market-driven alternative preparation delivery options (Schneider, 1998); arguments for reconceptualizing the work of school leaders (Short, 1998); and unambiguous observations that departments must either fundamentally change or face the very real prospect of being eclipsed by others (Dembowski, 1998). The common thread that is woven throughout the fabric of critiques is recognition of the need for content and instruction to align with changes taking place in schools and to produce high quality leaders to improve American education. The perceived inability of the field to deliver on that reasonable expectation is also fueling a deep sense of frustration. Although practitioners, professors, and policymakers have challenged the field to reform, the rhetoric of change appears greater than actual transformation (McCarthy, 1999).

TABLE 8.9 EVALUATION OF WHETHER CERTAIN ASPECTS OF THE SUPERINTENDENCY SHOULD BE TAUGHT DURING PRESERVICE EDUCATION OR INSERVICE EDUCATION

PRESERVICE

STRATEGIC PLANNING (18.1%)

STUDENT RIGHTS IN TERMS OF DUE PROCESS AND COURT-IMPOSED PROCEDURES (16.3%)

CHANGING DEMOGRAPHICS (16.1%)

PERSONAL TIME MANAGEMENT (16.0%)

SITE-BASED MANAGEMENT (14.9%)

EFFECTIVE PUBLIC RELATIONS SKILLS (14.3%)

STAFF RECRUITING / SELECTION (13.6%)

EMPOWERMENT OF STAFF (13.5%)

ADMINISTRATOR-BOARD RELATIONS (13.4%)

STAFF AND ADMINISTRATOR EVALUATION (12.8%)

INSERVICE

RESTRUCTURING OF DISTRICTS (32.6%)

DEVELOPING AND FUNDING INSTITUTIONAL PROGRAMS FOR CHILDREN AT-RISK (27.8%)

LEGISLATIVE AND LOCAL EFFORTS TO IMPLEMENT "CHOICE" PROGRAMS (24.4%)

AGING AND INADEQUATE FACILITIES (23.9%)

PARENT APATHY AND IRRESPONSIBILITY ABOUT THEIR OWN CHILDREN – INCLUDING CHILD ABUSE (21.5%)

GROWING PRESURE FOR PUBLIC SUPPORT OF NONPUBLIC SCHOOLS (21.2%)

CHANGING DEMOGRAPHICS (20.3%)

OBTAINING TIMELY/ACCURATE INFORMATION (20.2%)

CHANGING PRIORITIES IN CURRICULUM (20.2%)

STAFF RECRUITING / SELECTION (20.0%)

BOTH

HIGH-STAKES, STATE-MANDATED ACOUNTABILITY TESTING (74.7%)

EFFECTIVE PUBLIC RELATIONS SKILLS (73.3%)

ASSESSING EDUCATIONAL OUTCOMES (71.5%)

ADMINISTRATOR-BOARD RELATIONS (71.4%)

STUDENT DISCIPLINE (70.7%)

DEMANDS FOR NEW WAYS OF TEACHING OR OPERATING THE EDUCATIONAL PROGRAM (70.0%)

CHANGES IN SOCIETAL VALUES AND BEHAVIORAL NORMS (69.5%)

STAFF AND ADMINISTRATOR EVALUATION (69.3%)

REFINANCING SCHOOLS TO MEET INCREASING EXPENDITURES AND CAPITAL OUTLAY (69.0%)

CHANGING PRIORITIES IN CURRICULUM (67.9%)

Over the past several decades (1977-2000), a number of studies have indicated that superintendents are being challenged by decidedly different conditions, and critics reported widespread dissatisfaction among individuals completing graduate degree or certification programs in educational administration. In other instances, researchers have found these same individuals are generally satisfied with their university-based preparation programs. In most instances, those responding to surveys have completed educational administration programs 10 to 20 years earlier, raising concern about the usefulness of this data in promulgating future public policy without reference to commission reports, research findings, and emerging developments in the field. Changes in professional preparation should be carefully thought out and focused on strengthening the capacity of the next generation of school leaders to support learning in large and increasingly complex school settings.

Cunningham and Hentges (1982) and Glass (1992), in their respective studies of superintendents, found that over 70 percent of respondents regarded their preparation as excellent or good, and over one-third of those responding to the Cunningham and Hentges (1982) survey indicated that the strongest aspect of their graduate education program was the high quality of university professors. Five years later, in 1987, a study conducted by the National Center for Educational Information (NCEI) found that superintendents were generally pleased with their university-based preparation. Chapman's (1997) study of beginning superintendents found that 86.7 percent rated their university-based preparation programs as "excellent" or" good," pointing out that, although the quality of instruction was high, they expressed the need for more field experiences. Although most agree that having a strong background in the field's knowledge base is essential, aspiring and veteran superintendents agree with the need for gaining first-hand, practical knowledge about administrative processes, strategies, and tactics used in everyday situations.

As noted previously, the majority of university-based superintendent preparation programs in the United States offer similar courses in school administration including school law, business and finance, personnel administration, school-community relations, human behavior, and organizational theory. Although professors concur on the importance of human relations, organizational development, leadership, and interpersonal communication skills, Glass (1993) found that there was some discrepancy between what practicing superintendents believed they needed and what they received in their preparation programs. Chapman (1996) also found that superintendents felt the need for better preparation in financial management, interpersonal relations and group dynamics, politics (district and state level), change methods (including content knowledge and implemen-

TABLE 8.10 OPINION OF USEFULNESS OF EDUCATIONAL RESEARCH

USEFULNESS	GROUP A: 25,000 OR MORE PUPILS		GROUP B: 3,000-24,999 PUPILS		GROUP C: 300-2,999 PUPILS		GROUP D: FEWER THAN 300 PUPILS		NATIONAL UNWEIGHTED PROFILE	
	No.	%	No.	%	No.	%	No.	%	No.	%
HIGHLY USEFUL	47	50.0	203	37.2	382	28.4	51	20.4	683	30.6
USUALLY USEFUL	39	41.5	242	44.4	626	46.5	104	41.6	1011	45.2
OCCASSIONALLY USEFUL	8	8.5	98	18.0	323	24.0	86	34.4	515	23.0
IS NOT USEFUL	0	0.0	1	0.2	12	0.9	8	3.2	21	0.9
NO OPINION	0	0.0	1	0.2	3	0.2	1	0.4	5	0.2
TOTAL	94	100.0	545	100.0	1346	100.0	250	100.0	2235	100.0

TABLE 8.11 EVALUATION OF SUPERINTENDENCY PREPARATION PROGRAMS: 1971, 1982, 1992, AND 2000

	1971	1982	1992	2000
EXCELLENT	NA	26.8	26.8	26.2
GOOD	NA	47.4	47.4	47.4
FAIR	NA	NA	22.0	22.2
POOR	NA	NA	4.6	3.6

tation strategies), school law (current court decisions that impinge on districts), and a knowledge of teaching, learning, and curriculum.

Notwithstanding widespread criticism of program weaknesses and slow progress, some departments of educational administration are taking these critiques seriously, are successfully altering programs in rather fundamental ways, and are contributing to the direction and legitimacy of change in the field. Although they are still considered "outliers" (McCarthy, 1999), these innovative programs hold considerable promise for the more hesitant majority. A number of studies have identified specific graduate program components, including cohorts, mentors, and problem-based learning (Clark, 1997; Murphy, 1993; Pounder, 1995). In addition, evaluations of the Danforth principal preparation program involving 21 UCEA institutions found that these components, as well as field-based internships, contributed to high levels of participant satisfaction and positive perceptions among colleagues of being effective leaders (Leithwood, Jantzi, Coffin and Wilson, 1996).

Critics question whether departments of educational administration have the interest and will to adequately serve practitioners, and are exploring alternative venues for delivering training. Over the past several decades, educational administration programs have been criticized for emphasizing the acquisition of knowledge and theory; "knowing about," rather than addressing issues of practice. Ascertaining whether departments of educational administration are responding to these concerns, and the strength of transformative efforts, is of fundamental importance to the debate on whether they will have a role in preparing future administrators. Although a definitive answer may not be possible, as there is wide variance in programs (McCarthy and Kuh, 1996) and change initiatives (Murphy and Forsyth, 1999), other indicators may prove useful in charting the direction of change of the field in general.

The Handbook of Research on Educational Administration (1988, 1999) and its predecessors have been an integral part of the professional knowledge base in the field since 1964, and tend to reflect emphases in the field at the time they are published. *The Handbook of Research on Educational Administration* (1988), edited by Norman Boyan, reflects a period in which the field placed considerable emphasis on empirical research and theory. It was an archival report to the scholarly community of research over the preceding 30 years, and its structure and content followed traditional areas of research and categories of administrative work. *The Second Handbook of Research on Educational Administration*

TABLE 8.12 EVALUATION OF GRADUATE PROGRAMS IN YOUR STATE IN EDUCATIONAL ADMINISTRATION

	GROUP A: 25,000 OR MORE PUPILS		GROUP B: 3,000-24,999 PUPILS		GROUP C: 300-2,999 PUPILS		GROUP D: FEWER THAN 300 PUPILS		NATIONAL UNWEIGHTED PROFILE	
	No.	%	No.	%	No.	%	No.	%	No.	%
EXCELLENT	14	14.9	59	10.9	180	13.5	34	13.8	287	13.0
GOOD	31	33.0	272	50.3	675	50.7	141	57.1	1119	50.5
FAIR	40	42.6	169	31.2	407	30.6	58	23.5	674	30.4
POOR	9	9.6	41	7.6	70	5.3	14	5.7	134	6.1
TOTAL	94	100.0	541	100.0	1332	100.0	247	100.0	2214	100.0

TABLE 8.13 EVALUATION OF GRADUATE PROGRAMS FOR SUPERINTENDENCY, ANALYZED BY AGE

	AGE 45-UNDER		AGE 46-50		AGE 51-55		AGE 56-60		AGE 61-ABOVE	
	No.	%	No.	%	No.	%	No.	%	No.	%
EXCELLENT	46	22.1	138	24.6	212	25.7	131	28.9	56	31.3
GOOD	105	50.5	268	47.8	384	46.5	210	46.3	86	48.0
FAIR	50	24.0	125	22.3	190	23.0	91	20.0	31	17.3
POOR	7	3.4	30	5.3	40	4.8	22	4.8	6	3.4
TOTAL	208	100.0	561	100.0	826	100.0	454	100.0	179	100.0

(1999), edited by Joseph Murphy and Karen Seashore Louis, however, was notably different in several respects, and reflects changes taking place in both the academic and practice arms of the profession. Its emphasis on core technology (teaching and learning) is a clear attempt to re-center the field on the education of children rather than continue to focus on managing schools.

The Second Handbook is organized around contemporary and emerging issues facing school and district administrators. Research findings relevant to these several areas are integrated into the discussion of problems and prospects. Editors and contributing scholars suggest that research and practice, rather than being mutually exclusive, are complimentary. In this new framework, notions of leadership are linked to teaching and learning, new decision-making and governance patterns, and accountability for the education of all children, particularly those at risk.

Re-centering the field may be characterized as moving from an emphasis on the acquisition of knowledge and "theory," "knowing about" administration, to "knowing for" school improvement. Although this shift sets the stage for bridging the gap between the academic and practice arms of the profession, it is incomplete. Professional preparation may also benefit from emphasis on "knowing why" changes are being made and "knowing how" to accomplish these goals in new school, district, community, and state policy contexts (Björk, Lindle and Van Meter, 1999).

The reform reports on educational administration released during the past decade confirm the importance of superintendents to school reform and persuasively argue that changes in schools require concurrent changes in administrator preparation programs. The education reform reports view university-based educational administration programs as indispensable to preparing aspiring and veteran administrators to work in restructured school contexts, master new roles, become proficient in new political situations, and serve as effective change agents. Students completing these programs, however, express the need for aligning course content with emerging demands and increasing opportunities for field-based experience (Björk, 1999). *The Second Handbook of Research on Educational Administration*, as one of several barometers for change in the field, indicates a shift toward addressing problems of practice and may serve as a point of reference for changing preparation programs.

Professional Associations, Preparation and Standards

Practitioner organizations, including AASA and NASSP, as well as professor-oriented organizations, including UCEA and NCPEA, have long histories of involvement in the improvement of professional preparation of school leaders. The innovations, policy initiatives, and persistence of these and other organizations contributed to laying the groundwork for restructuring professional preparation in the field.

UCEA. The UCEA, a consortium of 56 universities in the United States and Canada, took an active role in reforming educational administration programs. As mentioned previously, UCEA sponsored the National Commission on Excellence in Educational Administration (NCEEA) and issued a report, *Leaders for America's Schools*, in 1987 that called for doing away with at least 300 of the 500 programs in the nation that were considered inadequate. The report also recommended that the remaining programs adopt a professional school model similar to the characteristics of programs in medicine that place considerable emphasis on clinical experience, and enlist active participation of exemplary principals and superintendents. Furthermore, it suggested that a national policy board, comprised of professional associations that have long-standing interest in leadership preparation, provide a unified voice on policy issues affecting the field, improve preparation, and practice and monitor changes.

AASA. In addition to UCEA, AASA has been a strong advocate for improving the quality of preservice programs. AASA developed a set of performance guidelines (Hoyle, English, and Steffy, 1985, 1990) to help diagnose administrator problems, frame professional development plans, and assess performance outcomes. AASA used these guidelines to establish an innovative superintendent assessment center program in Kentucky. Several years later, in 1993, AASA formulated eight standards for superintendents focused on the areas of educational leadership; policy and governance; community relations; management; curriculum planning and instructional development; instructional leadership; and human resources and ethics (AASA Commission, 1993). AASA became a strong advocate for using these standards for improving university-based superintendent preparation. In 1999, AASA received support from the Office of Educational Research and Improvement (OERI), United States Department of Education, to establish the Center for Accountability and Solutions. The work of the Center is focused on enhancing the capability of superintendents in collecting, analyzing, and using data as diagnostic and decision-making tools, a fundamental element of the ISLLC performance standards.

NASSP and NAESP. NASSP has also been a strong advocate for improving professional preparation in the field. The NASSP's support of competency-based and then performance–based preparation for school administrators in the 1970s and 1980s called for educational administration programs to develop individualized programs for aspiring administrators based on a diagnosis of needs. They also called for programs to undertake self-analyses and abolish out-of-date courses, content and instructional practices.

In 1978, NASSP developed an assessment center designed to analyze skills of aspiring administrators using simulations and interviews in 12 skill areas viewed as essential to the success of school principals. This process was intended to be used to select principals; however, it was also used to screen prospective candidates into some educational administration graduate programs (Milstein and Kruger, 1993). In 1990, NASSP joined with NAESP and established the National Commission for the Principalship. It concurred with reports released by other commissions and task forces that professional preparation programs were not aligned with emerging needs of school administrators, and licensing requirements were no longer relevant to principals' work. They explored the notion of national licensure as a means of influencing changes in professional preparation.

NPBEA. NPBEA was established in 1988 and was viewed as a significant turning point in the profession. It brought together a number of professional associations concerned with leadership preparation after several decades of disjointed activities. In 1989, NPBEA released *Improving the Preparation of School Administrators: An Agenda for Reform,* which called for eliminating inadequate professional preparation programs; strengthening the content of those remaining; reducing student-faculty ratios; and using a practitioner-oriented doctorate, an Ed.D., as the basis for becoming a

TABLE 8.14 EVALUATION OF GRADUATE PROGRAMS IN YOUR STATE IN EDUCATIONAL ADMINISTRATION, ANALYZED BY AGE

	AGE 45-UNDER		AGE 46-50		AGE 51-55		AGE 56-60		AGE 61-ABOVE	
	No.	%	No.	%	No.	%	No.	%	No.	%
EXCELLENT	32	15.4	70	12.5	104	12.7	57	12.7	26	14.6
GOOD	104	50.0	276	49.4	402	49.0	235	52.2	102	57.3
FAIR	63	30.3	174	31.1	261	31.8	133	29.6	42	23.6
POOR	9	4.3	39	7.0	53	6.5	25	5.6	8	4.5
TOTAL	208	100.0	559	100.0	820	100.0	450	100.0	178	100.0

school administrator. This report was followed by a comprehensive set of recommendations released in 1993 that provided guidelines for improving recruitment, preparation, licensure, and selection of school administrators. The unified curriculum guidelines developed by NPBEA in 1994, regarding accrediting educational administration programs, were adopted by NCATE in 1996, and were used for educational administration program reviews in 1997. In 1993, NPBEA released *Principals for Our Changing Schools,* which codified the knowledge and skill base for the profession and served as a blueprint for improving educational administration programs in the nation.

In 1994, NPBEA established a consortium with the Council of Chief State School Officers (CCSSO) to formulate national licensure standards for school administrators. The premise underlying their work is that a uniform set of national standards would provide a powerful point of leverage for making needed changes in the field. The Interstate School Leaders Licensure Consortium developed six standards that were compatible with those promulgated by AASA in 1993, and NCATE in 1996, and were subsequently adopted by 24 states, with 7 additional states either adapting or using them in some other fashion. The ISLLC standards are intended to improve the quality of professional preparation, and shift the focus from administration to leadership and the centrality of student learning. The six standards focus on developing a shared vision within schools; creating cultures that support learning; ensuring safe, efficient, and effective learning; collaborating with the broad community; acting in a fair and ethical fashion; and understanding the socio-economic, legal, political, and cultural contexts in which schools are embedded.

The ISLLC standards are intended to influence changes in educational administration program content, instructional strategies, and clinical experiences. A sophisticated licensure portfolio, jointly developed by ISLLC and the Educational Testing Service (ETS), was released in 1999 and requires demonstration of knowledge, dispositions, and performances of ISLLC standards and indicators. In addition, a performance-based assessment instrument, The School Leaders Licensure Assessment (SLLA), based on the ISLLC standards and developed by ETS, has been adopted for use by eight states and will be used in combination with other methods for initial licensure of beginning school principals. The Collaborative Professional Development Process for School Leaders (CPDP) is performance-based and focuses on enhancing professional growth of school leaders consistent with

TABLE 8.15 SUPERINTENDENTS' EVALUATION OF GRADUATE PROGRAMS AS PREPARATION FOR SUPERINTENDENCY

	GROUP A: 25,000 OR MORE PUPILS		GROUP B: 3,000-24,999 PUPILS		GROUP C: 300-2,999 PUPILS		GROUP D: FEWER THAN 300 PUPILS		NATIONAL UNWEIGHTED PROFILE	
	No.	%	No.	%	No.	%	No.	%	No.	%
EXCELLENT	28	29.5	171	31.5	328	24.5	56	22.3	583	26.2
GOOD	49	51.6	241	44.4	632	47.3	129	51.4	1051	47.2
FAIR	16	16.8	107	19.7	315	23.6	51	20.3	489	22.0
POOR	2	2.1	24	4.4	62	4.6	15	6.0	103	4.6
TOTAL	95	100.0	543	100.0	1337	100.0	251	100.0	2226	100.0

TABLE 8.16 EVALUATION OF GRADUATE PROGRAMS FOR SUPERINTENDENCY, ANALYZED BY NUMBER OF YEARS SINCE ATTAINING HIGHEST DEGREE

	0-5 YEARS AGO		6-10 YEARS AGO		11-15 YEARS AGO		15+ YEARS AGO	
	No.	%	No.	%	No.	%	No.	%
EXCELLENT	98	29.5	140	26.6	130	26.9	220	24.5
GOOD	159	47.9	265	50.4	219	45.2	414	46.1
FAIR	67	20.2	96	18.3	116	24.0	212	23.6
POOR	8	2.4	25	4.7	19	3.9	53	5.9
TOTAL	332	100.0	526	100.0	484	100.0	899	100.0

ISLLC standards and school/district improvement needs. The development of the ISLLC-based School Superintendents Assessment (SSA) will be used in superintendent licensure.

Preliminary indications suggest that these initiatives not only are changing university-based educational administration programs, but that NCATE may use both the ISLLC standards and the SLLA as part of Performance 2000, an initiative intended to provide national recognition for professional preparation programs. The ISLLC initiative is a comprehensive licensure initiative directed toward revitalizing leadership preparation in the United States, establishing national licensure, and facilitating reciprocity among states. A "key recommendation is that states should eliminate barriers that keep licensed and experienced school leaders from moving among states" (Shipman and Murphy, 1999).

The Perception of Administrator Shortage

Over the past decade, NPBEA and its member associations have launched a series of initiatives focused on leveraging the improvement of quality in school and district leadership preparation in the United States. Accreditation of university-based professional preparation programs, the development of standards for practice, licensure examinations based on those standards, and the release of the codification of the knowledge and skill base for the profession provide a framework for improvement in the field. At a time when many of these efforts are beginning to have the desired influence, perceptions of widespread under-supply of administrator candidates are causing concern that policymakers will abandon the standards and the push toward improving the quality of school leaders in efforts to fill positions.

The issue of administrator supply and demand is complex. Anecdotal evidence and studies warn of impending shortages, including estimates that nearly one-half of principals in the nation will retire by 1999 (Muse and Thomas, 1991), and that superintendency positions are emptying faster than they are being filled (Brockett, 1996). Although the Bureau of Labor Statistics projects a 10 to 20 percent increase in the number of school administrator vacancies at all levels through 2005, data also suggest that there are adequate numbers of individuals currently licensed to fill positions.

A study commissioned by NASSP and NAESP, *Is There a Shortage of Qualified Candidates for Openings in the Principalship: An Exploratory Study* (1998), confirmed a shortage of qualified people seeking the principalship in slightly more than half (52 percent) of the 403 districts surveyed. Although superin-

TABLE 8.17 EVALUATION OF GRADUATE PROGRAMS FOR SUPERINTENDENCY, ANALYZED BY RACE

	NON-MINORITY		MINORITY	
	No.	%	No.	%
EXCELLENT	547	25.9	36	31.0
GOOD	1008	47.7	46	39.7
FAIR	461	21.8	28	24.1
POOR	98	4.6	6	5.2
TOTAL	2114	100.0	116	100.0

TABLE 8.18 EVALUATION OF GRADUATE PROGRAMS FOR SUPERINTENDENCY, ANALYZED BY GENDER

	MALE		FEMALE	
	No.	%	No	%
EXCELLENT	509	26.2	76	25.9
GOOD	923	47.5	132	45.1
FAIR	424	21.8	66	22.5
POOR	86	4.4	19	6.5
TOTAL	1942	100.0	293	100.0

tendents were not dissatisfied with the applicants hired, they were concerned about diminishing numbers of candidates in the search pools. The *Occupational Outlook Handbook* (1998 - 1999) published by the federal government indicates that the job is getting increasingly difficult. Pay incentives have not increased commensurate with heightened job demands, resulting in declining competition for assistant principal and principal positions.

A recent study, *Career Crisis in the School Superintendency?*, conducted with cooperation and assistance from the American Association of School Administrators and the National Center for Educational Statistics (NCES), explores issues related to superintendents' perception of a career crisis and related issues, including job mobility, role satisfaction, and future life plans. "The popular perception is that of an impossible job where superintendents confront escalating and competing demands, find themselves besieged by confusing and conflicting interest groups, and enjoy little or no security" (Cooper, Fusarelli, and Carella, 2000).

The study reports that 92 percent of superintendents surveyed are concerned with high turnover, and that 88 percent believe there is a shortage of applicants and concur that there is a serious crisis facing the profession. These findings are contrary to findings of an increase in the mean years experience in one position to seven years, up from 6.2 years in 1992 (Glass, Björk, Brunner, 2000). Cooper, Fusarelli, and Carella recommend that meliorating several factors would open the market and reduce the "shortage" in the superintendency. The job market appears to be segmented by the lack of superintendent mobility. Mobility is restricted by their preference for working in a "good" district of similar size, and the inequitable distribution of advanced degrees of superintendents in districts of varying size. For instance, superintendents in small districts constitute an overwhelming majority of CEOs in the nation, but they hold fewer advanced degrees (43 percent) than colleagues do in medium-sized districts (75 percent) or large districts (79 percent). The lack of advanced degrees may restrict the majority of superintendents in the nation from being considered for suburban or urban districts. In addition, unattractive pay and benefits and non-portability of pensions restrict mobility. Moving toward a system of regional or national reciprocity for pension plans that

TABLE 8.19 EVALUATION OF CREDIBILITY OF EDUCATIONAL ADMINISTRATION PROFESSORS, ANALYZED BY AGE

	AGE 45-UNDER		AGE 46-50		AGE 51-55		AGE 56-60		AGE 61-ABOVE	
	No.	%	No.	%	No.	%	No.	%	No.	%
EXCELLENT	41	19.7	70	12.5	113	13.7	64	14.1	25	13.9
GOOD	107	51.5	296	52.7	419	50.9	226	49.8	102	57.0
FAIR	52	25.0	157	27.9	235	28.6	132	29.1	42	23.5
POOR	8	3.8	36	6.4	54	6.6	30	6.6	9	5.0
NO OPINION	0	0.0	3	0.5	2	0.2	2	0.4	1	0.6
TOTAL	208	100.0	562	100.0	823	100.0	454	100.0	179	100.0

TABLE 8.20 EVALUATION OF CREDIBILITY OF EDUCATIONAL ADMINISTRATION PROFESSORS

	GROUP A: 25,000 OR MORE PUPILS		GROUP B: 3,000-24,999 PUPILS		GROUP C: 300-2,999 PUPILS		GROUP D: FEWER THAN 300 PUPILS		NATIONAL UNWEIGHTED PROFILE	
	No.	%	No.	%	No.	%	No.	%	No.	%
EXCELLENT	7	7.4	58	10.8	198	14.8	48	19.1	311	14.0
GOOD	42	44.2	272	50.6	710	52.9	132	52.6	1156	51.9
FAIR	39	41.1	168	31.2	352	26.2	56	22.3	615	27.6
POOR	7	7.4	40	7.4	78	5.8	11	4.4	136	6.1
NO OPINION	0	100.0	0	100.0	4	0.3	4	1.6	8	u.4
TOTAL	95	100.0	538	100.0	1342	100.0	251	100.0	2226	100.0

allows pensions to follow superintendents, similar to what has been done in higher education with the TIAA-CREF pension model, may contribute to superintendent mobility.

In the fall of 1998, NPBEA convened a symposium, The School Administrator Supply Crisis, hosted by the Education Commission of the States in Denver, Colorado. Association members, scholars, practitioners, and foundation representatives conveyed constituent concerns of the perception of an administrator shortage, particularly the decline in the number and quality of applicants available for administrative positions in the United States (Forsyth, 1999). Historical documents show that that many individuals who complete professional preparation programs, and are licensed, do not practice. In the field of educational administration, unlike the field of medicine, there is an imperfect correlation between supply and demand.

Participants at NPBEA's Denver symposium discussed a complex set of factors contributing to administration being viewed as an unattractive profession that may prevent those who otherwise might seek principal and superintendent positions from applying. These discussions raised a number of important policy questions about supply and demand, the reasons for non-practice, and how professional preparation may be configured to serve the best interest of the state and the profession (Forsyth, 1999, p. 4).

Although anecdotal evidence suggests the existence of a "shortage," the absence of comprehensive, credible data on the number of individuals licensed, but not entering search pools, makes it uncommonly difficult to understand the scope and urgency of the issue or develop coherent policy alternatives. A series of state and national studies are needed to understand the dimensions and characteristics of the problem and produce an adequate supply of highly qualified school and district level administrators.

A Look at the 2000 Study Data

All of the previous 10-Year studies of the American superintendency have explored the characteristics of superintendent preparation and training. Surveys of professionals in the field conducted since 1923 have collected information about the graduate degrees, major fields of study in college, types of graduate programs taken for degrees, state licensure, and years of experience. Several of the studies posed value questions, such as whether practicing superintendents thought that training programs were adequately preparing them for their jobs. In the 1982 study, new questions were

TABLE 8.21 MAJOR STRENGTHS OF SUPERINTENDENTS' GRADUATE STUDY PROGRAMS

MAJOR STRENGTHS	GROUP A: 25,000 OR MORE PUPILS		GROUP B: 3,000-24,999 PUPILS		GROUP C: 300-2,999 PUPILS		GROUP D: FEWER THAN 300 PUPILS		NATIONAL UNWEIGHTED PROFILE	
	No.	%	No.	%	No.	%	No.	%	No.	%
HIGH-QUALITY PROFESSORS	58	23.4	269	18.7	655	18.3	122	18.5	1104	18.6
QUALITY OF EDUCATIONAL ADMINISTRATION COURSES	47	19.0	294	20.4	692	19.4	131	19.9	1164	19.7
QUALITY OF OTHER COURSES IN EDUCATION	14	5.6	79	5.5	182	6.1	40	6.1	315	5.3
ABILITY OF PROFESSOR TO RELATE CONTENT TO PRACTICE	56	22.6	284	19.7	737	20.6	122	18.5	1199	20.2
DISCUSSION OF CURRICULUM, INSTRUCTION, &TESTING ISSUES	33	13.3	203	14.1	513	14.4	92	14.0	841	14.2
AVAILIBILITY OF TECHNOLOGY	3	1.2	14	1.0	46	1.3	13	1.9	76	1.3
OPPORTUNITY FOR HANDS-ON	17	6.8	129	8.9	259	7.2	43	6.6	448	7.6
CONVENIENT SCHEDULE FOR PROFESSIONALS	20	8.1	169	11.7	489	13.7	96	14.6	774	13.1

introduced concerning challenges and issues superintendents thought should be covered in their training and preparation. Questions also were asked about superintendents' needs for continuing education, an important concern in the development of the profession.

The 1992 study introduced the notion of performance areas as an additional topic area for discussion regarding superintendent training and preparation. In 1982, an AASA task force completed a report entitled *Guidelines for the Preparation of School Administrators*, which focused on what superintendents should know and be able to do. The 1992 Study asked superintendents to indicate which of the eight "performance areas" contained in the guidelines are "most essential" to effective performance in the superintendency. These performance areas and specific skills needed to be an effective superintendent are elaborated in AASA's publication *Skills for Successful 21st Century School Leaders: Standards for Peak Performers, 3rd edition* (1998), written by John Hoyle, Fenwick English, and Betty Steffy.

The 2000 Study, however, replaced the set of questions focused on the usefulness of the eight performance areas with a series of questions directed toward identifying non-university-based organizations and agencies providing professional development and training and evaluation of superintendent experiences. These questions, in many respects, parallel questions focused on university-based professional preparation. In addition, questions focused on method of payment (self-financed, sabbaticals, assistantships, fellowships, and other forms of financial support from districts and other sources) were dropped. The overwhelming majority of respondents to the 1971, 1982, and 1992 surveys indicated that they had not received financial assistance, suggesting these questions were not relevant to professional preparation in the field. The following is an analysis of the 2000 Study data regarding superintendents' professional preparation and training.

Formal Academic Preparation and Degrees

Administrators enter the superintendency by completing academic degree programs and meeting state licensure requirements. Most states require a bachelor's degree for teacher certification, and a master's degree in educational leadership for administrator licensure.

Meeting Needs for Continuing Education

Many states mandate additional graduate level coursework, professional development, and inservice training to maintain administrator licensure. These continuing education needs are typically focused on maintaining the currency of administrators' knowledge in technical, regulatory,

TABLE 8.22. MAJOR WEAKNESSES OF SUPERINTENDENTS' GRADUATE STUDY PROGRAMS

MAJOR WEAKNESSES	GROUP A: 25,000 OR MORE PUPILS No.	%	GROUP B: 3,000-24,999 PUPILS No.	%	GROUP C: 300-2,999 PUPILS No.	%	GROUP D: FEWER THAN 300 PUPILS No.	%	NATIONAL UNWEIGHTED PROFILE No.	%
LOW-QUALITY PROFESSORS	22	9.4	143	10.5	346	10.1	63	9.7	574	10.1
ADMINISTRATION COURSES	29	12.3	143	10.5	375	11.0	61	9.4	608	10.7
FAILURE TO LINK CONTENT TO PRACTICE	42	17.9	235	17.2	548	16.0	110	16.9	935	16.5
tOO MUCH EMPHASIS ON pROFESSORS' pERSONAL eXPERIENCES	28	11.9	190	13.9	478	14.0	85	13.0	781	13.8
iNADEQUATE ACCESS TO TECHNOLOGY	43	18.3	269	19.6	643	18.8	120	18.4	1075	18.9
lACK OF HANDS-ON APPLICATION	48	20.4	266	19.4	668	19.5	140	21.5	1122	19.8
INCONVENIENT SCHEDULE FOR PROFESSIONALS	23	9.8	122	8.9	362	10.6	72	11.1	579	10.2

and specific skill areas. They are frequently met through short-term, highly focused workshops and seminars sponsored by a combination of providers, including institutions of higher education, state education agencies, the private sector, and professional associations, including AASA, ASBO, NSBA, and ASCD. These professional development and inservice programs tend to suffer from the same limitations as university-based graduate education programs. They tend to be instructor-centered and classroom-bound, rather than being student-centered, with field-focused experiences that are relevant to adult learning styles and that enhance transference of new knowledge and skills to other settings.

Education Prior to the Superintendency

Graduate Degrees Held

In the 1992 Study, about 96 percent of superintendents held a master's degree, specialist certificate, or doctorate. In 2000, nearly 100 percent of respondents hold a combination of those graduate degrees. A comparison of data on the highest degree attained by superintendents contained in the 1971, 1982, 1992 and 2000 reports indicates a trend toward superintendents completing graduate degree programs at higher levels. For example, superintendents in 1971 and 1982 indicated the highest degree attained was the master's degree at 55 percent and 43 percent, respectively. In subsequent years, 1992 and 2000, only 4.5 percent and 8.1 percent of superintendents indicated the master's degree was their highest degree attained. It appears that an increasing number of superintendents are pursuing master's degrees plus additional coursework (24 percent) as well as specialist (22 percent) and doctorates (45 percent), than was the case over the past 30 years. One reason for the increase in the number of degrees possessed by superintendents since the 1971 Study is that many older superintendents who had been "grandfathered" in state certificate programs had retired by 1992. In most instances, states require about 30 semester hours of coursework beyond the master's degree to qualify for superintendent licensure. Many older, practicing superintendents who held a master's degree, completed additional course credits to qualify them to hold that administrative position (see **Table 8.1**).

In 1982, 28 percent of sampled superintendents indicated that they possessed a doctoral degree. In 1992, that number increased to 36 percent, and then rose to 45.3 percent in 2000. These degrees were attained between 6 – 15 years ago, a period that roughly coincides with their careers in the superintendency. It appears that many superintendents are pursuing advanced graduate degrees while concurrently serving as chief executive officers (see **Table 8.2**). The larger the district, the more likely the superintendent is to have a doctoral degree (see **Table 8.3**). This is particularly evident in districts with more than 25,000 students, as well as in districts with 3,000 to 24,999 students, where 83 percent and 72 percent, respectively, of superintendents hold doctorates.

Undergraduate Degree Majors

There is a wide range of undergraduate academic majors held by superintendents. However, 27 percent of respondents indicated that their major was education, increasing from 25.3 percent in 1992. The second largest concentration of undergraduate majors is in the social sciences (23 percent).

TABLE 8.23 MENTORED BY A PRACTICING OR RETIRED SUPERINTENDENT, ANALYZED BY DISTRICT SIZE						
	YES		NO		UNCERTAIN / DON'T KNOW	
	No.	%	No.	%	No.	%
GROUP A: 25,000 OR MORE	62	65.3	31	32.6	2	2.1
GROUP B: 3,000-24,999	343	62.8	198	36.3	5	0.9
GROUP C: 300 – 2,999	769	57.2	567	42.2	9	0.6
GROUP D: LESS THAN 300	135	54.0	115	46.0	0	0.0

Superintendents' undergraduate majors also included biological/ physical sciences (9.5 percent) and physical education (10.8 percent). Although the nature of superintendents' work tends to emphasize management tasks, only 5 percent of superintendents had business as an undergraduate major (see **Table 8.4**).

Master's Degrees

State licensure requires the completion of an approved program of study that is typically embedded in master's degree programs. As expected, the prevalent master's degree major for superintendents is educational administration/supervision. In 1992, nearly 60 percent of reporting superintendents possessed a master's degree in educational administration. In 2000, 89.2 percent hold a master's degree in this major. In 1992, 11.7 percent of superintendents held a master's degree with secondary education majors, which is reflective of, at that time, many superintendents were former secondary teachers (see **Table 8.5**). In 2000, only 2.2 percent indicated secondary education as a major. These changes may reflect increasing requirements for administrator licensure enacted by state legislatures since the early 1980s.

Certificates

The specialist certificate (CAS or EdS) is a mid-level program between the master's and doctorate degrees. Typically, it consists of 30 semester hours of advanced graduate study in the field of educational administration, and may include courses in other closely aligned subjects or areas of professional study. In many states, certification requirements for the superintendency include 30 semester credit hours beyond the master's degree. This 30 hours of graduate work are often are organized as a specialist degree program. As shown in **Table 8.3**, only 22 percent of superintendents hold the specialist degree.

Doctorates

As noted previously, 45.3 percent of superintendents responding to the 2000 Study survey hold a doctorate, with 89.2 percent indicating that the major of their highest degree is in educational administration (see **Table 8.3 and 8.5**).

TABLE 8.24 MENTORED BY A PRACTICING OR RETIRED SUPERINTENDENT, ANALYZED BY AGE

	YES		NO		UNCERTAIN / DON'T KNOW	
	No.	%	No.	%	No.	%
30-35	9	52.9	8	47.1	0	0.0
36-40	27	67.5	13	32.5	0	0.0
41-45	103	68.2	47	31.1	1	0.7
46-50	373	65.6	193	33.9	3	0.5
51-55	488	58.7	334	40.2	9	1.1
56-60	230	50.2	227	49.6	1	0.2
61-65	71	45.2	84	53.5	2	1.3
66+	8	36.4	14	63.6	0	0.0
TOTAL	1309	58.3	920	41.0	16	0.7

TABLE 8.25 MENTORED BY A PRACTICING OR RETIRED SUPERINTENDENT, ANALYZED BY RACE

	YES		NO		UNCERTAIN / DON'T KNOW	
	No.	%	No.	%	No.	%
NON-MINORITY	1236	58.2	874	41.1	15	0.7
MINORITY	70	59.3	47	39.8	1	0.9
TOTAL	1306	58.2	921	41.1	16	0.7

Part–time Preparation

Most students in educational administration programs are commuter students who pursue graduate degree and licensure programs on a part-time basis, and attend classes after work or during summer school (McCarthy, 1999). These characteristics are often criticized as limiting the opportunities for gaining formal knowledge of superintendents' work, or incisive, first-hand knowledge through extended field experiences (Björk, 1999; Clark, 1989; Finn and Petersen, 1985).

Most aspiring and veteran administrators are mature, at mid-career, and have family obligations. Attending graduate school on a full-time basis would require giving up their full-time positions as teachers or administrators. Full-time study is precluded by the lack of adequate financial assistance. In 1992, only 12.8 percent of aspiring administrators received assistance while completing their master's degrees, with only 5.3 percent being awarded by school districts — the entities most likely to benefit from individuals completing administrator preparation programs (Glass, 1992). These percentages are consistent with levels of support reported in AASA's 1971 and 1982 studies of the superintendency. Although North Carolina created a unique system to support the enrollment of highly talented individuals in university-based principal licensure programs, the $20,000 annual stipend is less than half of the annual salary of senior classroom teachers with advanced graduate education — those most likely to pursue administrative careers. Those pursuing the superintendency do not have a comparable financial assistance program.

Age and Experience

The majority of individuals interested in pursuing an administrative career (75.6 percent) do not decide to enter the profession until having served as a classroom teacher for 10 years, and half of those become an administrator before they have completed 5 years of teaching. Since 1971, those spending five years or fewer in the classroom before becoming an administrator has declined (see **Table 8.6**). Individuals working in districts with more than 25,000 students and districts with between 3,000 - 24,999 students were more likely to enter administration within 5 years, 60 percent and 44.6 percent respectively, than those in smaller districts (see **Table 8.7**). Men have a tendency to enter administration with five or fewer years of teaching experience (40 percent). Women, however, tend to make that decision later in their careers, after 10 – 15 years of experience in the classroom (see **Table 8.8**). As discussed in Chapter 3, **Personal Characteristics**, individuals aspiring to the superintendency do not make that decision until mid-career. Superintendents spend an average of 8 years as a classroom teacher, obtain their first administrative position between the ages of 25-35, move to a central office position in their late thirties, and enter the superintendency early to mid-forties.

TABLE 8.26 MENTORED BY A PRACTICING OR RETIRED SUPERINTENDENT, ANALYZED BY GENDER

	YES		NO		UNCERTAIN / DON'T KNOW	
	No.	%	No.	%	No.	%
MALE	1099	56.3	837	42.9	15	0.8
FEMALE	211	71.1	85	28.6	1	0.3
TOTAL	1310	58.3	922	41.0	16	0.7

TABLE 8.27 SERVED AS A MENTOR TO AN ASPIRING ADMINISTRATOR, ANALYZED BY DISTRICT SIZE

	YES		NO		UNCERTAIN / DON'T KNOW	
	No.	%	No.	%	No.	%
GROUP A: 25,000 OR MORE	86	90.5	6	6.3	3	3.2
GROUP B; 3,000-24,999	477	87.4	59	10.8	10	1.8
GROUP C: 300 – 2,999	1034	76.9	268	19.9	43	3.2
GROUP D: FEWER THAN 300	145	57.3	96	37.9	12	4.8
TOTAL	1742	77.9	426	19.1	68	3.0

In general, teachers aspiring to be building level administrators and superintendents decide on their own (i.e., self-select) to enroll in graduate level educational administration courses. They bear the costs for graduate school without financial assistance from the district, state, or foundations, and typically do not receive release time to attend classes, participate in extended field-experiences or training, and rarely attend graduate school on a full-time basis (Clark, 1989). In 1992, Glass reported that 93.2 percent received no help in the form of graduate assistantships, and only 9 percent received sabbatical leave or district support for pursuing their specialist degree required for superintendent licensure. Superintendents pursuing doctoral studies, however, received more financial assistance (38 percent) and sabbaticals (26.5 percent) from their districts. Approximately one-quarter of superintendents attended graduate school on a full-time basis for a least one year to fulfill graduate school residency requirements. While more superintendents are completing graduate degree programs, and national commission reports stress the importance of substantive field-based experience, support for individuals to pursue these activities remains static.

Issues and Challenges Facing the Superintendency Today

Superintendents were asked to rank the most significant challenges facing the profession today. Although some were ranked as having great significance (see **Table 5.24**), over three-quarters of all superintendents believed most issues listed were significant, illustrating the intensity of district contexts in which they are currently working. It is not surprising that an overwhelming majority of superintendents view financing schools to meet increasing expenditures and capital outlay (97 percent), assessing/testing for learner outcomes (93 percent), accountability/credibility (87 percent), and demands for new ways of teaching or operating the educational programs (86 percent) as being of uncommon importance to them. These issues, as are all those listed, are inextricably linked to society's press for school reform. Aside from long-standing concern for adequate district finances, superintendents' emphases on curriculum, teaching, learning, and student performance on standardized tests have eclipsed traditional management areas.

Emphasis of Preservice and Inservice Education Programs

An integral part of understanding professional preparation for the superintendency is to ascertain how practitioners would organize instruction. As part of the series of questions directed toward evaluating their professional preparation, superintendents were asked to determine where specific areas might best be taught. Although it is difficult to group content into several categories that allow generalizations, there is an overwhelming sense that both university-based and non-university-based preparation programs should cover a number of content areas. In addition, there is not a clear differentiation as to where specific content areas should be taught, as there is some overlap. These key areas are highly related to areas of primary concern; issues they indicated as being of great significance. The top four areas include: testing and accountability (75 percent); public relations (73 percent); assessing educational outcomes (72 percent); and administrator-board relations (71 percent) (see **Table 8.9**).

Areas thought to be most appropriate for inservice training, those that build upon the foundation established in their professional degree program, tend to be the more technical, district-rooted areas of administrators' work. These areas include restructuring of districts (33 percent), developing/funding programs for children at risk (28 percent), legislative and local efforts to implement "choice" programs (24 percent), and aging and inadequate facilities (24 percent) (see **Table 8.9**).

Areas regarded as being most appropriate for preservice professional preparation include strategic planning (18 percent), law (16 percent), and personal time management (16 percent) (see **Table 8.9**). Although superintendents have generally differentiated between the type of content that may be more appropriately taught in one instructional setting than another, all of the content appears to be regarded as utilitarian.

Educational Research

In 1992, Thomas Glass observed that, even though education is an important social endeavor, less than 1 percent of education spending is dedicated toward research. The 1980s saw a considerable reduction in educational research funds available at the federal and state levels. Introduction of new program initiatives, materials, and techniques in public education frequently originated in federally sponsored projects or in projects affiliated with a college or university. Little research that is widely disseminated is sponsored by states, districts, or local schools. There is a very plausible reason for this: most of these organizations neither have the resources, nor the long-term policy perspectives, needed to sustain major, longitudinal research studies.

Most superintendents not only believe that educational research is useful, but their opinion as to *how* useful has increased over the past several years. The 1992 Ten-Year Study reported that 24.2 percent of superintendents said it is "highly useful," 41 percent said it is "usually useful," and 33.1 percent said it is "occasionally useful" (See Glass, 1992, p. 79). A decade later, 30 percent regard educational research as highly useful. In addition, nearly 45 percent regard it as "usually useful" and 23 percent said it was occasionally useful. Less than 1 percent (0.9 percent) indicated that it was "not useful" (see **Table 8.10**). The tendency of superintendents to regard research as either "highly useful" or "usually useful" (75 percent) corresponds to an increase of advanced graduate degrees. It may also reflect increasing need for using research to respond effectively to demands for reform as well as working in contentious environments.

Quality of Educational Administration Programs

Critics of educational programs frequently cite surveys of practicing administrators who have completed degree and licensure programs 10 - 15 years earlier, and cite them as evidence of the current lack of rigor and relevance of university-based programs. Many factors contribute to the current condition of professional preparation programs. Although simplistic answers to complex problems are seductive, they are frequently wrong. The commonality among historical studies and contemporary findings points to problems characteristic of preparation in the field, rather than a single failed strategy. Should the mix of providers be changed, problems endemic to the field would

TABLE 8.28 SERVED AS A MENTOR TO AN ASPIRING ADMINISTRATOR, ANALYZED BY AGE

	YES		NO		UNCERTAIN / DON'T KNOW	
	No.	%	No.	%	No.	%
30-35	7	41.2	8	47.1	2	11.8
36-40	27	67.5	13	32.5	0	0.0
41-45	102	67.5	46	30.5	3	2.0
46-50	430	75.8	119	20.9	20	3.5
51-55	672	80.9	137	16.5	22	2.6
56-60	361	78.8	83	18.1	14	3.1
61-65	128	81.5	23	14.6	2	3.8
66+	18	81.8	3	13.6	1	4.5
TOTAL	1745	77.7	432	19.2	68	3.0

remain. This suggests the need for a radical reconceptualization of how administrators are prepared, rather than tinkering at the edges of the problem.

Collaborative efforts among key stakeholders are laying much of the groundwork needed to forge promising new directions in preparation, practice, and licensure and have established a model for continued work on this complex task. Some of these problems result from constraints on individuals, which force them to prepare for professional careers on a part-time rather than a full-time basis. Other problems arise from the unwillingness or inability of school districts to support the development of leaders by providing financial assistance, paid sabbaticals, and opportunities to work with exemplary superintendents. Despite the wisdom of state standards, approval and oversight, they often inhibit restructuring programs and course content. Still other problems derive from deliberate, yet painfully slow, academic review processes and academic regulations that are incompatible with the fundamental purposes of professional school programs: preparing individuals to confront the problems facing schools (Björk, 1999; Björk and Ginsberg, 1996).

Embedded in these efforts are efforts to restructure programs, course content, and instructional methods that help students meet national standards (ISLLC) for the profession; increase relevance, rigor, and collaboration with districts; provide financial assistance and sabbaticals to allow individuals to participate in clinical experiences as is the case in medicine and law; reconstitute colleges of education as professional schools; and view preparation as a joint responsibility among professional associations, state departments of education, and universities.

Institutional Differences

There are between 400 and 500 educational administration programs in the nation. While in many respects these programs are becoming increasingly similar in terms of degrees, programs, content, and faculty (McCarthy and Kuh, 1997), there is also great variation in curriculum, course content, degree requirements, and academic rigor. These variations affect program quality and may be partially explained by dissimilar institutional missions among research universities, doctoral granting institutions, and comprehensive campuses that deliver these programs. For example, one of UCEA's requirements for institutional membership is that departments of educational administration have a minimum of five full-time faculty to ensure the breadth and depth of instruction and experiences essential for preparing school and district administrators. Although many other institutions may be approved by state certification agencies, they may have only one, or even no, full-time faculty members in educational administration.

In addition, course and credit requirements dictated to universities by state education agencies largely determine the general content of courses and the experiences administrators receive in their educational administration programs. If those institutions are not required to include specific program content or experiences by state departments of education, or national or regional accrediting bodies, then they usually do not appear in the graduate program requirements (Clark, 1989). Full-time or part-time internships are infrequently included as program requirements.

Program rigor may also be affected by institutional mission. Graduate research universities may place greater emphasis on the acquisition of a professional knowledge base to inform school and district leadership, while comprehensive institutions may tend to stress technical and craft knowledge related to practice. Murphy (1995) views the gap between the professional knowledge base (theory) and practice (technical knowledge) as the product of the emphases of administrator preparation in two preceding historical eras. One focused on providing prescriptions based on personal experience for doing administration and the other was preoccupied with research and generating theory, frequently without the benefit of conversations with practitioners.

Both strategies of administrator preparation are overly simplistic, and distort the complex realities of schools, administration, and leadership (Hoy and Miskel, 1996). Neither approach is adequate for preparing the next generation of school and district leaders. Björk (1999), however, suggests that professional knowledge (research and theories of practice) and technical, craft knowledge gained through field experiences are not mutually exclusive, but highly complimentary. This utilitarian perspective of administrator preparation acknowledges the value of practitioners using knowledge and theories of practice for identifying and solving real world problems, and using technical knowledge of how schools work to take corrective action. Robinson's (1998) and Bridges and Hallinger's (1992) problem-based learning approaches place a high value on an integration of theory and practice as a way for professors and practitioners to think about events, and to reframe professional preparation programs.

Quality of Programs

The 1982 AASA survey asked a question about superintendents' overall appraisal of the graduate program that prepared them for the superintendency. About one-quarter (26.8 percent) said their preparation program was "excellent." About half (47.4 percent) said it was "good." The 1992 Ten-Year study also asked respondents to provide an overall appraisal of their preparation program. There were negligible differences in responses, with 26. 2 percent indicating "excellent," 47.4 percent "good," and 22.2 percent "fair." Only 4.6 percent indicated it was "poor." The 2000 Study was very similar, with 26.2 indicating their preparation was "excellent," 47.4 percent "good," and 22.2 percent "fair." Only 3.6 percent indicated their professional preparation program was "poor" (see **Table 8.11**). Over the past 20 years, superintendents have been remarkably consistent in their evaluation of their graduate programs. Nearly three-quarters of all superintendents regard their professional preparation as either "excellent" or "good."

When individuals completing professional programs are asked to evaluate the quality of those programs, their typical response is "good" or "excellent" regardless of other indicators. Many link their own self-worth with their professional preparation program, and most would not like to admit they made a mistake in choosing a given program. This tendency may be reflected in the question of how sampled superintendents appraise educational programs in their state. In this case, responses were much more critical. Only 13 percent appraised preparation programs in their state as "being excellent"; however, 50.5 percent rated them as "good," and 30. 4 percent indicated they are "fair" (see **Table 8.12**).

TABLE 8.29 SERVED AS A MENTOR TO AN ASPIRING ADMINISTRATOR, ANALYZED BY RACE

	YES		NO		UNCERTAIN / DON'T KNOW	
	No.	%	No.	%	No.	%
WHITE	1639	77.1	419	19.7	67	3.2
OTHER	106	89.8	10	8.5	2	1.7
TOTAL	1745	77.8	429	19.1	69	3.1

TABLE 8.30 SERVED AS A MENTOR TO AN ASPIRING ADMINISTRATOR, ANALYZED BY GENDER

	YES		NO		UNCERTAIN / DON'T KNOW	
	No.	%	No.	%	No.	%
MALE	1503	77.0	388	19.9	60	3.1
FEMALE	247	8.2	41	13.8	9	3.0
TOTAL	1750	77.8	429	19.1	69	3.1

By Age

Superintendents younger than age 45 are more critical of educational administration programs than are older superintendents. Although 26.8 percent of all superintendents view their preparation as being "excellent," only 22.1 percent of superintendents under the age of 45 view them as being "excellent." A large majority of superintendents (74.5 percent) under the age of 45, however, regard them as "good" or "fair." Superintendents over the age of 61 regard their preparation differently. Over 31 percent view their preparation as "excellent" (see **Table 8.13**).

When asked to appraise preparation programs in their states, superintendents tended to be more critical. Only 14.6 percent of all superintendents view preparation programs in the state as being "excellent." Those between the ages of 46 - 60 are the most critical, with only 12.6 percent viewing these programs as "excellent." Nearly 81 percent, however, regard state programs being either "good" or "fair" (see **Table 8.14**). It is evident that superintendents have a tendency to be more critical of programs in the state in contrast to the preparation program they attended.

By District Size

Superintendents in large districts view the program they attended more favorably than their counterparts in smaller districts. Nearly 30 percent of superintendents in districts with more than 25,000 students and 32 percent of those in districts with between 3,000 – 24,999 students viewed their graduate program as "excellent" (see **Table 8.15**).

By the Number of Years Since Attaining Highest Degree

Superintendents who received their highest degree within the past 5 years viewed their preparation more favorably than those who attained their degree more than 5 years prior to the administration of the survey. Nearly 30 percent regarded their preparation as "excellent," compared to 26.6 percent of those who received it between 6 - 10 years, and 26.9 percent who received it between 11 - 15 years ago. Nearly 78 percent of those who completed their professional preparation within the past 5 years regard it as being "excellent" or "good" (see **Table 8.16**). This suggests that a vast majority of recently certified superintendents are satisfied with their superintendency preparation.

By Race

Survey data indicate that minorities are inclined to view their graduate preparation more favorably than whites. Thirty-one percent of minorities view their preparation as "excellent," compared to 25.9 percent of whites. Whites were more likely to view their program as "good." However, when combined, nearly three-quarters of whites (73.6 percent) view their graduate program as "excellent" or "good," and 71 percent of minorities regard it in the same way. Overall, a majority of minorities and non-minorities are satisfied with their superintendent program (see **Table 8.17**).

By Gender

Women and men rate their superintendent preparation programs in a similar fashion. Roughly 26 percent of men and women view their program as excellent. Nearly 74 percent of male superintendents consider their preparation as being "excellent" or "good" in comparison to 71 percent of female superintendents (see **Table 8.18**).

Quality of Instructors

In the past, educational administration professors often were accused by practitioners as being too "theoretical" and removed from the realities of operating school districts. In a 1989 study, Michael Sass found, in a sample of 480 professors of educational administration, that exactly two-thirds had never served in the superintendency. Of the third who had been superintendents, a large majority were between 50 and 65 years of age, meaning that being a professor was a capstone of their careers.

Although Sass (1989) found that few younger professors have ever been superintendents, there is a trend to hire new faculty that have administrative experience. McCarthy and Kuh (1997) found that one-third of faculty in educational administration programs had previously served as school administrators before joining the professorate. A closer look at the findings reveals that 45 percent of all new faculty hired, 35 percent of mid-level, and 28 percent of senior faculty, had prior experience as principals and superintendents. Diverse institutional missions are also reflected in hiring pattern differences. Over 51 percent of new faculty hired by non-UCEA institutions had administrative experience compared to 25 percent of new faculty hired at UCEA institutions. UCEA institutions have well-defined research missions, and the characteristics of the faculty hired understandably reflect these.

Faculty content specialization reflects the core areas of preparation programs. The top five areas identified by McCarthy and Kuh (1997) include leadership (16 percent), law (13 percent), organizational theory (9 percent), principalship (8 percent) and economics and finance (8 percent). Only 2 percent of faculty indicated the superintendency as their primary area of specialization. Most professors of educational administration, however, are viewed as generalists having several areas of expertise. Departments often hire practitioners as adjuncts to handle courses when full-time faculty are committed to teaching in master's level, principal preparation programs, or when departments do not have content area specialists such as in the superintendency. Although the criticism that faculty lack administrative experience is being remedied, it is only a gesture in the direction of fundamentally reconfiguring professional preparation in the field. Including internships, embedding field-based assignments in coursework, and establishing clinical professorships and involving principals and superintendents as instructors and mentors may enhance field-relevance and academic rigor.

Most educational administration professors were rated "good" or "fair," regardless of the age of the respondent (see **Table 8.19**) or district size (see **Table 8.20**). Superintendents assessed the credibility of educational administration professors in their graduate programs, indicating 14 percent as "excellent," 52 percent as "good," and 28 percent as "fair." Overall, two-thirds of superintendents regarded their professors as "excellent" or "good." Only 6 percent of superintendents regarded educational administration professors as "poor." More than 19 percent of superintendents in dis-

TABLE 8.31 PARTICIPATION IN PROFESSIONAL DEVELOPMENT/TRAINING OFFERED BY ORGANZATIONS/AGENCIES

ORGANIZATION	GROUP A: 25,000 OR MORE PUPILS No.	GROUP B: 3,000-24,999 PUPILS No.	GROUP C: 300-2,999 PUPILS No.	GROUP D: FEWER THAN 300 PUPILS No.	NATIONAL PROFILE No.
AASA	77	438	791	86	1392
ASBO	14	67	242	33	356
ASCD	47	287	489	35	858
NAESP	11	36	105	20	172
NASSP	19	102	262	42	425
NSBA	42	228	321	26	617
PRIVATE SECTOR	36	214	359	68	677
STATE AASA	54	349	853	116	1372
STATE EDUCATION AGENCY	53	317	887	166	1423
OTHER	15	96	265	68	444

tricts with fewer than 300 students viewed professors as "excellent," compared to 7.4 percent of superintendents in districts with more than 25,000 students. Also, superintendents under the age of 45 evaluated the credibility more favorably (19. 7 percent), compared to older superintendents (see **Table 8.20**).

University-Based Professional Preparation Programs

Strengths

Superintendents indicated that the ability of professors to relate course content to practice (20.2 percent); high-quality of educational administration course content (19.7 percent); high-quality professors (18.6 percent); and discussion of curriculum, instruction, and testing issues (14. 2 percent) were the major strengths of their graduate study programs (see **Table 8.21**). It should be noted that few programs have extensive, practical, field-based practicums and internships that were supported by release time or salary. In all likelihood, if educational administration programs had more extensive internships and practicums, superintendents might have given this category a much higher rating. In 1992, superintendents indicated that high quality of professors (24.9 percent) and quality of educational administration courses (22.2 percent) were the major strengths of their superintendent preparation programs.

Weaknesses

The major weakness of educational administration programs, according to superintendents, includes the lack of hands-on application (19.8 percent); inadequate access to technology (18.9 percent); failure to link content to practice (16.5 percent); and too much emphasis on professors' personal experiences (13.8 percent). In both the 1982 and 1992 studies, the major weakness was poor and irrelevant coursework, as identified by more than 20 percent of respondents in each survey. The category of "low quality of professors" dropped from 14 percent in 1982 to 9 percent in 1992. It then rose slightly to 10 percent in 2000. The category of poor and irrelevant course offerings dropped from 20.5 percent in 1992 to 10.7 percent in 2000 (see **Table 8.22**).

Mentoring and Coaching

Mentoring has served as a powerful developer of human potential throughout the centuries, and has assisted novices being inducted into, and succeeding in, their professions. Numerous authors have addressed the issue of administrator preparation and have identified mentoring as a key component of induction programs (Murphy, 1991). Mentors can provide assistance for aspiring superintendents as they progress in the profession from induction to independence. Mentors and

TABLE 8.32 PARTICIPATION IN PROFESSIONAL DEVELOPMENT/TRAINING OFFERED BY ORGANZATIONS/AGENCIES, ANALYZED BY AGE

ORGANIZATION	AGE 30-35 No.	AGE 36-40 No.	AGE 41-45 No.	AGE 46-50 No.	AGE 51-55 No.	AGE 56-60 No.	AGE 61+ No.
AASA	6	21	76	343	514	307	126
ASBO	2	5	20	100	134	74	25
ASCD	2	4	42	208	343	199	65
NAESP	1	2	13	45	63	27	20
NASSP	7	6	24	106	156	85	40
NSBA	3	6	27	143	244	141	52
PRIVATE SECTOR	2	13	40	160	262	154	48
STATE AASA	8	24	84	328	527	289	111
STATE ED. AGENCY	11	27	81	352	543	293	112
OTHER	2	7	29	117	176	85	35

interns work best when they establish a professional relationship based on trust. Mentors, who are typically practicing superintendents, often serve as role models, share information, provide insights, and guide individuals in practicums and internships. These relationships often continue after the internship experience, as new administrators build professional networks. Coaching of superintendent proteges often involves on-site assistance and demonstrations related to technical tasks, as well as timely and substantive feedback. A coach may collaborate with mentors and interns in planning, developing, and evaluating field-based experiences; providing consultation to interns; participating in training workshops; and facilitating how interns connect theoretical knowledge with field experiences

As an example, Kentucky incorporated mentoring into its principal intern program (KPIP) and is effectively using coaches in the Kentucky Leadership Academy (KLA) initiative. These experiences are directed towards supporting aspiring principals and superintendents in learning how to do administration and how to lead in reform contexts.

Despite the tendencies of school boards to select male candidates almost exclusively, research on women and minorities in the superintendency provides irrefutable evidence that they successfully perform tasks required of anyone in the role, and furnish important role models that are necessary for those aspiring to the position. Recent research suggests that the women's movement and equity legislation may be positively influencing the attitudes of male administrators, increasing frequency of encouragement, support, and mentoring (Edson, 1988); and may have also increased the number of women in the principalship and district office administrative positions. The number of women appointed to superintendencies, however, remains remarkably low (AASA, 1993a).

The absence of mentor relationships, role models, and networks is frequently cited in the literature as a primary reason why more women and minorities do not go into the superintendency (Campbell, 1991; Edson, 1988; Lynch, 1990; Marshall, 1989; Schmuck, 1975; Shakeshaft, 1979, 1989; Tyack and Hansot, 1982; Whitaker and Lane, 1990). Thus, using mentors and coaches as integral parts of professional preparation is of central importance in building the capacity of aspiring superintendents, and meeting specific needs of women and minorities entering the profession.

The majority of superintendents (59 percent) have been mentored in their careers by a practicing or retired superintendent, regardless of district size, age, race, or gender. Nearly two-thirds of superintendents in urban districts with more than 25,000 students (65. 3 percent), and those in districts with 3,000 - 24,999 districts (62.8 percent) have been mentored, compared to much smaller numbers of superintendents in districts with fewer than 3,000 students (see **Table 8.23**). Similarly, two-thirds of superintendents between the ages of 36 - 50 have been mentored (see **Table 8.24**). There is very little difference between non-minority (58.2 percent) and minority superintendents (59.3 percent) with regard to being mentored by a practicing or retired superintendent (see **Table 8.25**). It appears that

TABLE 8.33 OPINION OF USEFULNESS OF NON-UNIVERSITY-BASED PROFESSIONAL DEVELOPMENT/TRAINING

USEFULNESS LEVEL	GROUP A: 25,000 OR MORE PUPILS		GROUP B: 3,000-24,999 PUPILS		GROUP C: 300-2,999 PUPILS		GROUP D: FEWER THAN 300 PUPILS		NATIONAL UNWEIGHTED PROFILE	
	No.	%	No.	%	No.	%	No.	%	No.	%
VERY USEFUL	34	35.8	154	28.5	390	29.2	64	25.5	642	28.9
USEFUL	23	24.2	137	25.4	322	24.1	66	26.3	548	24.7
SOMEWHAT USEFUL	37	38.9	237	43.9	550	41.2	99	39.4	923	41.5
NOT USEFUL	0	0.0	4	0.7	26	1.9	4	1.6	34	1.5
NO OPINION	1	1.1	8	1.5	48	3.6	18	7.2	75	3.4
TOTAL	95	4.3	540	24.3	1336	60.1	251	11.3	2222	100.0

non-minority superintendents are willing to mentor others, regardless of race. Female superintendents appear to be mentored more frequently (71.1 percent) than their male colleagues (58.2 percent) (see **Table 8.26**). This suggests that male superintendents are not gender-biased with regard to providing mentoring to female colleagues.

It is interesting that superintendents responding to the survey are more likely to mentor others in the field (78 percent) than they were to receive mentoring during their careers (58 percent), regardless of district size, age, race, or gender. Over 90 percent of superintendents in urban districts with more than 25,000 students and 87 percent of those in districts with 3,000 - 24,999 students mentored other superintendents (see **Table 8.27**). Although a vast majority (78 percent) of superintendents mentored others, those older than 51 years of age (80 percent) tended to mentor colleagues more often (see **Table 8.28**). Although over three-quarters of non-minority superintendents (77 percent) mentor colleagues, a significantly larger proportion of minority superintendents (90 percent) mentor others (see **Table 8.29**). Male superintendents (77 percent) mentor colleagues, however, very few women (8 percent) serve as mentors. This may be explained by the fact that there are very few women in the superintendency and women seldom have the opportunity to mentor other women. In addition, the superintendency, as a male-dominated profession, may carry a cultural bias against males being mentored by a female colleague (see **Table 8.30**), while the reverse is not the case (see **Table 8.26**).

Non-University-Based Professional Development and Training

Professional associations are playing a major role in developing and delivering professional development and inservice training to school and district administrators throughout their careers. These activities reflect roles played by professional associations in other fields, including medicine, law, and dentistry, that are focused on maintaining currency of technical skills and licensure.

The vast majority of superintendents participated in professional development and training activities sponsored by AASA, their state affiliates, or state education agencies. The next largest number of superintendents attended sessions sponsored by ASCD and NSBA, or delivered by the private

TABLE 8.34 EVALUATION OF NON-UNIVERSITY-BASED PROFESSIONAL DEVELOPMENT, ANALYZED BY AGE

AGE	VERY USEFUL		USEFUL		SOMEWHAT USEFUL		NOT USEFUL	
	No.	%	No.	%	No.	%	No.	%
30-35	2	14.3	8	57.1	4	28.6	0	0.0
36-40	6	15.8	15	39.5	16	42.1	1	2.6
41-45	29	20.0	48	33.1	67	46.2	1	0.7
46-50	160	29.5	136	25.0	239	44.0	8	1.5
51-55	239	30.1	202	25.4	340	42.8	14	1.8
56-60	151	34.3	93	21.1	187	42.5	9	2.0
61-65	55	36.9	41	27.5	51	34.2	2	1.3
66+	2	9.5	5	23.8	14	66.7	0	0.0
TOTAL	644	30.0	548	25.5	918	42.8	35	1.6

TABLE 8.35 EVALUATION OF NON-UNIVERSITY-BASED PROFESSIONAL DEVELOPMENT, ANALYZED BY RACE

RACE	VERY USEFUL		USEFUL		SOMEWHAT USEFUL		NOT USEFUL		NO OPINION	
	No.	%	No.	%	No.	%	No.	%	No.	%
WHITE	605	28.7	517	24.5	882	41.9	35	1.7	68	3.2
OTHER	40	34.8	30	26.1	38	33.0	0	0.0	7	6.1
TOTAL	645	29.0	547	24.6	920	41.4	35	1.6	75	3.4

sector (see **Table 8.31**). Individuals between the ages of 46 - 60 tend to participate more frequently than those younger or older (see **Table 8.32**).

General Usefulness

Nearly 29 percent of superintendents found professional development and training activities as "very useful," 25 percent viewed them as "useful," and 42 percent said they were "somewhat useful." Superintendents in districts with more than 25,000 students were more likely to find professional development and training delivered by associations "very useful" (36 percent), than colleagues in smaller districts (see **Table 8.33**).

Evaluation by Age

Superintendents between the ages of 46 - 65 tended to find professional development and training "very useful" more so than those individuals who are younger or older. In addition, there appears to be a tendency of individuals to regard association-sponsored training more favorably as they get older. A smaller percentage of younger superintendents, those most likely to have recently completed graduate degree programs, found these training sessions "very useful" (see **Table 8.34**).

Evaluation by Race and Gender

Minorities (35 percent) were more likely to regard professional development and training delivered by professional associations as being "very useful" than non-minorities (29 percent) (see **Table 8.35**). A similar pattern is evident in the differences between how men and women view association-sponsored professional development and training. Over 39 percent of women tend to regard it as "very useful," whereas only 27 percent of men regard it in the same way (**see Table 8.36**).

TABLE 8.36 EVALUATION OF NON-UNIVERSITY-BASED PROFESSIONAL DEVELOPMENT, ANALYZED BY GENDER

GENDER	VERY USEFUL		USEFUL		SOMEWHAT USEFUL		NOT USEFUL		NO OPINION	
	No.	%	No.	%	No.	%	No.	%	No.	%
MALE	530	27.4	494	25.5	812	42.0	31	1.6	68	3.5
FEMALE	115	39.4	55	18.8	111	38.0	4	1.4	7	2.4
TOTAL	645	29.0	549	24.7	923	41.4	35	1.6	75	3.4

TABLE 8.37 MAJOR STRENGTHS OF NON-UNIVERSITY-BASED PROFESSIONAL DEVELOPMENT/TRAINING

MAJOR STRENGTHS	GROUP A: 25,000 OR MORE PUPILS		GROUP B: 3,000-24,999 PUPILS		GROUP C: 300-2,999 PUPILS		GROUP D: FEWER THAN 300 PUPILS		NATIONAL UNWEIGHTED PROFILE	
	No.	%	No.	%	No.	%	No.	%	No.	%
HIGH-QUALITY INSTRUCTORS	48	18.8	262	17.5	581	15.8	97	14.6	988	16.2
QUALITY OF SESSION CONTENT	68	26.7	387	25.8	904	24.5	136	20.5	1495	24.5
ABILITY OF INSTRUCTOR TO RELATE CONTENT TO PRACTICE	62	24.3	373	24.9	902	24.5	156	23.6	1493	24.5
DISCUSSION OF CURRICULUM, INSTRUCTION, & TESTING ISSUES	29	11.4	176	11.8	429	11.6	100	15.1	734	12.0
USE OF TECHNOLOGY IN TRAINING	6	2.3	38	2.5	102	2.8	21	3.2	167	2.7
OPPORTUNITY FOR HANDS-ON	16	6.3	110	7.3	279	7.6	47	7.1	452	7.4
CONVENIENT SCHEDULE FOR PROFESSIONALS	24	9.4	143	9.6	445	12.1	94	14.1	706	11.6
NO STRENGTHS	2	0.8	9	0.6	39	1.1	11	1.7	61	1.1

Evaluation by Number of Years Since Completing Highest Degree

Superintendents who completed their highest degree within five years tend to be more critical of the usefulness of professional development and training delivered by professional associations. There is a tendency for superintendents to regard training more favorably as the number of years since they attained their highest degree increases. For example, only 22 percent of those who completed their degree within five years regard their training as "very useful," in comparison to 34 percent who completed it between 11-15 years ago.

Major Strengths

Superintendents were asked to evaluate the major strengths of non-university-based professional preparation and training. Nearly 25 percent regarded session content and the ability of the instructor to relate content to practice as being the greatest strengths. More than 16 percent identified the high quality of instructors, and 12 percent recognized inclusion of instruction and testing issues as strengths. In general, superintendents in districts with more than 25,000 students (19 percent), and those with between 3,000 - 24,999 students (18 percent), regarded the quality of instructors more highly than did colleagues in smaller districts (see **Table 8.37**).

When asked to evaluate their university-based preparation programs along these same lines, superintendents indicated that the ability of professors to relate course content to practice (20.2 percent); the high quality of educational administration course content (19.7 percent); high-quality professors (18.6 percent); and discussion of curriculum, instruction, and testing issues (14.2 percent) as the major strengths of their graduate study programs (see **Table 8.21**). It appears that superintendents regard non-university-based course content more highly, and find instructors more able in relating program content to practice than their counterparts in university-based programs, even though they regarded the quality of instructors and other areas more favorably.

Weaknesses

Superintendents were asked to identify areas of weakness in their non-university-based training. They indicated that the lack of opportunity for hands-on application (18 percent), the lack of use of technology in training (16 percent), the tendency of instructors to place too much emphasis on personal experiences (12 percent), and the inability of instructors to relate content to practice (10 percent) were the major weaknesses in non-university-based training programs (see **Table 8.38**).

TABLE 8.38 MAJOR WEAKNESSES OF NON-UNIVERSITY-BASED PROFESSIONAL DEVELOPMENT/TRAINING									
	GROUP A: 25,000 OR MORE PUPILS		GROUP B: 3,000-24,999 PUPILS		GROUP C: 300-2,999 PUPILS		GROUP D: FEWER THAN 300 PUPILS		NATIONAL UNWEIGHTED PROFILE	
MAJOR WEAKNESSES	No.	%	No.	%	No.	%	No.	%	No.	%
LOW-QUALITY INSTRUCTORS	21	10.3	124	10.3	303	10.2	44	7.9	492	10.0
LOW QUALITY OF SESSION CONTENT	19	9.3	120	10.0	295	9.9	63	11.4	497	10.1
INSTRUCTOR DID NOT RELATE CONTENT TO PRACTICE	20	9.9	127	10.5	296	10.0	63	11.4	506	10.3
LACK OF DISCUSSION OF CURRICULUM, INSTRUCTION & TESTING ISSUES	17	8.4	120	10.0	288	9.7	51	9.2	476	9.6
LACK OF TECHNOLOGY IN TRAINING	37	18.2	191	15.8	484	16.3	86	15.5	798	16.2
NO OPPORTUNITY FOR HANDS-ON APPLICATION	35	17.2	209	17.3	527	17.7	107	19.3	878	17.8
INCONVENIENT SCHEDULE FOR PROFESSIONALS	20	9.9	131	10.9	349	11.8	53	9.6	553	11.2
TOO MUCH EMPHASIS ON INSTRUCTOR'S PERSONAL EXPERIENCES	28	13.8	163	13.5	353	11.9	70	12.6	614	12.4
NO STRENGTHS	6	3.0	21	1.7	75	2.5	17	3.1	119	2.4
TOTAL	203	4.1	1206	24.5	2970	60.2	554	11.2	4933	100.0

When superintendents were asked to identify weaknesses in their university-based programs, they included: the lack of hands-on application (19.8 percent); inadequate access to technology (18.9 percent); failure to link content to practice (16.5 percent); and too much emphasis on professors' personal experiences (13.8 percent) (see **Table 8.22**).

The debate on the relative strengths and weaknesses of university-based and non-university-based professional preparation programs has increased in intensity over the past decade. Unfortunately, these discussions have often produced more heat than light. It is clear that both university- and non-university-based professional preparation programs share similar weaknesses that emerge from similar constraints on the nature of delivery. They tend to be instructor-centered and class-room-based. These deficiencies may be corrected in part by integrating course content and instruction more closely with field-based experiences.

Summary

In the coming decade, thousands of individuals will complete superintendent preparation programs. There are a considerable number of interrelated issues regarding how the next generation of superintendents should be prepared, which entities are best suited to provide education and training, and whether emerging national standards for licensure (ISLLC) may contribute to ensuring the rigor and quality of those who will lead schools in the 21st century. Although many individuals who complete preparation programs may not actually become superintendents, the knowledge and skills acquired are invaluable to building the capacity of districts to improve the education of children, particularly those at risk. In addition, it is becoming evident that an increasing number of superintendents are viewing the position as "impossible," and the salary and benefits as inadequate, contributing to many highly qualified professionals deciding not to enter candidate pools. In addition, the weaknesses of both university- and non-university-based programs are similar, which refocuses the often-heated debate from research and practice to addressing a common problem and finding shared solutions.

The most promising area for corrective action appears to lie in the integration of knowledge with practice, by relying on instructors who have a sense of the reality of superintendents' work and engagement with the contexts of schooling. The acquisition of professional knowledge ("knowing about"), and how it relates to improving schooling ("knowing for"), provides a clear purpose and direction for superintendents' work. Preparing the next generation of superintendents, however, must include ways to extend thinking beyond "doing administration" to "knowing why" they are doing it and effectively communicating that purpose to others. In addition, superintendents must become more adept in "knowing how" to accomplish their goals in decidedly different, more democratic contexts. "Knowing how" will require continual "retooling" of administrators' skills as the nature of work evolves and changes in the coming decades. The most serious obstacle to achieving truly excellent superintendent preparation programs is the lack of will and money to provide internship experiences for highly qualified aspiring superintendents. These issues cut across the full spectrum of those who presently provide professional preparation and those who may join the enterprise in the future.

Bibliography

Achilles, C. (1998). "How long?" *The AASA Professor* 22,1: 9-11.

American Association of Colleges of Teacher Education. (1988). *School Leadership Preparation: A Preface to Action*. Washington, DC: Author.

Ashe, J., J. Haubner and N. Troisi. (1991). "University preparation of principals: The New York Study. *NASSP Bulletin* 75,536: 145-150.

Barnett, B., M. Basom, D. Yerkes and C. Norris. (2000). "Cohorts in educational leadership programs: Benefits, difficulties, and the potential for developing school leaders." *Educational Administration Quarterly* 36,2.

Barnett, B. and I. D. Muse. (1993). "Cohort groups in educational administration: Promises and challenges." *Journal of School Leadership* 3, 400-415.

Björk, L. (April 1999). "Integrating formal and experiential knowledge: A superintendent preparation model." Paper presented at the annual meeting of the American Educational Research Association. Montreal, Canada.

Björk, L. (April 1996). "Impact and response: The implications of school restructuring on university-based professional preparation programs." Paper presented at the Annual Meeting of the American Educational Research Association. New York.

Björk, L. (May 1993). "Effective schools; effective superintendents: the emerging instructional leadership role." *Journal of School Leadership* 3, 246-259.

Björk, L., and R. Ginsberg. (April 1992). "Principals of reform and reforming principals: A South African perspective." Paper presented at the Annual Meeting of the American Educational Research Association. San Francisco.

Björk, L., J. C. Lindle and E. Van Meter. (1999). "A summing up." *Educational Administration Quarterly* 35,4: 658-664.

Boyan, N. (1988). *Handbook of Research on Educational Administration*. New York: Longman.

Brent, B. and E. Haller. (Spring 1998). "Who really benefits form graduate training in educational administration? Prompting the debate." The *AASA Professor* 22,1: 1-7.

Bridges, E. and P. Hallinger. (1992). *Problem-Based Learning for Administrators*. Eugene, OR: Clearinghouse on Educational Management (EA 023 722).

Brockett, D. (1996). Boards find fewer superintendent candidates. *School Board News*. 16, 10:1.

Cambron-McCabe, N. (1993). Leadership for democratic authority. In J. Murphy (1993*). Preparing tomorrow's leaders: Alternative designs* (p. 157-176). University Park, PA: University Council for Educational Administration.

Campbell, T. (1991). "Perspectives of women and minorities in the principalship." Paper presented at the Annual Meeting of the American Educational Research Association. Chicago.

Carnegie Forum on Education and the Economy (1986). *A nation prepared: Teachers for the 21st century*. Washington, DC: Author.

Carver, F. D. (June 1988). "The evaluation of the study of educational administration." Paper presented at the EAAA Allerton House Conference. University of Illinois at Urbana-Champaign.

Chapman, C. H. (1997). *Becoming a superintendent: Challenges of school district leadership.* Upper Saddle River, NJ: Merrill.

Clark, D. (March 1997). "The search for authentic educational leadership: In the universities and in the schools." Division A address presented at the annual meeting of the American Educational Research Association. Chicago.

Cooper, B. and W. L. Boyd. (1988). "The evolution of training for school administrators." In D. Griffiths, R. Stout and P. Forsyth (Eds.), *Leaders for America's Schools.* Berkeley: McCutcan.

Cooper, B., L. Fusarelli and V. Carella. (2000). *Career crisis in the superintendency? The results of a national survey.* Arlington, VA: American Association of School Administrators.

Council of Chief State School Officers. (1996). *Interstate School Leaders Licensure Consortium: Standards for School Leaders.* Washington, DC: Author.

Cunningham, L. and J. Hentges. (1982). *The American School Superintendency 1982: A Summary Report.* Arlington, VA: American Association of School Administrators.

Crowson, R. L. (1988). "Editor's introduction." *Peabody Journal of Education* 65, 4: 18.

Daresh, J. and M. Playco. (1995). "Alternative career formation perspectives: Lessons for educational leadership from law, medicine, and the priesthood." Paper presented at the Annual Meeting of the University Council for Educational Administration. Salt Lake City.

Danforth (1987). *The Danforth program for professors of school administration.* St Louis: Danforth Foundation.

Dembowski, F. (1998). "What should we do now? Suggested directions for school administration." *The AASA Professor* 22,1: 19-22.

Downey, C. (Spring 1998) "Is it time for us to be accountable too?" *The AASA Professor* 22,1: 12-17.

Douglas, D. (1992). "Challenging the conventional assumptions about the preparation programs for aspiring superintendents." In F. Wendel (Ed.). *Reforming Administrator Preparation Programs.* University Park, PA: The University Council for Educational Administration.

Edson, S. (1988). *Pushing the Limits: The Female Administrative Aspirant.* New York: State University of New York Press.

Erlandson, D. A. and L. Witters-Churchill. (March 1988). *"The Texas NASSP study."* Paper presented at the annual meeting of the National Association of Secondary School Principals. Anaheim, CA.

Forsyth, P. (1999). "The school administrator supply." Columbia, MO: National Policy Board for Educational Administration.

Glass, T. (1993). "Point and counterpoint: What is in the context of what might be?" In Carter, D., T. Glass, and S. Hord *Selecting, Preparing and Developing the School District Superintendent.* London: Falmer Press.

Glass, T. (1992). *The 1992 Study of the American School Superintendency: America's Education Leaders in a Time of Reform.* Arlington, VA: American Association of School Administrators.

Griffiths, D. E. (1988). *Educational Administration: Reform PDQ or RIP* (Occasional paper #8312). Tempe AZ: University Council for Educational Administration.

Haller, E. J., B. O. Brent and J. H. McNamara. (1997). "Does graduate training in educational administration improve America's schools?" *Phi Delta Kappan* 79,3: 222-227.

Hill, M. S. (1995). "Educational leadership cohort models: Changing the talk to change the walk." *Planning and Changing* 26,3/4: 179-189.

Holmes Group. (1986) *Tomorrow's Teachers*. East Lansing, MI: Author.

Hoy, W.K. and Miskel. (1977). (3rd edition). *Educational Administration: Theory, Research and Practice*. New York: Random House.

Hoyle, J., F. English, and B. Steffy. (1998). *Skills for Successful 21st Century School Leaders*. Arlington, VA: American Association of School Administrators.

LISA (*Leadership Institute for School Administrators*) update. (December 1996). Arlington, VA: American Association of School Administrators.

Leithwood, K., D. Jantzi, G. Coffin, and P. Wilson. (1996). "Preparing school leaders: What works?" *Journal of School Leadership* 6: 316-342.

Lynch, K. (August 1990). "Women in school administration: Overcoming the barriers to advancement." *Women's Educational Equity Act Publishing Center Digest*: 1-5.

Marland, S. P. (1960). "Superintendents' concerns about research applications in educational administration." In R. F. Campbell and J. M. Lipman (Eds.), *Administrative Theory as a Guide to Action*. Chicago: University of Chicago, Midwest Administration Center.

Marshall, C. (1989). "More than black face and skirts: New leadership to confront major dilemmas in education." *Agenda* 1,4: 4-11.

McCarthy, M. (1999). 'The evolution of educational leadership preparation programs." In Murphy, L. and K. S. Louis. *Handbook of Research on Educational Administration, 2nd edition*. San Francisco, Josey-Bass, 119-139.

McCarthy, M. and G. Kuh. (1997). *Continuity and Change: The Educational Leadership Professorate*. Columbia, MO: University Council for Educational Administration.

McCarthy, M., G. Kuh and J. Beckman. (1979). "Characteristics and attitudes of educational administration doctoral students." *Phi Delta Kappan* 61: 200-203.

McCarthy, M., G. Kuh, L. Newell, and C. Iacona. (1988). *Under Scrutiny: The Educational Administration Professorate*. Tempe, AZ: University Council for Educational Administration.

Miklos, E. (1983). "Evolution of administrator preparation programs." *Educational Administration Quarterly* 19,3: 153-177.

Milstein, M. (1993). *Changing the Way We Prepare Educational Leaders: The Danforth Experience*. Newbury Park, CA: Corwin.

Milstein, M. (1990). "Rethinking the clinical aspects in administrative preparation: From theory to practice." In S.L. Jacobson and J. Conway (Eds.), *Educational Leadership in an Age of Reform*. New York: Longman.

Milstein, M. and J. A. Krueger. (1993). 'Innovative approaches to clinical internships: The New Mexico experience." In J. Murphy, (Ed.). *Preparing Tomorrow's Leader: Alternative Designs*. University Park, PA: University Council for Educational Administration.

Murphy, J. (Spring 1987). "Notes from a beginning professor of educational administration." *UCEA Review* 28,3: 14-22.

Murphy, J. (1992). *The Landscape of Leadership Preparation: Reframing the Education of School Administrators.* Newbury Park, CA: Corwin Press.

Murphy, J. (Ed.). (1993). *Preparing Tomorrow's School Leaders: Alternative Designs.* University Park, PA: UCEA.

Murphy, J. (1995). "Restructuring schooling: The changing role of the superintendent and the district office." In K. Leithwood (Ed.), *Effective School District Leadership.* Albany, NY: State University of New York Press.

Murphy, J. and P. Forsyth (Eds.). (1999). *Educational Administration: A Decade of Reform.* Thousand Oakes, CA: Corwin.

Murphy, J., and P. Hallinger. (1993). "Restructuring schooling: Learning from ongoing efforts." In J. Murphy and P. Hallinger (Eds.), *Restructuring Schooling: Learning from Ongoing Efforts.* Newbury Park, CA: Corwin/Sage.

Murphy, J. and K. S. Louis. (1999). *Handbook of Research on Educational Administration, 2nd Edition.* San Francisco: Jossey-Bass.

Muse, I. and G. J. Thomas. (1992). "The rural principal: Select the best." *Journal of Rural and Small Schools* 4,3: 32-37.

National Association of Elementary School Principals (1998). *Is There a Shortage of Qualified Candidates for Openings in the Principalship? An Exploratory Study.* Alexandria, VA: Author.

National Association of Elementary School Principals (1990). *Principals for 21st Century Schools.* Alexandria, VA: Author.

National Association of Secondary School Principals. (1985). *Performance-based Preparation of Principals: A Framework for Improvement.* Reston, VA: Author.

National Association of Secondary School Principals. (1990). *Assessor's Manual: NASSP Principals Assessment Center.* Reston, VA: Author.

National Commission on Excellence in Educational Administration. (1987). *Leaders for America's Schools.* Tempe, AZ: University Council for Educational Administration

National Governors' Association. (1986). *Time for Results: The Governors' 1991 Report on Education.* Washington, DC: Author

National Policy Board for Educational Administration. (1989). *Improving the Preparation of School Administrators: An Agenda for Reform.* Charlottesville, VA: Author.

National Commission on Excellence in Education. (1983). *A Nation at Risk: The Imperative for Educational Reform.* Washington, DC: U.S. Government Printing Office.

Norton, S. (1995). "The status of student cohorts in educational administration preparation programs." Paper presented at the annual convention of the University Council for Educational Administration. Salt Lake City, UT.

Occupational Outlook Handbook (1996-1997). Bureau of Labor Statistics. http://stats.bls.gov/oco/ocosoo7.htm.

Odden, A. (1992). *Education Policy Implementation.* Albany: SUNY Press.

Peterson, K. D., and C. E. Finn. (Spring 1985). "Principals, superintendents and administrator's art." *The Public Interest*, No. 79, pp. 262.

Pitner, N. (1982). *"Training of the school administrator: State of the art"*(occasional paper). Eugene, OR.: Center for Educational Policy and Management.

Pohland. P. and L. Carlson. (Fall 1993). "Program reform in educational administration." *UCEA Review*, 4-9.

Pounder, D., (1995). "Theory to practice in administrator preparation: An evaluation study." *Journal of School Leadership* 5: 151-162.

Prestine, N. (1992). "Preparation of school leaders can emphasize learning in context." *Leadership and Learning* 4,2: 23.

Robinson, V. (1994). "The practical promise of critical research in educational administration." *Educational Administration Quarterly* 30,1: 56-76.

Sass, M. (1989). "AASA performance goal and skill areas: Importance to effective superintendency performance as viewed by practicing superintendents and professors of educational administration." Unpublished dissertation, Northern Illinois University.

Schmuck, P. (1975). *Sex Differentiation in Public School Administration*. Arlington, VA: American Association of School Administrators.

Schneider, J. (Spring 1998). 'University training of school leaders isn't the only option." *The AASA Professor* 22,1: 7-8.

Shakeshaft, C. (1979). *"Dissertation research on women in educational administration: An analysis of findings and paradigm for future research."* Unpublished doctoral dissertation, Texas A & M University, College Station.

Shakeshaft, C. (1989). "The gender gap in research in educational administration." *Educational Administration Quarterly* 25: 324-337.

Shipman, N. and J. Murphy. (Spring 1999). "ISLLC update." *UCEA Review*, p. 13, 18.

Short, P. (1998). "Leader preparation: A reflection and response to the Haller article." *The AASA Professor* 22,1: 17-19.

Thompson, S. D. (1989). "Troubled kingdoms, restless natives." *Phi Delta Kappan* 70,5: 371-375.

Tyack, D. and E. Hansot. (1982). *Managers of Virtue: Public School Leadership in America, 1820-1980*. New York: Basic Books

Van Meter, E. and J. Murphy. (1997). *Using ISLLC Standards to Strengthen Preparation Programs in School Administration*. Washington, DC: Council of Chief State School Officers.

Weller, L. D. Brown, C.L. and Flynn, K. J. (1991). "Superintendent turnover and school board member defeat: A new perspective and interpretation." *Educational Administration Quarterly* 29,2: 61-71.

Whitaker, K. and Lane, K. (February 1990). "Is a women's place in school administration? Women slowly open the door to educational leadership." *The School Administrator*: 8-12.

Zheng, H. (1996). "School contexts, principal characteristics, and instructional leadership effectiveness." Paper presented at the Annual meeting of the American Educational Research Association. New York.

Index of Tables

Date Due